DO-IT-YOURSELF

Build Your Own PC

FOR

DUMMIES®

DO-IT-YOURSELF

Build Your Own PC

FOR

DUMMIES®

by Mark L. Chambers

WILEY

John Wiley & Sons, Inc.

Build Your Own PC Do-It-Yourself For Dummies®

Published by
John Wiley & Sons, Inc.
111 River Street
Hoboken, NJ 07030-5774

www.wiley.com

Copyright © 2009 by John Wiley & Sons, Inc., Hoboken, New Jersey

Published by John Wiley & Sons, Inc., Hoboken, New Jersey

Published simultaneously in Canada

For general information on our other products and services, please contact our Customer Care Department within the U.S. at 877-762-2974, outside the U.S. at 317-572-3993, or fax 317-572-4002.

For technical support, please visit www.wiley.com/techsupport.

Wiley publishes in a variety of print and electronic formats and by print-on-demand. Some material included with standard print versions of this book may not be included in e-books or in print-on-demand. If this book refers to media such as a CD or DVD that is not included in the version you purchased, you may download this material at http://booksupport.wiley.com. For more information about Wiley products, visit www.wiley.com.

Library of Congress Control Number: 2008940688

ISBN 978-0-470-19611-3 (pbk); ISBN 978-0-470-46216-4 (ebk); ISBN 978-0-470-46218-8 (ebk); ISBN 978-0-470-46219-5 (ebk)

Manufactured in the United States of America

10 9

WILEY

About the Author

Mark L. Chambers has been an author, a computer consultant, a BBS sysop, a programmer, and a hardware technician for more than 20 years — pushing computers and their uses far beyond normal performance limits for decades now. His first love affair with a computer peripheral blossomed in 1984 when he bought his lightning-fast 300bps modem for his Atari 400. Now he spends entirely too much time on the Internet and drinks far too much caffeine-laden soda.

With a degree in journalism and creative writing from Louisiana State University, Mark took the logical career choice: programming computers. However, after five years as a COBOL programmer for a hospital system, he decided there must be a better way to earn a living, and he became the Documentation Manager for Datastorm Technologies, a well-known communications software developer. Somewhere in between writing software manuals, Mark began writing computer how-to books. His first book, *Running a Perfect BBS*, was published in 1994 — and after a short decade or so of fun (disguised as hard work), Mark is one of the most productive and best-selling technology authors on the planet.

Along with writing several books a year and editing whatever his publishers throw at him, Mark has also branched out into Web-based education, designing and teaching a number of online classes — called *WebClinics* — for Hewlett-Packard.

His favorite pastimes include collecting gargoyles, watching St. Louis Cardinals baseball, playing his three pinball machines and the latest computer games, supercharging computers, and rendering 3-D flights of fancy with TrueSpace — and during all that, he listens to just about every type of music imaginable. Mark's worldwide Internet radio station, *MLC Radio* (at www.mlcbooks.com), plays only CD-quality classics from 1970 to 1979, including everything from Rush to Billy Joel to *The Rocky Horror Picture Show.*

Mark's rapidly expanding list of books includes *MacBook For Dummies; iMac For Dummies; Mac OS X Leopard All-in-One Desk Reference For Dummies; Scanners For Dummies; CD & DVD Recording For Dummies; PCs All-in-One Desk Reference For Dummies; Mac OS X Tiger: Top 100 Simplified Tips & Tricks; Microsoft Office v. X Power User's Guide; BURN IT! Creating Your Own Great DVDs and CDs; The Hewlett-Packard Official Printer Handbook; The Hewlett-Packard Official Recordable CD Handbook; The Hewlett-Packard Official Digital Photography Handbook; Computer Gamer's Bible; Recordable CD Bible; Teach Yourself the iMac Visually; Running a Perfect BBS; Official Netscape Guide to Web Animation;* and the *Windows 98 Troubleshooting and Optimizing Little Black Book.*

His books have been translated into 14 languages so far — his favorites are German, Polish, Dutch, and French. Although he can't read them, he enjoys the pictures a great deal.

Mark welcomes all comments about his books. You can reach him at mark@mlcbooks.com, or visit MLC Books Online, his Web site, at www.mlcbooks.com.

Dedication

This book is posthumously dedicated to my friend and teacher, LSU journalism professor Jim Featherston. Jim taught me everything I need to know — now I can put ideas to paper.

Author's Acknowledgments

I find that writing the acknowledgments is always the easiest part of any book because there's never a shortage of material. I always have a big group to praise.

First, a well-earned round of thanks to my knowledgeable technical editor, Jim Kelly, who checked every word for accuracy (while enduring every bad joke and pun).

As with every book I've written, I'd like to thank my wife, Anne, and my children, Erin, Chelsea, and Rose, for their support and love — and for letting me follow my dream!

Finally, I send my heartfelt appreciation to the hard-working editors at Wiley Publishing, Inc., who were responsible for the launch and completion of this new *Do-It-Yourself* edition — it takes a ton of work to produce a completely new edition, and they did an incredible job. Thanks are due to my project editor, Mark Enochs, my copy editor, Teresa Artman, and my acquisitions editor, Bob Woerner. They're talented, dedicated people, and I count myself very lucky that I had their assistance for this project — and many to come, I hope!

Publisher's Acknowledgments

We're proud of this book; please send us your comments through our online registration form located at http://dummies.custhelp.com. For other comments, please contact our Customer Care Department within the U.S. at 877-762-2974, outside the U.S. at 317-572-3993, or fax 317-572-4002.

Some of the people who helped bring this book to market include the following:

Acquisitions, Editorial, and Vertical Websites

Senior Project Editor: Mark Enochs

Executive Editor: Bob Woerner

Senior Copy Editor: Teresa Artman

Technical Editor: James F. Kelly

Editorial Manager: Leah Cameron

Vertical Websites Project Manager:
Laura Moss-Hollister

Vertical Websites Assistant Project Manager:
Jenny Swisher

Vertical Websites Assistant Producers:
Angela Denny, Josh Frank, Kit Malone, and
Shawn Patrick

Editorial Assistant: Amanda Foxworth

Sr. Editorial Assistant: Cherie Case

Cartoons: Rich Tennant (www.the5thwave.com)

Composition Services

Project Coordinator: Katie Key

Layout and Graphics: Carrie A. Cesavice,
Reuben W. Davis, Shane Johnson,
Jennifer Mayberry, Christine Williams

Proofreaders: Laura Albert, Amanda Graham,
Linda Quigley

Indexer: Sharon Shock

Publishing and Editorial for Technology Dummies

    Richard Swadley, Vice President and Executive Group Publisher

    Andy Cummings, Vice President and Publisher

    Mary Bednarek, Executive Acquisitions Director

    Mary C. Corder, Editorial Director

Publishing for Consumer Dummies

    Kathleen Nebenhaus, Vice President and Executive Publisher

Composition Services

    Debbie Stailey, Director of Composition Services

Contents at a Glance

Table of Contents

Part IV: Advanced PC Options................................207

Introduction

You've decided to build your own computer. Congratulations! That statement might seem a little like "You've decided to fly a 747" or "You've decided to teach yourself accounting" — but I'm here to tell you that this book was especially written to make it both *easy* and (believe it or not) *fun* to build your own multimedia computer with an Intel or AMD processor. (Oh, and don't forget that you're likely to save a significant chunk of cash as well, especially if you're building a powerful PC for applications such as gaming and video editing.)

To sum up, I explain the mysterious parts in the box in honest-to-goodness English, with a little humor and without the jargon — and then help you build the PC that's perfect for you!

Why Build Your Own?

Buying a PC from a retail computer store or a big mail-order company is easy: Out comes the credit card, the boxes arrive at your house, and installation is as simple as plugging in the keyboard, mouse, speakers, and monitor. Even the most experienced PC hardware junkie will have to admit that a novice can save time and potential headaches by buying a retail PC.

Therefore, you might be asking yourself, "Why don't I just travel the retail PC route like most people? Why go to the trouble of building my own computer?" There are several doggone good reasons why you should assemble your own machine:

It just plain costs less to build your own PC!

The first reason — and, for some people, the most important reason — for building a computer is to save as much money as possible over the cost of a retail PC (especially if you're buying a PC from a local retail store, or if you're building a super-fast gaming system). When you build your own computer, you're not paying for all the overhead tacked on to the original price of a computer, including a storefront, advertising, and a salesperson's paycheck.

Many retail PC packages don't include a monitor, so often the price that you see isn't for a complete system. And yes, you can save a hundred dollars or more over the price of a complete PC offered by a big mail-order company. It's simply a matter of searching for the right companies that sell computer components at rock-bottom prices. Remember, using a Web site such as www.pricewatch.com can bring you — in just a few seconds — the best prices available *anywhere*!

Even if you have to buy every single component from your computer case to your mousepad, you're still likely to save a considerable amount of cash by assembling your own computer.

Exercise your freedom of choice!

When you build your own computer, you can select special components that don't kowtow to the cookie-cutter mold of retail PCs. For example, don't expect to find specialized pointing devices (such as trackballs) on most retail PCs at your local computer store. If you buy a retail PC and you want to use a trackball rather than a mouse, you'll have to buy one separately (and then you're stuck with a mouse that you don't need). That might not seem like much of a hassle, but consider other specialized components, such as a high-end sound card with Dolby Digital support, a gamer's 3-D video card with 1GB of video RAM, or a TV/video capture card. Buying one of these adapter cards, removing the case, and substituting the adapter card that you *really* wanted in the first place becomes a big deal.

When you design and assemble your own computer, you buy precisely what you need, including any specialized hardware or peripherals. Even if the perfect computer that you were considering at the computer store doesn't have a FireWire port and a Blu-ray recorder, you can certainly build a computer that does have these extras! If you're considering buying a PC from a direct vendor (such as Dell or Gateway) and you need special hardware, the vendor can usually supply it — although you'll pay substantially more for the vendor's version of the part than you would have paid for the part through a mail-order catalog. Having a custom PC is nice, but unless you build it yourself, you'll *always* pay more.

Enjoy the learning experience

What do you learn when you buy a retail PC? The answer: Not much. Sure, you get a crash course in removing Styrofoam and plugging in cables, but most owners of a retail PC are still afraid to remove the case from their computer. If you buy a retail PC, you'll be left in the dark when the time comes to upgrade your system to extend its useful life or replace a broken component. (And you're likely to invalidate what's left of your warranty if you crack the case.)

On the other hand, when you build your own computer, you *know* what makes it tick. You'll blossom into a bona fide techno-wizard! With your assembly experience and your knowledge of PC hardware, you'll be better prepared to fix problems and upgrade hardware and peripherals. The technicians at your local PC repair shop will wonder what happened to you; perhaps you should visit them from time to time just to swap hard drive specifications.

Spare yourself the shipping and repair hassles

When you buy a retail PC from a store (or even from one of the big-name mail-order companies), you'll probably be presented with a technical support number and assurances that your computer will be promptly repaired if it breaks. You'll find that the word *promptly* has many meanings: waiting several minutes (or even an hour) to speak to a technical support representative, finding out that you'll be without your PC and the data that you need for several weeks, or making an appointment with a service representative to eventually drop by your house and bring a replacement part. Oh, and don't forget that this coverage usually lasts for only a year, unless you paid big bucks for the extended service contract when you bought your PC.

When you build your own PC, you can buy parts locally. And, if a part breaks, you don't have to pick up the telephone and start waiting. You'll never find yourself repacking your computer to send it halfway across the country. Instead, you can bring the faulty component back to the store for an immediate replacement.

Dodge bundled software costs and get what you want

Retail PC salespeople like to crow about the cool software that's included with their computers. You usually get a productivity suite (which includes a word processor, some sort of database application, and a spreadsheet program), a few Internet applications, and free hours on an online service. If you're lucky, you might also get a year-old game or two with your computer. Generally, these programs are stripped-down versions of larger packages.

Read between the lines when a PC manufacturer touts its bundled software. For example, you might get baby sister Microsoft Works preloaded instead of its full-featured, big sister Microsoft Office, which most retail PCs sold in stores don't include — unless you pay more for it.

Unfortunately, bundled software isn't free at all: You pay for it along with your hardware, the documentation is usually sparse, it's rarely exactly what you need, and you usually can't subtract it from the total price of your computer if you don't want it. Often, you won't even receive the original program installation discs, so you can't reinstall the software. In fact, many new computer owners end up uninstalling the bundled software to make room for the programs that they really want to run. If you build your own PC, you can select your own full versions of your favorite applications later and save additional money.

Avoid the computer sales experience

Although used-car salespeople seem to rank the lowest on the social totem pole, computer salespeople aren't much better. Many salespeople who I've encountered in retail computer stores either consider the customer an idiot or have little idea of exactly what they're selling (making them the perfect target for a few well-placed techno-questions — nothing's funnier than an embarrassed clueless salesperson who treated you like a computer novice just a few seconds before)! Others try to pass off a computer that's been returned as near the quality of a brand-new machine. (Look closely for the word *refurbished* the next time you shop for a computer, and you might see this technique in action.)

By building your own PC, you can circumvent your computer retail store and all the techniques that salespeople use to try to talk you into a specific computer. You end up with a better computer that is less expensive and *perfectly* suits your needs.

Select the brands that you prefer

Are you looking for specific brand-name components in your computer, such as a Western Digital Raptor SATA hard drive or a Sound Blaster X-Fi Titanium sound card from Creative Labs? If you buy a retail PC, you end up with whatever hardware the manufacturer deems satisfactory (and you'd be surprised by how many big-name manufacturers of retail PCs use no-name parts). Often the only way that you can determine what you're getting is to open the computer's case on the sales floor (or, if you used a mail-order shop, when you receive it).

Even if you're buying a computer from a direct vendor that offers customized PCs, it's unlikely that you'll be able to ask for a specific brand for most of the components used to assemble your computer. Typically, these vendors do use brand-name parts but only those brands and models the vendor prefers. If you need a different model, you're no better off than you would be buying a computer in a chain store.

When you build your own computer, *you* select the parts required to build it, including any specific brand-name preferences.

About This Book

You'll find that each chapter in this book acts as a reference for each type of computer hardware that you can add to your computer; some are required components, and others are optional devices that add extra functionality to your PC. You can start at any point — each chapter is self-contained. The book also includes a glossary of computer terms and an appendix about what's on the DVD in the back of this book.

Each chapter also provides the general information you need to make a buying decision between different flavors of the same component. For example, in Chapter 10, I discuss both bare-bones and advanced sound cards (without resorting to engineer-speak).

If you're interested in buying and installing a particular component, such as a DVD drive or a video adapter card, you can jump directly to the chapter that describes the device and start reading. Most chapters end with general instructions that familiarize you with the installation process. (They don't replace the specific documentation that accompanies each component, although the generic steps that I provide give you an idea of what's involved.)

On the other hand, if you're interested in building a computer from scratch, start with Chapter 1 and follow the chapters in order; you can also skip to other chapters whenever necessary for information that you might need.

Conventions Used in This Book

From time to time, I might ask you to type a command within Windows (or whatever operating system you're using). That text often appears in bold like this: **Type me**. Press the Enter key to process the command.

I list menu commands with this format: File⇨Open. For example, this shorthand indicates that you should click the File menu and then choose the Open menu item.

From time to time, I mention messages you should see displayed onscreen by an application or the operating system. Those messages look like this: `This is a message displayed by an application.`

Although you don't really need to know a great deal of technical information to build a computer, you might be curious about the technical details that surround computers and the components that you're using. This technical information is usually formatted as a sidebar (in a separate box) to separate it from the stuff that you really *have* to know.

Introducing Colossus

Throughout this book, I recommend a number of specific components by brand and model number. If I were building my own PC at the time of this writing (and I actually do build this PC on the companion DVD), I'd pick these parts, and I'll always let you know why I chose them.

I should note, however, that time marches on, as does computer technology. The components I name in this edition will (of course) be supplanted soon enough with newer models, so make sure you check the manufacturer's Web site to see whether a new device with more features or better performance is available.

I named my dream PC *Colossus,* after the truly awesome sentient supercomputer that takes over the world in the cult 1970 film *Colossus: The Forbin Project.* (If you don't name your PC while building it, I strongly urge that you name it after it's completed. Consider it the human side of the assembly process!) This outstanding movie has a sizable following among techno-types. If you enjoy a good science fiction film about artificial intelligence, don't miss this flick.

Foolish Assumptions

Here's a friendly warning: You might run across one or two doubting Thomases when you announce that you're building your own PC. Those folks probably make lots of foolish assumptions about what's involved in building a PC, and you just might want to burst their bubble by telling them the following truths:

- ✔ You *don't* have to be a computer technician with years of training, and you don't need a workshop full of expensive tools. In this book, no assumptions are made about your previous knowledge of computers, the Internet, programming your DVD player, or long division.

- ✔ No experience? Don't let that stop you! I introduce you to each of the systems in your computer, what they do, and how you install them, including advanced technology that would make a technoid green with envy. (I can't fix spaghetti by myself, so you know that building a PC must be easier than it first appears!)

✔ Some people still think that you don't save a dime by building your own PC. If that's the case, why are there locally owned computer stores in your town building custom PCs? By assembling your own computer, you can save hundreds of dollars (and take advantage of used parts like a keyboard or modem from an older computer).

✔ Finally, some people might ask you what you plan to learn by building your own PC — and that's an easy one! By the time that you're finished, you'll be ready to add and upgrade parts yourself so that you'll save money in the future — and computer-repair techs will growl when you meet them.

Now that I've put those myths to rest, it's time for the good stuff!

How This Book Is Organized

I divided this book into five major parts, all made up of a number of chapters, and each chapter is further divided into sections. You'll find all the nasty acronyms and abbreviations, part names, and relevant items in the index; important topics and information that appear elsewhere in the book are cross referenced to make them easier to find. And do not overlook the companion DVD at the back of the book!

Part 1: Preparations and Planning

In Part I, I introduce you to the tool (yes, only one tool) of the PC assembly trade (a screwdriver, which tells you how complex the hardware *really* is), what components make up a PC, and how they work together within your computer. You also determine what type of computer you should build by examining your current and future needs.

Part II: Assembling the Basics

In Part II, you assemble the required components to build a bare-bones PC — it won't play the latest 3-D shoot-'em-up game with all the visual bells and whistles, but it will have all the basic features that you need. You'll be able to load your choice of operating system after you finish this part.

Part III: Adding the Fun Stuff

In Part III, I cover the addition of hardware that makes a multimedia PC fun to use — such as a digital stereo sound card, a DVD drive, and a DSL/cable modem. After you've completed this part, you can use your new PC to access the Internet or watch a DVD movie while you work. Or you can finally play that latest 3-D shoot-'em-up game with every last audio-visual bell and whistle turned on.

Part IV: Advanced PC Options

In Part IV, I introduce you to advanced hardware that pumps up the performance of your PC, including home networking (both the wired and the wireless type), digital scanners, and USB devices. (If the acronyms sound like Egyptian hieroglyphics, read all about them here.) Not every computer owner needs the technology found in this part, but after you've read these chapters, you'll be familiar with the enhancements that you can add to create a power user's PC — including the ultimate gaming PC, which I cover in Chapter 14.

Part V: The Part of Tens

The four chapters in Part V are a quick reference of tips and advice on several topics related to the assembly of PCs. For example, you'll find a chapter devoted to potential problems.

Appendixes: About the DVD and the PC Builder's Glossary

Read about the companion DVD in the first Appendix. Then, the glossary lists all the computer components, terms, abbreviations, and acronyms you need to know about.

Icons Used in This Book

Some things that you encounter while building your PC are just too important to miss. To make sure that you see certain paragraphs, they're marked with one of the following icons.

These are important. Consider my maxims to be the stuff you'd highlight in a college textbook — these facts and recommendations would make a good tattoo because they're universal and timeless in scope. (You'll see!)

Information marked with this icon is the printed equivalent of those sticky notes that decorate the front of some PCs. You might already know this stuff, but a reminder never hurts.

The Tip icon makes it easy to spot information that will save you time and trouble (and sometimes even money).

As you can imagine, the Warning icon steers you clear of potential disaster. *Always* read the information under this icon first!

Where to Go from Here

Before you turn the page, grab yourself a pencil and some scratch paper for taking notes — or throw caution to the wind and write directly in the book. If you need help on a particular component, jump to the right chapter; if you need to start from the beginning, start with Part I. And check out the DVD if you want to see me install a component.

Enjoy yourself and *take your time.* Remember Mark's First Maxim of PC Assembly:

You're not running a race!™

(I told you that maxims were universal and timeless, didn't I?) Although the process of building your own PC might seem a little daunting now, it *really is* easy. Plus, nothing is more satisfying than using a computer that you built yourself or answering PC questions from friends and relatives because "you're the computer expert!"

Part I
Preparations and Planning

The 5th Wave   By Rich Tennant

"The way the clown tells it, he was hired to deliver a balloon bouquet to the victim, who's this big computer nut — got all the equipment you can imagine. Well, it may have just been static electricity, but we're taking the clown in for questioning."

In this part . . .

I introduce you to the various components used to build a computer, and you find out what task each component performs. I also cover some of the basic rules of computer assembly. Finally, you act as your own consultant and determine which type of custom computer you should build to fit your needs. (It won't hurt, I promise.)

Chapter 1

A Screwdriver Is All You Need

Ask most people what they know about computers, and they'll tell you that a PC is a complex, sealed box full of confusing parts that you need an engineering degree to understand — something like a cross between an unopened Egyptian pyramid and a rocket engine. Ask those same people whether they want to try their hand at actually *building* a computer, and they'll probably laugh (or cry) out loud. Even if you did buy all the mysterious electronic parts (which techno-types affectionately refer to as computer *components*), where would you start? Where do you buy everything? How do you fit the components together? Nobody but an honest-to-goodness computer nerd could possibly put a computer together!

Well, ladies and gentlemen, I have great news: If you can handle the lone tool shown in Figure 1-1 — yes, the humble Philips screwdriver — you can safely assemble your own computer (and even enjoy doing it!). After you discover how to build your own computer and start to use it, you'll probably agree with me: Building a computer is *much* easier than figuring out how to use some of the complicated software that the computer can run. The idea that building a computer is as difficult as building or repairing a car is just a myth (probably encouraged by computer salespeople).

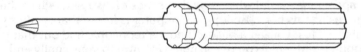

Figure 1-1: The tool of choice for computer builders.

In this chapter, I introduce you to the standard electronics and peripherals that you can use to build your computer, and then I show you how they fit together. (And after you successfully build your first computer, drop me an e-mail at mark@ mlcbooks.com with the subject "I Did It Mark!", and I can congratulate you personally!)

Assembly 101

You might have heard a horror story or two about someone who tried to build a PC and ended up being sucked through a black hole into another dimension. When you announce to the world that you're going to build your own computer, you're likely to face a number of common myths:

- ✔ **"Why, you have to be practically psychic about how machinery works to stick your hands inside a computer!"** Wrong. In fact, you don't have to know how any of the components work, so you don't have to be an expert in laser optics, magnetism, or electronic theory. You just need to connect the parts together correctly and attach them to the motherboard and computer case.

- ✔ **"You can't build a computer on a card table, you know. You're going to need an airstrip, a complete toolkit, and a warehouse full of parts."** Nope. You can not only assemble a computer on your dining room table but also do so with no special tools. Find your favorite screwdriver, and you're a lean, mean, computer-assembling machine.

- ✔ **"It's going to take you years to put together a computer. Heck, by the time you're finished, your computer will already be out of date."** Depends on how long it takes. No, no — just kidding! This myth is *definitely* false. If you have all your components ready to go, assembling a PC is a first-time project that you can easily finish during a long weekend.

- ✔ **"Something's not going to work with something else. You'll see."** Wrong again. (Geez, who *are* these people? They probably still think that airplanes will never get off the ground.) Today's computer components are designed to work with each other. Regardless of what brand name you buy or how much you spend, if you buy a standard computer device, it should join in that big cooperative team effort that makes a working computer.

What's the secret to building a PC? Time for the first Mark's Maxim for this book:

There really isn't a secret to building a PC.™

That's why many people have started their own home businesses building custom computers in their spare time — and why many thousands of my readers have built their own computers using this book. Building a computer is fun — that is, after you conquer your initial fear. Plus, you get a big ego boost after people find out that you built your own computer. Suddenly, you're a genuine PC guru to your family and friends, so be prepared to handle those technical support questions at your next party.

Building a better computer

Over the past few years, I've developed a simple rule for myself, which applies perfectly to building anything from a mousetrap to a computer. I call this rule *CA* — or, for those who can't stand abbreviations, *commonsense assembly.* The idea is a simple one: You can prevent most mistakes while assembling a PC by using a little common sense.

Keep the following CA rules in mind when handling and connecting computer components:

✔ **Give yourself plenty of empty space and adequate lighting.** If you're building a computer on the dining table, make sure that your work area is covered with newspaper to avoid scratches. I also recommend keeping an adjustable desk lamp handy to shine light where you need it.

✔ **Don't start without all the necessary components.** If you don't have everything that you need to follow a project from beginning to end, don't start yet (only to find you have to stop halfway through). It's too easy to miss a step or forget something if you leave your computer's bedside and come back the next day.

✔ **Treat your components carefully.** This commonsense rule doesn't mean that you need to wear gloves when handling cables or that you need to refrigerate your adapter cards. Just don't drop a part on the floor or toss it to a friend. Keep components in their antistatic packaging until you're ready to install them.

✔ **Follow the Three Absolutes of Component Care and Feeding.**

1. *Never* bend a circuit board or an adapter card.

2. *Always* make sure the cables that connect your parts aren't pinched.

3. *Never* try to **make** something fit. Take the component out, check the instructions again, and try it a different way if possible.

Installing adapter cards on your motherboard can sometimes take a little longer or require a little more force than plugging a game cartridge into a video game. But determining whether a card is aligned correctly with the slot is usually easy because the slot is keyed to the shape of the corresponding card.

✔ **Read any documentation that comes with each computer component.** Although I provide step-by-step assembly instructions throughout this book, one of your components might require special switch settings or some other unique treatment.

✔ **Keep all your parts manuals together for easy reference.** Store all your component manuals for a particular PC that you've built in a separate binder. After your computer is running, you can refer to your manuals quickly if you need to change any settings. In the future, if you want to sell the old device and upgrade, it's considered good manners to provide the original manual with the component. (*Complete with manual* makes a better impression on eBay.)

✔ **Save your boxes and receipts.** Although it's rare, you might find yourself stuck with a brand-new defective item, and you'll need the original packaging to return it.

✔ **Use a box to keep your small parts.** Loose screws, jumpers, and wires have a habit of wandering off if left on their own. If you end up with extra screws or doodads after successfully assembling a PC, put these parts in a box and start your own spare-parts warehouse. Trust me: They'll come in handy in the future. If you're a true techno-nerd, get thee hence to a hardware store and buy one of those wall racks with all the little compartments — they're perfect for organizing everything from screws to wires and jumpers.

✔ **Keep a magnetic screwdriver handy.** It *never* fails. Sooner or later, you end up dropping a screw inside your computer case. If no loose components are in the case, feel free to pick up the case, turn it upside down, and let gravity do its thing. However, if you've installed a component that's not screwed down yet, I recommend using a magnetic screwdriver for picking up wayward screws.

✔ **Check *all* connections after you install a component.** I can't explain this phenomenon (other than to invoke Murphy's Law), but you'll often connect a new component firmly only to discover later that you somehow disconnected some other connector accidentally.

✔ **Never forget the common foe: static electricity.** I'll show you how you can easily ground yourself before you touch any circuitry or adapter cards — *grounding* sounds painful, but it's not! Unless you ground yourself, you run the risk of damaging a component from the static electricity that might be lurking on your body. Chapter 3 covers grounding in more detail. It's a good habit to adopt from the very beginning.

✔ **Leave the computer cover off during assembly.** There's no reason to replace the case's cover immediately after installing a part. After all, what if you connected a cable upside down? Instead, test your newly installed device first, if possible. As long as you don't touch any of the circuit boards inside the case, you'll be fine.

By the way, nothing inside your machine will explode or spew nasty radiation, so you don't have to step behind a lead screen when you fire it up. Simply make sure that you don't touch any circuit boards inside while the machine is running. Personally, I replace the case's cover on a work-in-progress only at the end of the day (to fend off dust, felines, and small fingers).

The primary, number-one, all-important, absolutely necessary, required rule

Do not panic!

There's very little chance that you can destroy a component simply by connecting it the wrong way. Take your time while you build your computer and move at your own pace — you can avoid mistakes that way. Here's an important Mark's Maxim:

Building a computer is not a contest, and there is no time limit.™

After you gain experience by building a few machines, you can work on speed records; for now, just try to schedule as much uninterrupted time as possible. For example, I know several supertechs who can assemble a complete PC in a single hour. Of course, people often laugh at them at dinner parties. (Being a techno-nerd does have its dark side, I guess.)

The other primary, number-one, all-important, absolutely necessary, required rule

Liquids are taboo!

If you even so much as think of parking your soda or mineral water next to your computer (even just for a *second*), you might remind yourself of Chernobyl or Three Mile Island. If you spill beverages or other liquids on your computer components, that liquid will ruin every exposed circuit that it touches — period. You can't salvage anything from such a spill.

PCs Are Built with Standard Parts

Computers are practically appliances these days — one computer is put together pretty much like another. Ever since IBM introduced the IBM PC, computers have been built using standard components with the same connectors and dimensions, so you no longer need the experience of an electronics engineer to assemble one. And the parts are self-contained, so you don't need to worry about soldering (or gears and springs, either). Everyone uses the same building blocks that fit together the same way.

In fact, assembling standardized computer components is how popular mail-order and direct-sale computer manufacturers build their machines. Like you, they order standard computer components and peripherals and then follow a procedure (much like the ones that I describe in this book) to assemble the computer according to your specifications.

Introducing the Major Parts

Before you find out more about where to buy the parts that make up a computer, allow me to introduce you to each of the major components. I describe each component in general, although you can find out all the details about each computer part in other chapters of this book.

The metal mansion

Your computer's *case* is its home, complete with a power supply, the various buttons and lights on the front, and the all-important fans that keep the inside of your computer cool. Today's high-power gaming machines have three or four fans, depending on how many devices inside are generating heat — heck, the fastest PCs that gamers build these days are liquid-cooled, just like your car!

You might notice several large, rectangular cutouts on the front of your case. Don't worry — your computer case isn't defective; it's supposed to have them. These holes, called *drive bays,* enable you to add components, such as a DVD-ROM drive. An unused drive bay is usually covered by a plastic insert. Or the front of your case might have a door that swings open for access to the bays. Figure 1-2 illustrates a custom "modded" case. Gamers and PC techno-jocks swear by unique cases, just like how owners of custom cars love fancy paint jobs and flames galore. This case has additional air vents at the front and room for more fans at the back, as well as colorful paint and chrome accents.

You can get computer cases in various sizes. The size that you choose depends on how many toys (usually called *peripherals*) you want to add to your computer. See Chapter 3 for a more detailed discussion of your computer's case.

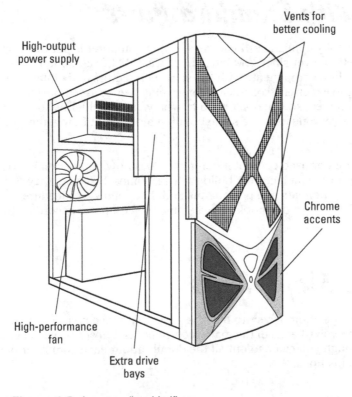

Vents for
better cooling

High-output
power supply

Chrome
accents

High-performance
fan

Extra drive
bays

Figure 1-2: A custom "modded" case.

The big kahuna

A number of different circuit boards are inside a computer, but only one is big enough, complicated enough, and important enough to be called your computer's *motherboard*. Your computer motherboard holds

- ✔ **The CPU chip:** This acts as the brain of your PC.
- ✔ **The RAM modules:** These act as your computer's memory while it's turned on.
- ✔ **All sorts of connectors:** You connect lots of things to your motherboard, such as hard drives, a DVD drive, and power cables.

In fact, the motherboard holds just about everything, as you can see in Figure 1-3. (PCI slots are covered in Chapter 4, and your motherboard's BIOS makes an appearance in Chapters 3 and 7.)

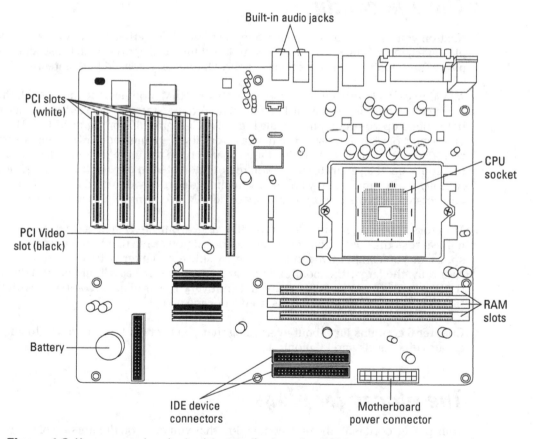

Figure 1-3: Your computer's main circuit board, affectionately called the *motherboard*.

If you enjoy acronyms and abbreviations, you'll be happy to know that CPU stands for *central processing unit,* and RAM stands for *random access memory.*

Computer CPUs come in different speeds, measured in gigahertz (GHz), such as 3 GHz. Sometimes, the CPU speed is mentioned after the processor name, such as Pentium 4 3.06 GHz. In general, the faster the CPU speed, the faster your computer.

The most popular brand of CPU these days is the Intel Core 2 series, which includes the Core 2 Duo and Core 2 Extreme Edition, but you can also find processors from Advanced Micro Devices, which everyone calls *AMD.* AMD's alternative CPUs are usually less expensive and often run as fast and efficiently as the Core 2 series. I discuss the most popular processors and their advantages later in Chapter 4.

For all the details on your motherboard, see Chapter 3. I discuss CPU chips and RAM modules in Chapter 4.

The eye candy

Next on your list are the video card and the monitor. Together, these two parts display everything from your e-mail to your latest financial figures to all those killer Web pages (and don't forget those flashy enemy Quarkians you need to disintegrate).

All video cards have their own special, onboard RAM modules; the more RAM, the more colors and detail the card can display. Today's state-of-the-art video cards also help speed up your computer while it displays 3-D graphics or digital video. The video card performs most of the display work itself, giving your CPU a well-deserved rest. (Note that many of today's motherboards have a built-in video card, so you might not need a separate card if you're not interested in playing the latest games.) Although you can certainly find many manufacturers of video cards, the actual chipsets used in the cards are built by either AMD (originally ATI) and NVIDIA.

Monitors have screen areas that typically range from 15–24 inches (measured diagonally across the case). You can go even larger if you crave that much onscreen space, or you can put two monitors side by side for a larger virtual desktop. Naturally, the larger the monitor, the more expensive. Today's liquid crystal display (LCD) monitors use less electricity and emit very little radiation compared with the "antique" CRT (or tube) monitors used a decade ago.

Chapter 6 contains just about everything that you ever (or never) wanted to know about video cards and PC monitors.

The places for plugs

Your power cord isn't the only connection that you need on the outside of your computer. For example, you also need to attach a mouse and a keyboard (unless you go wireless), and you might also want to access a portable MP3 player, a gamepad, a digital camera, a printer, or a scanner. These days, virtually all the *ports* (the connectors so proudly displayed on the back of your PC) are built into the motherboard, but you can install new ports for external devices separately.

You can point and click with things other than a mouse, such as a trackball, a touchpad, or a drawing tablet. A mouse is practically a requirement for Windows (although you can still navigate strictly from the keyboard if necessary).

Even the traditional keyboard has changed. Ergonomically shaped keyboards are designed to make typing easier on your hands, wrists, and forearms. And both Windows XP and Windows Vista recognize two or three Windows-specific keys to activate the Start button and display menus in an application. (Thank goodness Bill Gates can't add new letters to the alphabet.)

Your computer also needs at least one universal serial bus (USB) port to use many external devices. For example, most digital cameras connect via USB ports, as do virtually all printers on the market today. (Need the complete rundown on ports? Jump to Chapter 5.)

Oh, and don't forget your Ethernet network port. Just about every motherboard available today has a built-in Ethernet card, and some even include built-in wireless network hardware. For all the details on building your own network (or connecting your new PC to an existing network), swing by Chapter 12.

You might also see a FireWire port. Although these are more common on a Mac than on a PC, you could run into them from time to time.

As a quick and handy primer, Figure 1-4 shows what the three ports look like in comparison. Even if the shape throws you, they're typically marked with a symbol.

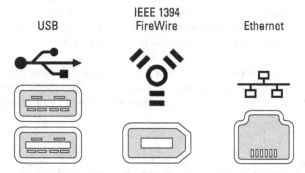

Figure 1-4: Ports ahoy: USB, FireWire, and Ethernet.

The data warehouse

Earlier in this chapter, I mention that your RAM modules act as your computer's memory while the computer is running. However, when you switch off your computer, it forgets the data in RAM, so you need a permanent place to store Uncle Milton's Web page address or your latest stock report. This permanent storage comes in three forms: hard drive, removable storage drive (for example, a DVD/Blu-ray recorder or a USB Flash drive), and (maybe) a floppy disk drive.

Some PCs still include one floppy drive. (You know the one. It still uses a 3½-inch disk that holds a paltry 1.44MB.) If you like, you can skip the installation of a floppy drive, seeing as they are as unnecessary as an appendix to a cutting-edge PC running Windows Vista. (A USB Flash drive is far superior in every way to the venerable floppy.)

You need at least one hard drive. Today's hard drives hold gigabytes (GB) of data (that's 1,000 megabytes), or even a terabyte (TB) of data (that's 1,000 gigabytes). At the time of this writing, typical hard drives range in capacity from 80GB to more than 1TB — and those figures are constantly rising, while costs are constantly dropping. (You've gotta love that free-market competitive model!)

Buy as much data territory as possible. Chapter 7 is your guide to hard drives — and there's even a section on floppy drives.

The bells and whistles

Today's multimedia PCs have almost more extras, add-ons, and fun doodads than any mere mortal can afford (well, except for Bill Gates, that is). If you want to be able to install and run today's software, though, you need at least a DVD-ROM drive. Multimedia applications and games also need a sound card (or built-in audio hardware on your motherboard), along with a set of speakers or headphones. In Chapter 9, I tell you more about DVD drives, and Chapter 10 has the skinny on PC sound cards.

Another common addition to a PC is a printer. If you need the lowdown on today's printer technology, jump to Chapter 13. If a high-speed cable or DSL Internet connection is available in your area, you can jump on the Internet broadbandwagon. (That's so bad it doesn't even qualify as a pun.) Otherwise, you can still use a dial-up modem for connecting your computer to other computers across telephone lines, especially if you're an Internet junkie. (I cover modems in Chapter 11.)

In later chapters, I also discuss advanced stuff for power users, such as network hardware and scanners. You don't have to read those chapters, and you won't be tested on them. But they're there in case you feel adventurous (or you really need them).

Connecting Your Computer Components

You might be wondering how to connect all the various components that make up a computer. "What happens if I connect something wrong? Am I going to light up like a Christmas tree? Will I burn up an expensive part?"

I admit that when I built my first computer in the early 1990s, I had these same concerns. To reassure you, consider these facts:

 Most connectors for computer components are marked to help you plug them in correctly. In fact, some connectors are designed so that you can install them in only one direction, with many using color to indicate where they connect.

✔ **Ruining a computer component simply by plugging it in the wrong way is almost impossible.** At the worst, the device simply won't work. Just connect the component properly, and it should work just fine.

✔ **Although you connect your computer to a wall socket, unless you disassemble the power supply or monitor (which you are *not* going to do), you won't be exposed to dangerous voltage.**

Of course, it pays to take basic precautions — such as unplugging your PC each time you add or remove a component.

Most components within a computer are connected with cables. For example, Figure 1-5 shows a power cable (a perfect illustration of a connector that can only work The Right Way). Of course, I give you instructions on how to make sure that you're connecting cables properly.

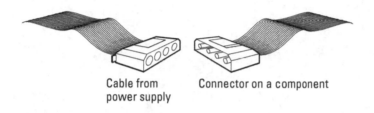

Cable from
power supply

Connector on a component

Figure 1-5: A PC power cable — can you ever have too many?

You'll also be adding *adapter cards*. These circuit boards plug into your computer, much like how a game cartridge plugs into a video game. Adapter cards provide your computer with additional features. For example, you can add a sound card (see Chapter 10) to provide better audio than the built-in sound hardware that came with your motherboard. Adapter cards are arranged in rows at one end of a computer, as shown in Figure 1-6.

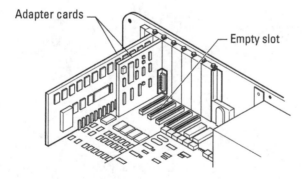

Adapter cards

Empty slot

Figure 1-6: Adapter cards installed in a computer.

Depending on the type of motherboard that you install, you'll use PCI, PCI-Express, or AGP adapter cards. In Chapter 3, I explain how to select the right type of adapter card as well as what all those NASA-inspired abbreviations mean. Make sure that you get the right kind of adapter card because the wrong type of card won't fit.

Chapter 2

What Type of PC Should I Build?

When you walk into an oh-so-hip, retail electronics store these days to buy a PC, the salesperson is supposed to help you choose the right one for your needs. If you build your own computer, however, you need to figure out for yourself what type of computer is best for you. Take it from me — you're likely to come up with something *far* better than many so-called experts who sell computers.

In this chapter, I show you how to figure out what type of computer fits your needs, and I suggest three basic configurations. I tell you what parts you need to buy. I also fill you in on the different sources for buying computer parts. I wrap up this chapter with some thoughts on choosing the best operating system for you.

Interrogating Yourself on Your Computer Needs

If every computer owner had the same needs, only a single model would be available. But because today's computers are used at home and at the office, for business and for pleasure, what works well for one person might not fit for another. Although most computers sold at the time of this writing are Intel-based computers, they're about as different from each other as the 30-odd flavors at your local ice cream parlor — or at least they should be.

To custom-build the computer that you need, you have to design it around who you are and what you plan to do. The easiest way to determine what type of computer you need is to ask yourself a series of questions. For those who enjoy TV shows about lawyers, here's a chance to cross-examine yourself. Grab a pen and a notebook and write your answers to the questions on this checklist:

- ✔ **Primary application:** What will be the main function of your computer? In other words, what will you be doing with it about 75 percent of the time you're using it? Do you plan to use the computer for word processing and drafting, or for Internet e-mail and Web surfing? Are you a big-time game player who likes to play the latest and hottest 3-D game releases? Jot down the main function of your computer under the heading "Primary application."

  If you're not quite sure what your primary application will be, just write a general descriptor, such as *Internet access, home use,* or *very expensive paperweight.*

- ✔ **Secondary application:** What will be the secondary function of your computer? In other words, what will you typically use it for if you're not performing the main function? Do you play games during the evening, or does your family use the computer for educational purposes or those hot eBay bargains? Write the secondary use for your computer under the "Secondary application" heading.

- ✔ **Family computer:** Will children be using your computer for educational games? If so, write that use under the "Family computer" heading.

- ✔ **High-quality video:** Will you be using your computer for heavy-duty graphics, such as the latest cutting-edge 3-D games; professional desktop publishing; home DVD theater; video editing (say, with a program such as Adobe Premiere Pro); or advanced image editing (say, with a program such as Corel Paint Shop Pro Photo X2)? If so, write *required* under the "High-quality video" heading.

- ✔ **Power user:** Are you going to run an entire suite of computer programs, such as Microsoft Office? Will you be running sophisticated, expensive applications, such as Adobe Creative Suite 4? If you're planning on using complex programs, write *yes* under the "Power User" heading.

  Some people just plain want the fastest possible computer. They hate waiting, and they're willing to pay extra to get the Cadillac of computers that's ready for anything. If you fit this description and you don't mind paying extra for many of your computer components, go ahead and write *yes* under the "Power user" heading. You'll spend more money than the typical person because you're buying more powerful and expensive parts, but you'll probably end up with the nicest computer on your block — and your PC will last longer before requiring an upgrade.

- ✔ **One last question:** Where were you on the night of the 15th? (Too bad Perry Mason didn't have a computer to keep track of all those details!)

See, that didn't hurt! You've now eliminated the salesperson and built a list of your computer tasks and activities. From this list, you can build your own description of your computer needs. Pat yourself on the back and pour yourself another cup of coffee or grab another soda. In the following section, you use this list to determine what type of components you need to build into your computer.

Answering Your Computer-Needs Questions

If you were buying a computer through a retail store, the salesperson's next move after inquiring about your computer needs would be to saunter over to one particular model and say something reassuring, like "Based on what you've told me, I'd recommend this as the perfect PC for you. Will that be cash, check, or charge?"

Whoa, Nellie! Chances are that the salesperson's choice *might* meet your needs, but when you're building your own computer, *you* get to decide which parts are more important than others. Are you looking for speed? Storage space? The best sound or the best 3-D graphics?

In this section, you use the description of your computer needs (which you created in the preceding section) to choose between three standard computer designs. I created each of these basic designs to fit a particular type of computer owner. Later in this chapter, you find out whether you need to add special stuff to your base model. (You might recognize this method as the same one used by savvy car buyers to get exactly the car they want at the lowest possible price.)

Look through the descriptions of each of the three designs that follow and then select one that can best serve as the base model for your computer. Of course, you can add or subtract parts, select more expensive parts for any of these designs, or just jot down extra parts that you want to add after your computer is up and running. The following computer designs aren't hard-and-fast specifications, just suggestions.

Design 1: The Jack Benny economy class

One of the reasons why you might want to build a computer is to save money. My first design is tailored for those who want to build a basic, no-frills computer for the least amount of money. (Fans of old-time radio, think about the penny-pinching Jack Benny.) You won't be piloting the latest 3-D shooting game on this computer . . . but then again, life doesn't begin and end with games. However, you can skip only certain pieces of hardware; for example, avoid asking, "Do I really need a keyboard?" (Hey, even a Maxwell needs wheels.)

This type of computer is suitable if the checklist description that you compiled in the preceding section fits this profile:

✔ Both your primary and secondary applications are word processing, home finance, keeping track of household records, Internet e-mail, or similar simple applications that don't require the fastest computer or a large amount of memory.

✔ According to your checklist, you have no entry under "Family computer," you do not require high-quality video, and you are not a power user.

In Table 2-1, I list the appropriate details about the computer components that you need to build this bare-bones, basic computer design. Although it has no bells and only a few whistles, it still qualifies as an entry-level PC. (Find more details on all these components in upcoming chapters.) This PC will run its best using Windows XP Home or Vista Home Basic.

Table 2-1	Requirements for a Bare-Bones Computer
Computer Component	*What to Look For*
Case	Standard "pizza-box," ATX minitower, or desktop model; single fan
CPU/motherboard	Intel Celeron or AMD Sempron; PCI slots
System RAM	512MB
Hard drive	One EIDE drive, 120GB minimum
Optical drive	16x internal DVD drive
Video card	Standard 128MB PCI/AGP adapter
Sound card	PCI audio card
Monitor	17-inch LCD
Ports	At least four USB 2.0 ports
Input	Standard keyboard; mouse

Design 2: The Cunningham family edition

Remember Richie Cunningham and his family from *Happy Days*? If home computers had been around in the 1950s, Richie and crew would have used this standard edition design. (Think of this model as the family sedan.) It's typical in every way, including the moderate amount of money that you'll spend building it. This computer can handle image editing and digital media without blinking, as well as most games.

This type of computer is suitable if your checklist description fits this profile:

✔ Your primary application involves browsing the Web, using Internet e-mail, working with more advanced productivity programs (such as spreadsheets and scheduling applications), using simple desktop-publishing software, or basic image editing with a program like Photoshop Elements.

✔ Your secondary application involves computer games or educational software.

✔ You don't require high-quality video, and you're not a power user.

Table 2-2 lists the requirements for the most important parts that you need for building this midrange design.

Table 2-2	Requirements for a Middle-Range Computer
Computer Component	*What to Look For*
Case	ATX minitower model; dual fan
CPU/motherboard	Intel Core 2 Duo or AMD 64 Athlon X2; PCI and PCI-Express slots
System RAM	1GB
Hard drive	One EIDE or SATA drive, 240GB minimum
Optical drive	16x internal DVD recorder
Modem	56 Kbps v.90 internal data/fax, cable/DSL modem for broadband
Video card	Standard 256MB PCI-Express 3-D video adapter with NVIDIA or ATI graphics chipset
Sound card	PCI audio card with Surround Sound
Monitor	19-inch LCD
Ports	Four USB 2.0 ports, digital media card reader, and one FireWire port
Input	Standard keyboard; mouse

Design 3: The Wayne Manor Batcomputer

"Holy microchips, Batman!" Design 3 is the power user's dream — everything is first class. This system can handle even the toughest jobs: creating 3-D artwork, putting games such as Spore through their paces, creating videos and editing images with Adobe Photoshop CS4. The Batcomputer that you build can be as good as any top-of-the-line computer that you can buy at That Big Store That Sells PCs — except, of course, that you'll spend hundreds of dollars less.

This type of computer is suitable if your checklist description fits this profile:

✔ Your primary application involves advanced or heavy computational work, such as computer-aided drafting, video editing, or 3-D animation. If your primary application is playing the latest and greatest computer games in all their glory, you should consider the Batcomputer, too.

✔ According to your checklist, you require high-quality video, and you are a power user.

✔ You simply want the best possible computer, which will last the longest time before it requires upgrading.

Table 2-3 lists the requirements for the most important components that you need for this design.

Table 2-3	Requirements for a Top-of-the-Line Computer
Computer Component	*What to Look For*
Case	Full-tower model; dual or triple fan
CPU/motherboard	The fastest doggone Core 2 Extreme Edition or Athlon Phenom processor available; PCI and PCI-Express slots
System RAM	2GB to 4GB
Hard drive	One SATA drive, 500GB minimum
Optical Drive	16x dual-layer Blu-ray/DVD recorder
Floppy drive	One 3½-inch, 1.44MB disk drive
Modem	Cable/DSL modem for broadband
Video card	PCI-Express 3-D adapter, 512MB minimum of video memory; NVIDIA or ATI graphics chipset with TV tuner
Sound card	PCI audio card with Surround Sound, 3-D positional sound, hardware MP3 encoding
Monitor	21-inch widescreen LCD display
Ports	Four to six USB ports, one FireWire port, digital media card reader, and one eSATA port
Input	Ergonomic keyboard with extra Windows keys, trackball

You might also need a secondary 12 volt, 4-pin connector to connect the power supply and motherboard to draw enough power for additional lights, fans, and some high-end video cards. After you select the best base-model computer that meets your needs, you're ready to identify any special add-ons (or, in the language of the techno-wizards, *peripherals*) you need to use with your applications.

If you're really serious about your graphics, you'll need to know about the GPU, or graphics processing unit. The minimum GPU speed (called the *core clock* in technospeak) I recommend for a midrange PC is about 500 MHz, with the high-end gaming cards turning in over 750 MHz. See Chapter 14 for more.

Getting Your Hands on the Special Stuff

If you plan to use your new computer almost exclusively for a particular purpose (composing music, or drafting, for example), you might already know what special stuff you need. In case you're a newcomer to your particular application, however, the following sections outline some of the special stuff that you might need.

Drafting, graphics, and pretty pictures

If you're an artist or you're interested in computer graphics, you might want to get your hands on some of the equipment in this list. The first two are peripherals, and the second two are upgrades to standard components:

✔ **Drawing tablet:** This computer peripheral is something like an electronic piece of paper. (Now there's a real technological advancement, right?) You can draw on the surface of the tablet, as shown in Figure 2-1, which in turn sends your drawing directly to the screen. Many freehand artists and drafting gurus prefer drawing with natural movements of the hand rather than trying to draw a line by using a mouse cursor. (For more information on the drawing tablet, jump to Chapter 5.) The drawing tablet is definitely a power user peripheral (usually used by professionals), and would be most likely found on a top-of-the-line system that features a larger monitor and plenty of system RAM.

✔ **Scanner:** A scanner (as shown in Figure 2-2) enables you to "read" pictures from printed material directly into a graphics program. You can also use a scanner to read (or *acquire*) text from a magazine article or book directly into your word processing program. Some scanners use a feature named OCR — an abbreviation that's actually easier to use than the full phrase, *optical character recognition*. OCR allows you to convert scanned text into editable text that you can modify in a word processor. (For all the details on scanner technology, head to Chapter 13.) Your scanner will demand a spacious hard drive of at least 120GB (the higher the resolution, the larger the image file). And the more system RAM you add to your machine, the faster your image-editing software will perform.

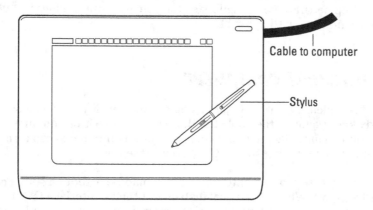

Cable to computer

Stylus

Figure 2-1: A drawing tablet — the tool of choice for graphic artists (and techno-nerds without scratch paper).

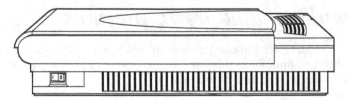

Figure 2-2: A flatbed scanner is great for acquiring graphics and text.

Home-office and small-business stuff

Are you going to get all businesslike on me? No problem — a computer can help you organize a home office so that you can find the right information when you need it. (Imagine that!) Consider these extras as company money well spent:

- ✔ **Printer:** Most home office computers need an inkjet or a laser printer. Both these printers have distinct advantages, and I explain the differences in detail in Chapter 13.

- ✔ **Scanner:** If you build your PC with a data/fax modem, you might consider adding a scanner. Besides the advantages that I mention in the preceding section, a scanner provides the "missing link" for your modem's fax capabilities. Without a scanner, you can fax only electronic documents that you create on your computer: You're stuck if you want to fax something from a paper copy. With a scanner, however, you can scan in the pages from your hard copy and then fax the images.

- ✔ **Data/fax/voice modem:** Speaking of modems, how would you like your computer to answer the phone for you? If you pick up a data/fax/voice modem, you can set up separate voice mailboxes for you and your business. I talk more about modems in Chapter 11.

Mozart's musical computer

Too bad Wolfgang Amadeus never got to jam using a computer. If you're a musician, you might already know some of the cool stuff that you can do with a computer. Whether or not you're a musician, the following computer components can turn your PC into a miniature recording studio. Check out these toys:

- ✔ **MIDI:** No self-respecting computer musician would be without a sound card with MIDI support. With the Musical Instrument Digital Interface (MIDI) standard, you can play music directly into the computer from your instrument and then edit the music. Or your computer can take control of a MIDI-capable instrument that you've connected to the MIDI port and play it automatically. (For the complete description of MIDI, visit Chapter 10.)

- ✔ **MP3:** Are you interested in riding the recent wave of MP3 popularity? These digital music files can be downloaded from the Internet and stored on your computer's hard drive, yet they sound exactly like you're listening to an audio CD. You can also transfer these files to one of the new generation of handheld MP3 personal players (like my favorite, the iPod from Apple) and listen while you're walking or working. (I serve up the MP3 details in Chapter 10.)

✔ **CDs:** Musicians and audiophiles can burn MP3 files to create custom audio CDs — any DVD recorder can do the trick — and your home-brewed CDs can sound as good as the music CDs you buy in a store. (For all the details on DVD drives, skip to Chapter 9.)

The ultimate bad-guy blasting box

Now, you might have to pretend with your friends and family, but you can relax around here: I know the *real* reason why you need a computer. If you haven't played some of today's best action, strategy, and simulation computer games, you're missing out on the chance to fly an Apache helicopter, play 18 holes with Arnold Palmer, or take over the entire galaxy, planet by planet!

Although I go into heavy-duty detail on building a game machine in Chapter 14, here's a quick introduction to the special stuff that you need to create your ultimate game machine:

✔ **Controller:** When you mention that you're ready to play games, most people think of a computer joystick (or its close relative, the PC gamepad) first. The traditional favorite for flight games, joysticks come in a wide range of styles: Some have two buttons and sell for less than $10, and others have 20 buttons that are programmable for every game and sell for more than $100. Joysticks aren't the only controller choice, though. You can find steering wheels and pedals for car racing, video-game-style gamepads, and even 3-D controllers for games such as Red Alert 3 and Frontlines.

If you're willing to spend the extra cash, you can even get a *force feedback* controller that shakes and rumbles when your F-16 (or your medieval warrior) gets hit.

✔ **3-D video card:** If you prefer 3-D games, you need an advanced 3-D video card that can help speed up the action. Today's top 3-D video cards use a PCI-Express slot. (Chapter 6 includes more info about video cards.)

✔ **Audiophile sound card:** A great game machine needs the same high-quality sound card demanded by computer musicians. Most games released these days have spectacular soundtracks, and the Dolby Digital sound from a good sound card enhances gameplay. Some games even use a technique called *stereo positioning* (which the more expensive sound cards can take advantage of). If a racecar passes you on the right, for example, you hear the sound of its engine through your right speaker. (If you're interested in sound cards, check out Chapter 10.)

✔ **Subwoofer speaker:** Speaking of speakers, if you want to feel like you're inside your game, consider a more expensive PC speaker system that includes a subwoofer. Audiophiles know that a *subwoofer* speaker provides the richest, deepest bass (even down to subsonics that you can't actually hear), and game players enjoy the rumble that it adds to special effects such as laser blasts, machine guns, and afterburners. (Chapter 10 has more details on speaker systems and subwoofers.)

Picking Up the Parts

"Okay, Mark, now I know what parts I need, but where am I going to find them?" As little as 15 years ago, you would have had a hard time locating all the individual components for a computer. But now that a personal computer has practically become a household necessity (and more people are building their own computers), you have several sources for the parts that you need.

Only buy brand-new components for your computer whenever possible. Why? Some components in a computer (for example, the hard drives, which are complex and have a large number of moving parts) can fail after a few years of use. In addition, prices for the fastest and most powerful components are constantly dropping. (Don't worry: The components you choose will work together fine, without the device conflicts many PC owners encountered in the days of Windows 98.)

In this section, I cover several likely sources for the components you need.

Researching before you buy

From time to time during your computer shopping, you might feel as though you're alone and that there's no one to help you decide between brands or make decisions on features. Not so! ("Everybody's a critic," as they say in show business.) If you feel that you need more information before deciding on parts to buy, consider these sources:

- ✔ **Computer magazines:** You need look no further than your local newsstand to find a half-dozen excellent magazines that specialize in product reviews, tips and tricks for the novice computer owner, and coverage of the newest and hottest computer technology. I recommend *PC Magazine* and *Maximum PC* for their hardware reviews.

Some magazines hand out awards for the hardware and software that they rate most highly. If the computer component that you're considering carries two or three of these awards on its box, you probably have a winner. For example, I personally rate the *PC Magazine* Editor's Choice Award as an indicator of a high-quality product.

- ✔ **The Web:** Most publishers of computer magazines also offer online versions of their printed material, and you can search through an entire site for product information, reviews, and product comparisons. Some good examples are PC Magazine (at www.pcmag.com), PC World (www.pcworld.com), Tom's Hardware (www.tomshardware.com), IDG.net (www.idg.net), ZDNet (www.zdnet.com), and other sites, such as CNET.com (www.cnet.com) and Pricewatch (www.pricewatch.com). Many online stores also offer reviews and ratings submitted by customers, like Newegg (www.newegg.com).

- ✔ **Internet newsgroups:** Although you need an Internet connection to read messages, newsgroups such as alt.comp.hardware.homebuilt and comp.hardware are chock-full of interesting reviews, hints, and tips. If you need to ask something specific, you can simply post a message to the newsgroup and receive an answer by e-mail or in a reply posting on the newsgroup. Visit Google Groups at `http://groups.google.com` to read these newsgroups using your Web browser.

✔ **Computer user groups:** Computer user groups come in handy! You'll likely find someone who has already traveled down the same road and bought a similar computer component. You can learn from that person's mistakes or success without spending a dollar.

I live for mail order

What's that you say, Bunkie? You need to buy some new parts, like a motherboard, hard drive, and video card? You say that you want to save money and don't want to pay the inflated prices at your local Maze O' Wires computer store? Or perhaps you live in a small town without a local computer store? Never fear — use mail order, and let the postal service (or, more likely, FedEx or UPS) leap to the rescue.

When you order parts from a reputable mail-order company, you can choose from a huge selection of computer parts, and you *always* save money over buying them from a retail computer store. Depending on where you live, you might also save money by avoiding local sales tax on your purchase.

If you've never ordered parts through the mail and you're not sure whether you're working with a reputable company, keep these guidelines in mind:

✔ **Check the specs.** Ask the salesperson for a detailed description of the part before you complete the order, just to make certain that you're buying the right item. Feel free to ask questions — for example, "Is that an AGP or a PCI video card?" If you like things in writing, ask the salesperson to mail or fax you the specifications and the price.

✔ **Research refunds.** Make sure that the company allows you to return a part for a full refund if it doesn't turn out to be what you need. If you return a component, some companies charge you a *restocking fee,* which is basically a charge that you pay the company for the hard work involved in sticking a returned box back on a shelf. (I wish I had a piece of *that* action!)

✔ **Choose to charge.** Personally, I always use a credit card, which provides me with additional leverage if there's a problem. Today's online Web stores are typically secure and easy to use.

✔ **Buy only what you want.** If you can't get exactly the part that you need from one company, you can *always* get it elsewhere. Beware of salespeople and online stores that tell you that they're out of the particular part that you're looking for but can sell you a better model of the same part for a higher price.

✔ **Keep your shipment grounded.** Some companies tack on an additional shipment charge, or they automatically charge you for next-day shipment unless you request regular shipment. Unless you really *do* need that part tomorrow, you can probably save ten dollars or more by choosing regular ground shipment.

Get the full warranty for each part

Even if you find a retail PC at the price that you want that includes many of the brand-name parts that you're looking for, beware the fine print when it comes to warranties. You're not necessarily receiving the full manufacturer's warranty on each component. Instead, brand-name components on many retail computers are covered by the computer company's warranty (typically one year for both parts and labor). Say your retail PC machine has a name-brand hard drive that breaks after two years. Even though that hard drive technically has a three-year warranty — if you buy it separately, that is — you might not be able to return it to the manufacturer for service or replacement when it comes as part of a package deal.

When you buy your own components and build your own PC, though, you're assured that each component is covered for the full length of the hardware manufacturer's warranty.

After you build your first computer, you'll develop a good relationship with at least one or two mail-order companies. I have several favorite companies, each of which is my first stop for a particular type of part. (It's always a good idea to find a monitor locally, though, because you can evaluate it with your own eyes and you won't pay a fortune on shipping.) For an updated list of my favorites in the world of mail-order companies, visit my Web site, MLC Books Online, at www.mlcbooks.com.

Ordering parts online

If you have access to the Internet, you can travel through the limitless world of cyberspace looking for computer parts.

If you need a start in online shopping, visit three of my favorite online computer stores: the Shopper.com site (www.computershopper.com), Newegg (www.newegg.com), and Price Watch (www.pricewatch.com).

All three of these Web sites enable you to search for computer goodies from many different manufacturers, and each offers specials on overstocked parts. You can display side-by-side comparison charts of different parts so that you can compare features and performance online. Then check for the site with the current lowest price — without leaving the comfort of that swivel chair you bought for the computer room.

Most of these Web sites accept only credit cards, although they offer secure connections if you're using Mozilla Firefox or Microsoft Internet Explorer — you can tell your connection is secure if a padlock icon appears in the browser's status line (as shown in Figure 2-3). The guidelines that I mention for mail-order purchases apply to online ordering, too.

Finding bargains in so-called obsolete computers

Most computers now being replaced or scrapped work just fine. For most of us, a computer generally doesn't become obsolete until it no longer has the performance to run the programs that you want to use. I have several friends who are still quite pleased with their Pentium-4-based computers — they're not technical wizards, and they don't use their computers very often.

You won't find any single answer to why a computer is deemed obsolete, but the answer doesn't matter all that much. The important point is that lots of people upgrade their computers, which gives you a great opportunity to scavenge perfectly functional, used equipment for your own computer. (Of course, if you're building a new system designed for high-performance applications, you should avoid any scavenged parts that would slow down the performance of your new PC. In that case, I'd recommend re-using only keyboards, pointing devices, and internal modems for parts.)

Look at the classified ads in your local newspaper (or check some of the resources mentioned in the section "Picking Up the Parts," elsewhere in this chapter). You're likely to find hundreds of people looking to unload their computer equipment — often at bargain-basement prices.

The lock icon indicates a secure Web site.

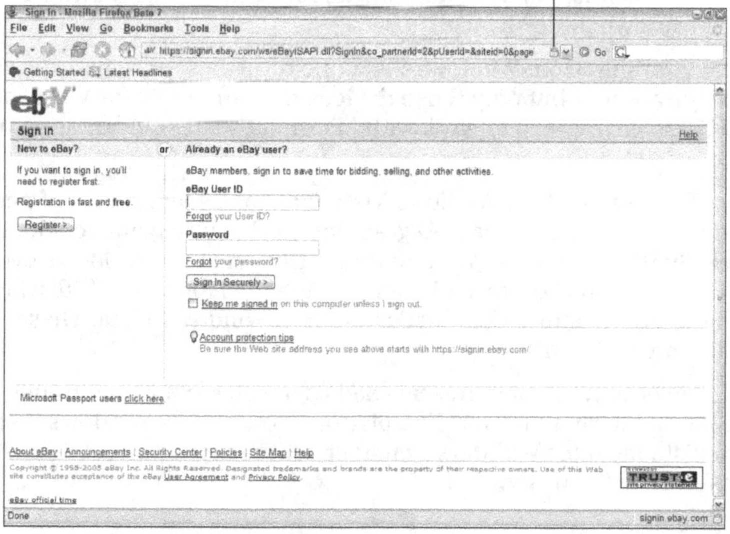

Figure 2-3: A secure Web site in Firefox.

Choosing an Operating System

You might be asking yourself, "Why don't I just run what everyone else runs?" True, today's common PC operating system of choice is Windows Vista, and it does a great job for many of the PCs around the world. But what if your needs are different?

That's why you need to become your own consultant to choose between Windows Vista and Windows XP. Heck, if you want to make things as authentic as possible, you can even charge yourself a tremendous amount of money. (Just don't try claiming it on your taxes.)

Consider these points when you're choosing an operating system:

- ✔ **Convenience:** Vista's the winner here, hands down. Microsoft has gone to a lot of trouble to make all sorts of actions as easy as possible in Vista, from burning a DVD to creating a wireless network. However, all that convenience requires at least 3GB of RAM and a Vista-capable video card to run smoothly!

- ✔ **Speed:** Are you looking for the fastest-performing operating system? If so, score one point for the older 32- and 64-bit operating systems: Windows XP and XP x64. These platforms load programs and data faster because they don't include many of the more graphics-intensive features of Windows Vista. (In other words, Vista's requirements for cutting-edge hardware may actually slow down performance.)

- ✔ **Hardware configuration:** Windows Vista offers the best automatic hardware configuration — but only those devices that are ready for Vista "out-of-the-box" are guaranteed to work with Microsoft's latest incarnation of Windows.

- ✔ **Graphics:** The eye candy in Windows Vista may take every ounce of performance out of that new super 3-D graphics card you're going to add, but Vista is easily the most attractive and futuristic version of Windows ever produced. (Note that the latest 3-D games might call for *DirectX 10,* which is the gaming graphics subsystem that's built into Windows Vista. These games run only on Vista.)

- ✔ **Security:** Will your new computer be used as a Web server, an intranet machine, or an Internet firewall? The platform to watch is Windows Vista. Windows Vista includes Windows Defender, which helps protect against malicious software and spyware.

Here's a checklist of preparations that should make your installation run more smoothly, no matter which platform you choose:

- ✔ **Back up your hard drive.** If you've saved any data or created any documents that you'd hate to lose, back up your computer completely before installing a new operating system. You can back up your system to DVD, or even offsite using a broadband (DSL or cable modem) connection and a subscription to an online backup service.

- ✔ **Read the installation instructions.** Sure, Windows Vista is designed to be installed by a kindergarten kid who's half asleep, but that doesn't excuse you from at least scanning the installation instructions.

✔ **Keep your driver disks handy.** Although you've installed parts under your previous operating system, you might need the specific drivers that came with your parts for your new operating system.

✔ **Impose on a friend.** Do you have a computer guru for a friend or a relative? Enlist an expert's help if you need it, especially if that person runs the same operating system that you're installing.

✔ **Yell for the cavalry.** What do you do if something goes horribly wrong and you can't find anything about it in the installation guide? Don't panic! Keep the tech support number for the operating system close at hand; it should be located in the manual or the additional literature that accompanied your installation discs.

Introducing Colossus

As I note in the Introduction, I recommend a number of specific components by brand and model number throughout this book. If I were building my own PC at the time of this writing, I'd pick these parts, and I'll always let you know why I chose them. (In fact, you can see me build this beast from start to finish on the DVD in the back of this book.)

Working with what I covered in this chapter, I can make two decisions about Colossus already:

✔ **I'll build a PC based on Design 3** (the Wayne Manor Batcomputer). Colossus will be the ultimate top-of-the-line PC, ready for the latest games, and video and image editing. The components I'm picking will cost more, but they'll deliver the best performance.

✔ **I'll use Windows Vista for my operating system (OS).** Vista offers the best compatibility with the cutting-edge components I'm choosing. (Oh, and my family would look forward to the graphics wonderland that is Vista.) 'Nuff said.

Part II
Assembling the Basics

The 5th Wave   By Rich Tennant

Okay, here's your problem. You've got warts on your motherboard.

In this part . . .

The real fun commences when you build a bare-bones PC from the motherboard up. You install the required stuff that every computer needs, such as RAM modules, a CPU, a hard drive, and a video card. I even have a chapter on choosing and installing an operating system. If that sounds a little frightening, don't worry; I explain each stage in detail, and each chapter ends with a general set of step-by-step installation instructions that gives you a good idea of what you can expect. After you're finished with this part, you'll be able to boot your new computer. *Remember:* All you need is a screwdriver!

Chapter 3

Building the Foundation: The Case and Motherboard

Topics and tasks in this chapter

- ✔ Choosing a case
- ✔ Selecting a motherboard
- ✔ Guarding against static
- ✔ Installing your motherboard
- ✔ Connecting the power supply
- ✔ Hooking up lights and buttons

You don't have to be an architect or a construction foreman to know that a building is only as good as its foundation. Build a skyscraper on sand, and it doesn't matter how well you wallpaper the bathrooms or how fast the elevators run. Eventually, a building with a weak foundation will fall, and it's certain to take everything with it.

In this chapter, you discover the various components that are common to all computer cases. I show you how to construct a sturdy foundation for your computer by selecting the right size and type of computer case, which provides the framework that houses the internal computer components. I introduce you to the geography of your motherboard; then you find out how to install the motherboard and connect it to the computer's power supply.

In later chapters, you continue your assembly project by finding out how to add components, such as a hard drive and a DVD recorder, to this chassis.

Choosing the Right Case

Selecting the proper case for your computer is very important, and here are the reasons why:

- ✔ **Your computer needs room to grow.** If you're a power user, you need room to expand. (A *power user* is someone with considerable computer experience or someone who needs a powerful computer for advanced applications; see Chapter 2 for more details.) Adding devices and other toys can easily lead you to outgrow a standard desktop case. Believe me, it's a royal pain to upgrade to a larger case because you basically have to disassemble your entire computer, remove the motherboard and other components, and move them all to a larger case. Keep this upgrade possibility in mind when you select your case and think about your future needs.

- ✔ **You need room on your desk.** If your desktop space is limited (by either the size of your desk or your work habits), you can save yourself some valuable real estate by selecting a tower (vertical) case and placing it under your desk. Or, you could choose a space-saver case.

Most cases have at least one or two rectangular cutouts in front of empty drive bays. You can use these open bays to hold components that need access to the outside world, such as a DVD drive or a removable cartridge drive. (After all, it's a little hard to load a DVD into a drive if it's buried inside the case.) When an open bay is empty, it's covered with a rectangular plastic piece that blends in with the outside of the case. Other drive bays remain hidden inside the case, with no access to the outside; these bays are usually reserved for additional hard drives, which don't need to be handled during routine use.

Virtually all cases also come with a single fan for cooling the components, but a case can also be designed to maximize airflow, with cutouts for additional fans, as well as more vents for moving more air through the case.

If coordinating your computer with your room is important, I bet those cases in designer colors and shapes are calling your name. Before you pick up an aerodynamic case in canary yellow or neon green, keep in mind that you'll probably find it difficult to find other parts in such exotic colors later on. And, exotic colors usually mean higher prices. Most computer components with external faceplates — such as DVD drives — come in only off-white and black, which tend to stand out like a sore thumb in an orange case. That's why the main colors for computer cases are still off-white and black, and I recommend that you stick with them unless you want a computer that looks like you assembled it at the junkyard.

If you must have a case in an exotic color, consider one with a hinged door that covers the drive bays — you can close the door when you're not loading a CD or DVD disc into your off-white DVD drive, and no one can tell that you're (gasp!) fashion-impaired.

Most new cases come with the mounting hardware necessary to attach your motherboard although it never hurts to ask when you order your case. You also need screws and plastic spacers, and they should be included with either the case or the motherboard. (You can also buy these screws and spacers at most larger electronics stores.)

You can choose from three standard types of cases: pizza- and shoe-box, desktop, and tower. You can compare their forms and sizes in Figure 3-1. Each has its merits as well as different amounts of elbow room for upgrading.

Space-saver cases: Pizza box and shoe box

Figure 3-2 illustrates a *pizza-box case,* which is very squat and thin. (And before you ask, it's not made of cardboard, nor does it contain Italian deliciousness inside. Sigh. I get that one all the time.) This case has only one or two open drive bays. Although you might not be able to add any adapter cards, this case does take up the smallest amount of space of any standard computer case. In fact, your friends might speculate that your svelte computer has been working out nights at the gym.

Pizza-box cases are typically used for network workstations or as simple terminals, so I don't recommend that you buy one of these for your home computer. However, if you're building an economy-class machine and want to save space as well as cash, the pizza-box case might be fine for your needs. (See Chapter 2 for details about what qualifies as an economy-class machine.)

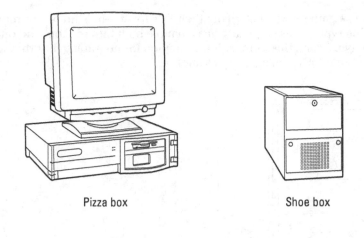

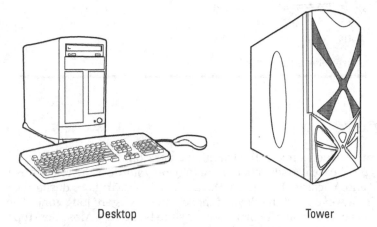

Figure 3-1: Choose your form to fit your needs.

Pizza-box cases don't offer much room for later upgrades.

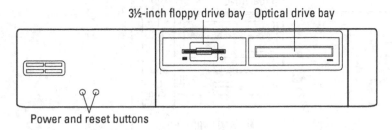

Figure 3-2: A slim and trim pizza-box case.

A derivative of the pizza-box case is the *shoe-box case,* which is roughly square and a little taller than a real-life shoe box. (*Shuttle box* is another name for a shoe-box case.) You can see its unique and compact design in Figure 3-3. These cases are favored by hard-core gamers who like to lug their PCs to a friend's house for multi-player gaming. This type of case typically has a handle built into the top, and offers only one or two bays. Again, this form isn't a champion for upgrading, but they are easily carried from one LAN gaming party to another.

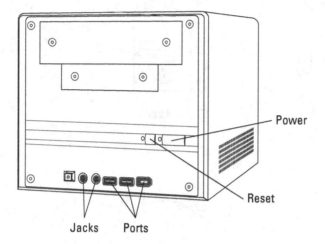

Figure 3-3: Shoe-box cases offer great portability.

Desktop case

The next case in our fashion show is the traditional desktop case, as shown in Figure 3-4. This type of case usually sits horizontally on your desk, just like those ponderous PC XT and AT cases did back in the ancient 1980s. Today's desktop case has gone on a diet, however, and the days of those behemoths are long gone. The desktop case isn't as compact as the pizza-box or shoe-box cases. Most desktop cases can switch between horizontal mode and vertical mode, depending on the orientation that you prefer.

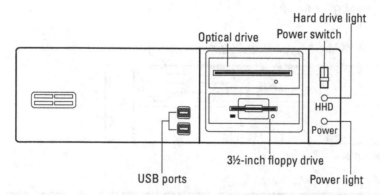

Figure 3-4: The standard desktop case: a middle-class computer castle.

The desktop case usually provides two or three open drive bays on the front, with one or two hidden bays. This case typically has room for six or seven adapter cards in the back, with at least two USB connectors on the front of the case. This setup is usually par for the course for a home computer. Unless you're a power user, the desktop case is your case of choice.

Tower case

For the techno-nerd or power user who has everything, we have the Ferrari of cases — the brawny tower case, which sits vertically like an old mainframe computer. As shown in Figure 3-5, many tower cases have four, or even five, open drive bays. If you're planning on stuffing your computer full of extras, this is the case for you. Like the desktop case, the tower case has room for a standard six or seven adapter cards in back. You're also likely to find at least two USB connectors on the front of the case. Because of the weight and size of a fully outfitted tower case, it is designed to sit upright on the floor under your desk, where you can comfortably reach all the buttons and the optical drive. The tower case is a favorite for gamers, which you can read about in Chapter 14.

Many manufacturers also produce a minitower case, which also sits vertically like a tower case but is designed to fit comfortably next to the monitor on top of your desk. An average minitower case has a drive bay capacity equal to that of a standard desktop case.

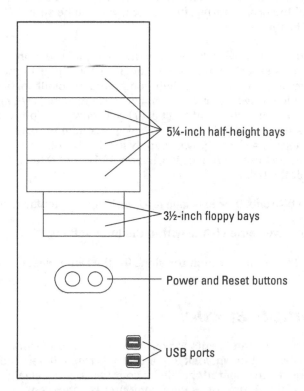

Figure 3-5: The professional wrestler of computer cases: the tower case.

Other Case Considerations

There are a few other case features to consider besides size and shape. From the fans that'll keep your machine cool to the lights that'll tell you what your PC's doing, keep these features in mind when deciding on your style of case.

Feeding power to your computer

Your new computer will be hungry for power, and the power supply takes care of that need by reducing the voltage from your wall socket to something more easily handled by your computer. The power supply then pumps the juice to the computer's components through a number of individual power cables.

While I'm on the subject of power supplies, don't forget that you shouldn't connect your chassis to AC power until Chapter 4, so put that cable away!

These cables end in a special connector that you can insert in only one direction, so it's well-nigh impossible to make a mistake and damage a hard drive or DVD drive because of an electrical short caused by a reversed connection. An ATX (Advanced Technology Extended) motherboard has only one power connector.

Most cases are now sold with the power supply already installed (yea!). A preinstalled power supply not only eliminates a step in building your PC but also ensures that you get a power supply of the proper rating. In addition, you can be sure that all the holes for the switches and cables match up.

The more powerful the CPU, the more power it generally draws — and the more powerful the case fan and the processor fan must be to cool it. (I cover fans in the following section.) Also, power users tend to stuff their computers full of all sorts of neat hardware toys, each of which draws its own power. For these reasons, I *strongly* suggest that you invest in a case that includes at least a 400-watt power supply, especially if you're going to add a slew of internal extras, such as a second hard drive. (In fact, AMD recommends at least a 400-watt power supply for the Athlon 64 series of CPUs. You can read all about processor choices in Chapter 4.) For anything less, 300-watt power supplies will fit the bill.

Never open a power supply to try to fix it or massage it to work in a particular case.

Live household voltage is not a welcome visitor within the human body.™

Leave a malfunctioning or broken computer monitor alone for the same reason.

Keeping your computer cool

Because all the various devices and components in your computer produce lots of heat, your computer can actually shut down, lock up, or return errors if it gets too hot. Extended overheating reduces the operational life of your parts — especially your CPU — and leads to early failure. How does your computer keep its cool through this heat wave?

The answer is nothing elaborate or high-tech. In fact, it's just a fan! Your computer's power supply uses a fan to continually circulate air through the inside of the case. Pizza-box cases and standard-size desktop cases are small enough to require only one fan. However, if you're thinking of buying a tower case and your computer will use the latest Intel or AMD processor, I highly recommend that you buy a case with at least dual fans. Multiple fans — I've seen uber-PCs with *four* fans onboard — are a definite requirement if this type of computer is going to stay on for many hours at a time or if it's jammed full of parts and devices. Ball-bearing fans are preferred because they last longer.

CPU chips now run so hot that they come equipped with their own dedicated fan, which sits on top of or beside the processor. This fan might be connected to one of the power cables leading to the power supply, or it might be connected to a special fan plug on the motherboard itself. If a CPU overheats, it generally locks up your computer or returns some strange results in your programs — and it will more than likely be permanently damaged. (Most motherboards now come with a CPU thermal-sensing feature that you can set in your PC's BIOS. If your CPU gets too hot, your system automatically shuts down. Check your motherboard manual for the settings you should choose to activate this shut-down feature.)

After your computer is running, place it where the fan exhaust isn't blocked by a wall or furniture. An open location provides better airflow.

Buttons, lights, and other foolishness

All cases today have a power light and a hard drive activity light. Your motherboard runs these components. Some new cases also feature a *digital readout* of the computer's internal temperature (or, in some cases, the temperature of the CPU itself). If you're building a cutting-edge PC with a super-fast processor and plenty of internal devices, I heartily recommend one of these cases, which allows you to monitor your PC's cooling (and help prevent the China Syndrome from occurring on your motherboard).

Another favorite case *modding* (slang for modification) is the addition of neon lights inside your case that look simply delicious in low light. Naturally, you'll need a case with transparent Plexiglas panels. (Remember the movie *The Fast and the Furious*?) I'm too old to need decals, special paint jobs, or neon finery on a case, but . . . kids today. Anyway, these lights typically need a standard internal power connector, so don't forget to reserve one if you're doing The Neon Thing. (More on modding in Chapter 14.)

Your case should also include a simple speaker, which looks just like the speaker in an inexpensive transistor radio. Although you'll definitely want a sound card and external speakers to take full advantage of today's software (see Chapter 10 for more about high-end sound), this little internal speaker still performs an important task: If something is wrong when you start your computer, the speaker alerts you with a number of beeps. (Chapter 4 explains what those beeps are telling you.)

Other than these standard items, your case can be as plain or as elegantly sculpted as you want. Naturally, designer cases from Gucci cost more, but you can subtly boast about your computer's good taste at parties, editors will want your picture in their fashion magazines, and you could become one of the "in crowd." It could happen.

Dust busting!

A computer needs at least one internal fan to keep its sensitive electronics cool. This circulating air has a drawback, though: All the internal parts within your new computer get dusty over time. *Hint:* Open your computer case every year or so to blow the dust off your motherboard, power supply, and all the various devices that you installed. Accumulated dust can act like an insulating blanket, causing chips and electrical parts to overheat. Consider it an anniversary of sorts. (Boy, I need to step away from the keyboard for a day or two.)

Before you open your case to upgrade or clear off the dust, head to your local computer store or photography shop and grab some *canned air* — one of those spray cans that shoots a compressed stream of air for dusting off cameras and computer parts. Techno-types swear by 'em. Take particular care when dusting off your motherboard and the fan intake on your power supply (which is likely to be filthy). Canned air is also handy for cleaning keyboards and adapter cards. Help out your planet by making sure that you choose a brand that doesn't deplete the ozone layer, and don't make the mistake of buying one of those air horns that the football types use at the game. (Take my word for it: They don't work, and they annoy the neighbors.)

Your Motherboard Is Your Best Friend

The *motherboard* holds most of the electronics and circuits that your computer needs to follow your orders. Depending on the type of processor that you've chosen, the top of your motherboard has a big square or slot socket to hold your computer's CPU chip and several rows of small slots to hold your RAM (memory) modules (as shown in Figure 3-6).

Fifteen years ago, buying a motherboard by itself was much more difficult. However, with the constant acceleration of CPU speeds and the requirements of today's software, folks in the mall are selling motherboards rather than ice cream. Some companies that advertise in *Computer Shopper* magazine or operate Web-based parts stores sell nothing but motherboards. And you can generally buy a bare motherboard at your local computer store if it has a repair shop.

Motherboard sizes

Today's motherboards follow the ATX standard size guidelines. You don't want a Baby AT or an AT motherboard; those are antiques now. Any new PC you're building should use an ATX motherboard and case (see Figure 3-7).

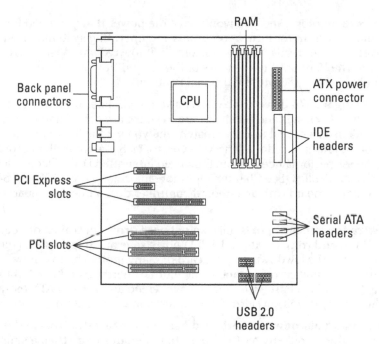

Figure 3-6: A typical motherboard and her parts.

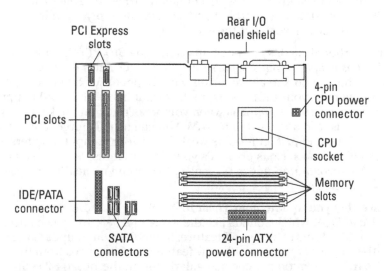

Figure 3-7: An ATX motherboard.

Motherboard features

While you're shopping for a motherboard, keep these guidelines in mind:

- ✔ **Stick with a minimum of a Core 2 Duo or an Athlon 64 X2.** You might have a strong temptation to jump on a great price for an older Pentium 4 motherboard. No matter what the processor speed, however, you'll be buying yesterday's technology, and you won't have the power that you need for running many current (or future) programs and operating systems. Even if the advertisement reads "A Good Pick for Windows XP and Vista," say good-bye to the Pentium 4 (as readers of the first edition of this book said good-bye to the 486 and the original Pentium).

✔ **Consider using a SATA drive controller.** As you might infer from the name, the *drive controller* sends and receives data to your hard drives and optical drive. (Think of a referee at a soccer match, and you get the idea.) Power users favor an onboard serial ATA (SATA) controller. SATA controllers provide you with faster performance than an Enhanced Integrated Drive Electronics (EIDE) drive controller. (See Chapter 7 for more information on EIDE and SATA drives.) A motherboard with an onboard controller doesn't need a separate controller.

✔ **Spend extra for onboard ports.** Like an onboard drive controller, onboard USB, FireWire, and eSATA (external SATA) ports save an adapter slot. (Jump to Chapter 5 for the lowdown on port cards.) Many motherboards now carry onboard sound cards. In fact, some motherboards even have built-in video cards, although I prefer to add my own video adapter. An ATX motherboard should (by definition) already have serial and parallel ports onboard.

✔ **Make sure that your new motherboard has at least two PCI slots and one PCI-Express slot.** Avoid any motherboard that includes more than a single Industry Standard Architecture (ISA) slot; peripheral component interconnect (PCI) technology provides better performance for your adapter cards (for example, a PCI video capture card or a hard drive controller card). Your PCI-Express slot, on the other hand, is dedicated to your video card. (Chapter 4 explains more about these different slots.)

Every motherboard carries a set of chips called the *BIOS.* (This silly acronym stands for *basic input-output system.*) Your BIOS determines much of what your computer can do and also controls what happens for different types of input. For example, your BIOS keeps track of what hard drives and floppy drives you can use, what happens when you press a key on the keyboard, and how data is read and written to RAM. You can usually forget about your computer's BIOS and just let it do its work, but if your computer suffers a hardware failure or a serious error, it's your BIOS that displays the error message. Most computers today use one of five brand-name BIOS chipsets: Intel, Award, Phoenix, NVIDIA, or AMI.

✔ **Make sure that you update your Flash BIOS.** Today's motherboards include *Flash BIOS,* which sounds like the name of a hero from a science fiction film. This is actually a good feature; it enables you to update the capabilities of your computer with new features and bug fixes from the motherboard manufacturer. I check regularly for motherboard BIOS updates on the manufacturer's Web site.

✔ **Choose more RAM.** All motherboards have a maximum amount of random access memory (RAM) that they can handle. Unless NASA has chosen you to control the next shuttle launch, a board that supports 3 to 4GB RAM should be sufficient. Real techno-nerds or ultra–power users might demand support for up to 6GB RAM.

Don't give me any static!

Before you install the motherboard in your case, it's time for a warning about the dangers of static electricity. Static can damage electrical components in the blink of an eye, and not even Thomas Edison himself could fix them. I won't launch into a terribly interesting discussion of how static was discovered in 400 B.C. by somebody we don't know with a piece of silk and a glass rod. For all I care, the discovery of static electricity could have been made by prehistoric man shuffling across a bearskin rug.

Instead, just remember this simple rule while handling motherboards, adapter cards, circuit boards, and other computer parts: Before installing any circuit board, adapter card, or part on your computer (or before removing it from the case), discharge any static electricity that you might be harboring by touching something else made of metal. (You can discharge static also by touching your spouse on the earlobe, although I don't recommend this method.)

Typically, the metal chassis of your computer is a good choice, although you can also touch a metal table or chair. If your computer is plugged in with the cover off (which happens quite often when you're installing a hard drive or an adapter card), you can touch the metal housing of your power supply for a perfect ground.

Antistatic strips are available for keyboards and wrist rests that discharge static. However, the only time that I ever worry about static is when I'm handling parts and circuit boards, so I don't use this item.

And for Colossus, 1 Pick . . .

Personally, I'm a tower man. A tower case provides me with the space for two optical drives and at least two hard drives, so the case I'm selecting would be a good pick for any high-performance PC. As I mention earlier, shopping for motherboards is a feature comparison fun-fest, and you'll see that reflected in my choice.

As of this writing, Colossus will enjoy

- ✔ **Antec Twelve Hundred full tower case:** In black (of course), this case can accommodate up to 12 drive bays accessible from the outside of the case as well as three internal (hidden) drive bays. Talk about room to expand! Front-mounted ports on the case include USB, analog audio, and eSATA. A whopping three cooling fans in front and two in the back assure great airflow. I'm also using an Antec NeoPower 650-watt power supply.

  This case will run you about $200. Find it online at www.antec.com.

- ✔ **ASUS P5N-D LGA775 motherboard:** This board supports the Core 2 Duo/Quad and Core 2 Extreme processors, with an NVIDIA chipset that allows me to use two NVIDIA video cards in SLI mode. (I discuss SLI mode in more detail in Chapter 14.) The ASUS board supports up to 8GB of memory, two PCI Express video card slots, SATA/EIDE/RAID controller, and a built-in surround sound audio hardware. Plus you'll get a huge selection of ports: USB, FireWire, SPDIF digital audio, and analog audio.

  This critter will set you back about $150. Read more online at www.asus.com.

Installing Slot Covers

Stuff You Need to Know

Toolbox:

↳ Phillips screwdriver

Materials:

↳ Slot covers
↳ Screws

Time Needed:
5 minutes

Your case has a number of holes on the back, which are meant for adapter cards. For each slot opening, you can screw in a bracket that attaches to an adapter card, holding the card firmly in place. If the adapter card has any external ports, they are also visible through the back of the case because they poke through the open slot.

Most cases have these slots open although the slots need to be covered. Adding slot covers involves a little manual labor. If your slots are already covered, scoot to the next section; or, if you'll be installing at least one or two adapter cards (I show you how in later chapters), leave one or two slots uncovered to save yourself the trouble of removing them again.

1. Check the parts that came with your case to find the *slot covers,* which are thin, metal strips with a bend at the top. You should also find a number of screws that fit into the screw holes at the top of each slot opening.

2. Lay your open case down on top of your work surface. You should be able to clearly see the screw holes and the slot openings at the back of your case.

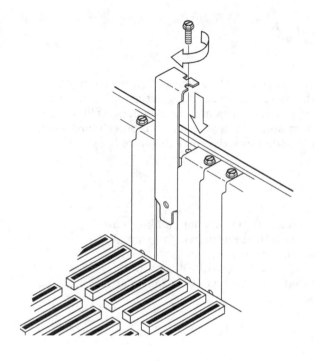

3. Slide a slot cover over one of the slot openings so that the screw hole lines up with the screw hole in the case, as shown in the figure.

4. Insert and tighten the screw to hold the cover over the opening.

5. Repeat Steps 3 and 4 until all the desired slot openings are covered.

Installing Your Motherboard

Stuff You Need to Know

Toolbox:
- Phillips screwdriver

Materials:
- Spacers
- Screws

Time Needed:
30 minutes

It's show time! Get ready to add your motherboard to your system case. This procedure is one of the most time-consuming in the entire PC assembly process, so be prepared to take things at your own pace. (Fifteen minutes can easily turn into 30 minutes while installing a motherboard — but as long as the installation is done properly, you can ignore the clock!)

1. Cover your work surface with newspaper and lay your open case down on top of the newspaper. You should be able to clearly see the screw holes and the plastic spacer guides where the motherboard will sit. Check the documentation that came with your case for any special instructions.

2. Protect your new motherboard from static electricity that you picked up from your lava lamp or from Trixie (the family Persian cat), and touch a metal surface beforehand.

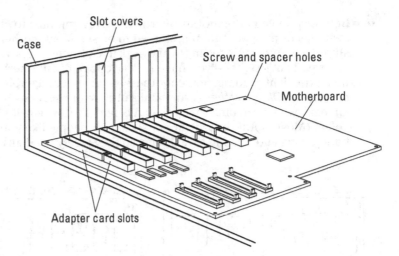

3. Hold the motherboard by the edges and lay it down inside the case to align it. All the electrical components (such as the CPU socket, memory sockets, and adapter slots) should be on top; the underside of the circuit board should have no components. To align the case, make sure that the adapter card slots line up with the slots cut into the back of the case.

4. Note which screw holes line up with the screw holes in your motherboard, and if necessary, write down their positions on a piece of paper. Most cases use only two to four screws to hold the board, and the rest of the board is supported and held rigid by plastic spacers. These spacers usually slide under a metal tab or a metal guide, which serve to keep your motherboard away from any possible dangerous contact with the metal of your computer case. You might find additional help in your motherboard manual on locating these holes.

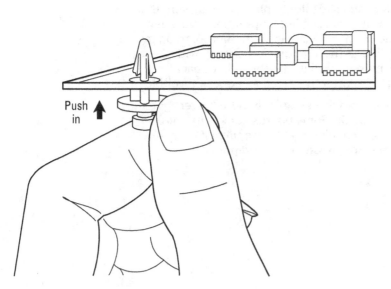

5. Remove the motherboard from the case and add the plastic spacers to the holes (in your motherboard) that need them. The figure illustrates how you push the spacers through the holes from the bottom of the board. The spacers should snap firmly into place.

6. Before you install the motherboard, take a few minutes to check for any switches or jumpers that might need to be set. Most motherboards are shipped with default settings that work fine although it pays to check anyway. That's right — you have to crack open the motherboard manual and do a little light reading. Some motherboards are configured with *dual inline packaging (DIP) switches* (little banks of slide or rocker switches) and *jumpers,* which are pins that you can connect with a small plastic-and-metal collar. (Most motherboards are designed for people like you and me who hate poking and moving tiny things, so they rarely need any configuration.)

DIP switches

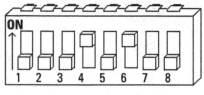

Sliders   Rockers   Jumper

If you need to set a DIP switch, use a pen to push the plastic sliders into the correct order. The edges of the switch are usually marked On and Off. (In the figure here, switches 4 and 6 have been set to On for two different types of DIP switches.) If you need to set a jumper (with an EIDE hard drive, for example), use your fingers or a set of tweezers to lift the plastic jumper and seat it into the correct position, as outlined in the component manual. (The figure here shows a jumper on pins 1 and 2.)

7. Pick up your motherboard by the edges and slide it into place, making sure that all the plastic spacers are correctly positioned. Don't get upset if it takes a few tries, and *don't bend or force anything.* I've never installed a motherboard on my first attempt. Once again, make certain that the adapter slots line up with the slots in the case as before. After the motherboard is in, gently check each corner of the board to make sure that it's correctly seated and doesn't wobble.

8. You're ready to lock it down. Add the screws to a snug fit, but don't overtighten them — circuit boards tend to crack if you do. Some boards come with thin, nonconductive washers for the screws, so don't forget to use them if they were included. That's it! Congratulations! See, that wasn't that hard, was it?

Connecting the Power Supply

Stuff You Need to Know

Toolbox:
- Your bare hands

Materials:
- None

Time Needed:
5 minutes

The hard part of installing your motherboard is over, but the process isn't complete. You still need to connect the wires from the power supply.

This is a good time to take care of this chore because your motherboard is easy to work with right now. You have unrestricted access to all the connectors on your motherboard, with no adapter cards or cables hanging around to interfere with your work

1. If your case is plugged into a wall socket, it shouldn't be! Unplug your PC first.

2. Locate the power connector on your motherboard. If you need help in finding the power connector, check your motherboard manual. Can you see why I recommend that you save all the documentation for your hardware? On an ATX motherboard, the two power cables are combined into one cable, and the plug is designed to connect only one way.

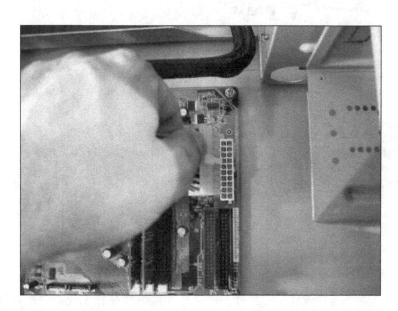

3. Align the connector with the socket and press down gently until the connectors snap in place. Connecting the power cable might seem kind of scary the first time that you do it, but take heart: Thanks to the ATX standard, you can't go wrong!

Connecting Lights, Switches, and the Speaker

Stuff You Need to Know

Toolbox:
✔ Your bare hands

Materials:
✔ None

Time Needed:
5 minutes

The final motherboard installation procedure involves connecting the wires to the buttons and lights on the front of your case, as well as the speaker that's buried somewhere in your PC chassis. Although most of the pins on your motherboard are marked, some of those markings can be pretty cryptic, so now is the time to grab your motherboard manual (and a good gooseneck lamp so that you can see those tiny labels).

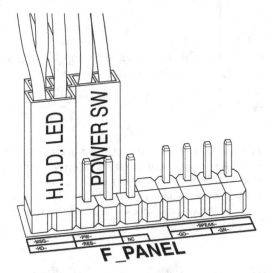

1. Check the documentation that came with your case to determine which wires lead to which lights and switches! Typically, you get to play "match the colors." For example, the connector on the green and white wires might be for the power button, and the red and white wires might be the PC speaker. The connectors on the ends of the wires are also be marked with a word or two (such as *power* or *reset*) that identifies them.

2. After you determine which connector is which, refer to your motherboard manual for the location of the following pins. On most motherboards, these words (or an abbreviation) are also printed right next to the pins, making it easier to locate them if you don't have a copy of the manual.

   ✔ **Power light or power LED:** This is the power light on the front of the case.

   ✔ **HDD light or HD LED:** This is the hard-drive activity light on the front of the case. It lights whenever your computer accesses your hard drive, so it's flickering just about all the time.

   ✔ **Reset:** This is the reset switch on the front of the case; you press it when your computer is locked up.

   ✔ **Speaker or Spk:** This wire should lead to your computer's internal speaker. Even if you plan on adding a sound card later, you need to connect the speaker because it provides audio error messages that can help you diagnose problems with your computer. In fact, you use these audio error messages in Chapter 4.

3. Attach each cable to its corresponding pins on the motherboard by pushing the connector onto the pins, as shown in the figure here. Generally, it doesn't matter which way the connector is facing, unless a specific direction or placement is mentioned in the motherboard documentation. If a connector needs to be reversed (because a light doesn't turn on when it should, or the Reset button doesn't work), you can fix it in the next chapter, when you run your first tests.

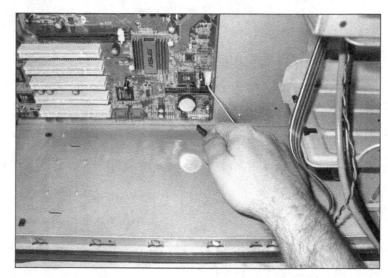

Chapter 4

A Bag of Chips: Adding RAM and a CPU

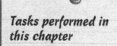
After you install the motherboard inside your computer's case, which I cover in Chapter 3, your PC might still be missing one or two very important parts: its brain (the central processing unit, or CPU) and its memory (random access memory, or RAM). When you run a computer program, your computer's CPU performs the calculations and executes the commands stored in that program. In tandem, your computer's RAM acts as a work area for the program: storing, changing, and retrieving data.

To reduce the amount of work, I recommend buying a motherboard with the CPU and RAM modules preinstalled (commonly called a *populated* motherboard, for some strange socio-engineering reason). For this book, I show you how to build a populated motherboard from the ground up. If you buy a populated motherboard, you don't need to worry about compatibility problems or installation hassles. (Differences exist in socket types, voltage requirements, and physical measurements in both the Intel and AMD lines of CPU chips, so not every motherboard accepts every CPU.) If the motherboard you're using comes with these chips preinstalled, you can skip most of this chapter and visit your local miniature golf course for a heady 18 holes. Don't forget, though — I need you back here to test the chassis in the last section of this chapter.

If you need to install your CPU or your memory — either before you install your motherboard inside your case or afterward — this chapter will attach itself to you like a suckerfish to the side of an aquarium. Just follow the appropriate steps and then test your chassis. You can feast your eyes on the to-be-completed deal in Figure 4-1.

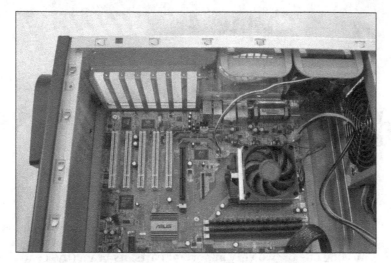

Figure 4-1: Your goal: The motherboard, CPU, and RAM all installed.

FYI about CPUs

You can choose from a number of CPU models these days, and you might be able to save a little money while shopping if you're faced with a decision between manufacturers and speeds. Therefore, review the general characteristics of the current crop of computer cranium components. I take them in order of price and power, starting with the low-end processors. Check out Table 4-1.

I mention this question elsewhere in this book, but the question bears repeating: What's the difference between a 2.4 GHz Pentium 4 CPU and a 2.8 GHz Pentium 4 CPU? No, it's not a trick question! Because the processors (Pentium 4) are the same type, it's the *speed,* which is expressed in megahertz (MHz) or gigahertz (GHz). When you're shopping for the processors that I describe in this section, make sure that you get the minimum speed for the type of computer you're building. (If you're not sure what that minimum speed or type is, see Chapter 2.) Note that if your CPU has multiple cores (dual or quad-core), it will perform faster and more efficiently than a single-core CPU of the same speed. However, you can also follow this simple Mark's Maxim:

Buy the fastest doggone possible processor you can afford!™

Adding plenty of RAM is just as important from a performance angle as buying the fastest CPU you can afford. With only 128MB of RAM, for example, Windows is still going to run slowly, even with a super-fast Intel Core 2 Quad Extreme processor. Later in this chapter, you'll find more details on how much RAM you should add.

While shopping, remember that the type of socket your motherboard has — think "connector that the CPU plugs into" — determines what type of processor you can use.

Why are bus speed and CPU cache important?

While shopping for a CPU, make sure you compare the amount of onboard cache memory included with each processor. *Cache memory* acts as a high-speed "workspace" for your CPU, storing data that the CPU is working with so that your processor doesn't have to perform calculations on data in system RAM (which is much slower). The more cache memory, the faster and more efficiently a processor performs.

Your motherboard communicates with the CPU and other components at a set *bus speed,* which you can think of as a speed limit for data throughout your system. Both your CPU and your motherboard must operate at the same bus speed. The higher the bus speed, the faster your PC operates.

Both of these important specifications vary with the type of processor (and might even vary within a specific model, depending on the manufacture date), so pay close attention to them while comparison shopping.

Table 4-1		CPU Comparisons	
CPU Make/Model	*Cores*	*Hyperthreading*	*Performance*
Intel Celeron	1	No	Light-duty family PC
AMD Sempron	1	No	Light-duty family PC
Intel Core 2 Duo	2	Yes	Casual gaming/family PC
AMD Athlon 64 X2	2	Yes	Casual gaming/family PC
Intel Core 2 Quad	4	Yes	Hard-core gaming/video editing
AMD Phenom	3 or 4	Yes	Hard-core gaming/video editing

Family PC choices: Intel Celeron and AMD Sempron processors

Celeron and Sempron are two processors designed for the price-conscious consumer. In other words, although you get lots of bang for your buck from these CPUs, they aren't as advanced and don't have the extra punch of their more expensive brethren. Don't get me wrong, though: Either of these two processors is still more than speedy enough to power a typical family PC. (Read about how I define a family PC in Chapter 2.)

Both Celeron and Sempron are single-core CPUs — unlike most other Intel and AMD CPU offerings, which offer anywhere from two to four cores. (More on multicore processors in a page or two.) Older single-core Pentium 4 CPUs are antiques, so avoid them.

The Intel Celeron: The darling of the low-cost crowd

The Celeron processor, designed by Intel as a cheaper alternative to the Pentium since the days of the Pentium II, works quite well if you're building a midrange computer for use with an office suite or if you plan to explore the Internet. The Celeron has a lower amount of cache memory than the rest of the Intel line, so it's not as efficient as an Intel Core 2 Duo CPU (more on this choice in a bit), and its raw megahertz speed rating is typically far slower. The Celeron also offers a slower bus speed.

The AMD Sempron: A bare-bones hot rod

Because AMD designed the Sempron processor to compete directly with the Celeron, the Sempron is usually neck-and-neck in performance benchmarks. Like the Celeron, the Sempron has less cache memory and a slower bus speed than the AMD Athlon 64 series (see the next section).

The Cunningham model: Intel Core 2 Duo and AMD Athlon 64 X2 processors

One step up the performance ladder, the Intel Core 2 Duo and the Athlon 64 processors are perfect for a midrange PC for home or office.

The Intel Core 2 Duo: Still king of the hill

The Core 2 Duo, a dual-core processor, is the most popular CPU on the market, and with good reason: It's a fantastic all-around CPU. The Core 2 Duo is often faster in raw speed than a corresponding Athlon 64 X2, and it runs with a wider range of motherboards. It's a great choice for just about any PC.

The AMD Athlon 64 X2: A reliable workhorse

Like the aging Pentium Extreme Edition, the AMD Athlon 64 X2 is no longer top dog, but it still offers excellent performance for a typical family or office PC. And it provides more efficient operation than first-generation Intel Core Duo CPUs. The Athlon 64 X2 is a dual-core processor.

By the way, that *64* in the Athlon 64 designation is no accident: All Athlon 64 processors support the latest 64-bit version of Windows — Windows XP Professional x64 Edition — as well as 64-bit Windows Vista. The dynamic duo of one of these operating systems and any Athlon 64-bit processor results in faster performance and support for up to an unbelievable 128 gigabytes of RAM.

Power user: Intel Core 2 Quad and AMD Phenom series processors

In this section, I cover the big CPU twosome dominating the current PC scene: the Intel Core 2 Quad series and the AMD Phenom series, which are both quite suitable for high-end power user systems. Either of these processors is my first recommendation for most folks playing the latest computer games, working with digital video or music, or using demanding business applications.

Today's processors include *hyperthreading technology,* which allows a single CPU to perform like multiple CPUs. (See the earlier Table 4-1.) In fact, Windows XP and Vista think that you're running a dual-processor motherboard! The adage "Two heads are better than one" is just as true when it comes to computer CPUs, and hyperthreading is a feature that you should ask for if you're building a new CPU. A PC using one of these chips is more efficient and runs significantly faster when you're running more than one application at a time.

The Intel Core 2 Quad: High-end horsepower

The Core 2 Quad Extreme Edition CPU is a super-fast processor that features Intel hyperthreading technology, providing the best performance for today's games, 3-D applications, and video editing. The latest versions of the Core 2 CPU are quad-core processors, so they excel at multitasking and number crunching.

The AMD Phenom: The tyrannosaurus rex of processors

The Phenom is AMD's fastest, most efficient, and most advanced CPU, offering four cores. The Phenom even outperforms the Intel Core 2 Quad four-core processor line, and it's a particular favorite with the gaming community. But wait: Before you close this book and head to your Web browser, you should know that the Phenom is not the right choice for everyone. Like a sports car, the Phenom is far more expensive than a standard Athlon 64 processor. Plus, fewer motherboards are approved for use with the Athlon Phenom. I would recommend it for techno-wizards who want absolutely the best performance available in a CPU or for those folks who want to look forward to three or four years of use before they plan to buy another motherboard or build another PC.

Add RAM to the Mix

If you bought RAM with your motherboard, it should come preinstalled. If you need to buy your RAM chips separately, here are the rules of the game:

- **DDR2 and DDR3:** The most common memory modules used with today's PCs are double data rate (DDR2) modules, which are effectively four times the speed of older synchronous DRAM (SDRAM) memory. The latest version of this type of memory is the DDR3 (Double Data Rate) module, which again increases the data transfer between RAM and your PC. However, the new DDR3 design is less common (and more expensive) than the older DDR2 standard at the time of this writing. DDR2 and DDR3 memory modules have one notch on the connector and two notches on each side of the module. Figure 4-2 illustrates a typical DDR module, just waiting for someone to reach out and install it.

Figure 4-2: Is it a potato chip? A chocolate chip? No, it's a DDR chip.

While you're out shopping for RAM, remember that DDR memory is assigned a speed rating as part of the name, so it's commonly listed as DDR266/PC2100 or DDR3 1066. As you might guess, the faster the memory speed, the better the performance, so the bigger numbers tell you that 333 (or 2700) is faster than 266 (or 2100). The speed rating that you choose should be determined by the memory speeds that your motherboard supports. Most of today's motherboards can accept two to four modules.

✔ **RDRAM:** Yet another high-performance variety of RAM, but this older species is on the decline. In fact, rambus dynamic random access memory (RDRAM) modules are now disappearing from the market as DDR3 memory grows more popular. (I know — the doggone acronyms are as bad as the full names.)

✔ **Compatibility:** To avoid mix-ups and stragglers, it's better to order all your RAM at one time from the same dealer. In general, RAM modules made by different manufacturers are *supposed* to work together as long as they're all rated at the same speed, although I've heard horror stories on the Internet about compatibility problems. Whenever you can, use one brand.

✔ **Amount:** Check the design that you created in Chapter 2 for the recommended amount of RAM that you should use, but don't forget this Mark's Maxim:

✔ **The more RAM, the merrier! This is especially true with Windows XP and Windows Vista. The more RAM you can add, the better and faster your system runs.**™

And for Colossus, 1 Pick . . .

I'm outfitting Colossus for the future, so I'm willing to invest the money in a CPU with performance to last me several years!

Inside the case, my super-PC will be powered by

✔ **Intel Core 2 Quad Core:** Although Intel's speed demon is expensive, it's worth it — the 2.66 GHz model (with included fan and heatsink) runs about $270 at the time of this writing.

✔ **Kingston HyperX 240-Pin DDR2 800 (PC2 6400) Memory:** I'm going with 4GB of RAM to start with (knowing that I can always add more RAM later on), so Colossus will enjoy two DDR2 modules. Each module carries 2GB, and I'll use two RAM slots on the motherboard.

Installing Your CPU

Stuff You Need to Know

Toolbox:
✔ Your bare hands

Materials:
✔ CPU
✔ Motherboard

Time Needed:
15 minutes

Suppose that someone who upgraded a PC donated an Athlon Phenom CPU to your cause — hey, it could happen, right? Or, more likely, you found a CPU for sale online at a great price. Anyway, you need to install your CPU on your motherboard. After all, that's where your processor belongs (it won't work by itself).

For a novice, the CPU installation process is probably one of the scariest moments in the entire project. The pins on a CPU can be damaged easily by small children, dogs, or a cat in an exceptionally bad mood. If you feel that you need professional help on this one, just bring your case (with motherboard installed) and CPU to your local computer repair shop or ask a computer guru whom you know to handle the CPU installation. Ask the expert to install the CPU, and watch the process closely. As I outline previously, most motherboards made for today's processors provide a square socket that accepts a flat processor chip.

1. Haul your open computer chassis onto your work surface. Don't plug the chassis in yet because nothing will happen. You'll plug in the power cord later in this chapter.

2. I'll bet that you just finished pulling a load of fuzzy socks out of your clothes dryer, didn't you? And rubbed a couple of balloons on your head? Don't handle anything until you touch a metal surface first. Get grounded. (If this makes no sense to you, read Chapter 1 for the importance of good grounding.)

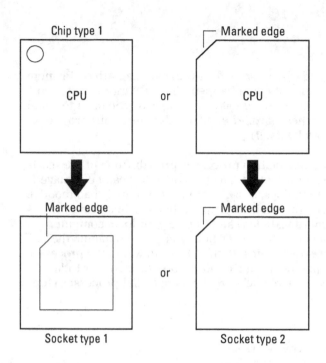

Chip type 1

or

Marked edge

Marked edge

or

Marked edge

Socket type 1   Socket type 2

3. Locate the CPU socket on your motherboard. The CPU socket is a big square that looks like it could hold two or three thousand pins. If you need help finding the CPU socket, refer to the schematic in your motherboard's manual. Today's motherboards typically feature special sockets called zero insertion force (ZIF) sockets for the CPU. ZIF sockets allow you to easily install or remove CPUs without requiring force.

Unfortunately, the CPU is not one of those parts that are cleverly designed to fit only one way, but at least the nice folks at the plant give you a marker to help during installation. Check out the figure here, which shows two typical CPU chips and two different types of sockets. See the stubby corner on the chip? That corner should point in the same direction as the socket's marker. Depending on the motherboard, the matching corner on the socket might be stubby as well, or it could have a small dot or a tiny groove. If you're the least bit unsure about how to line up the CPU chip, check your motherboard manual.

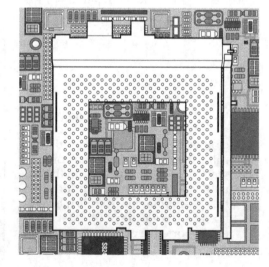

4. Raise the ZIF lever on the side of the socket. Your motherboard manual should show you how to lift the lever; this step unlocks the ZIF socket so that you can insert the chip.

5. Carefully place the CPU chip on top of the socket. The edges of the chip should match the edges of the socket, and the stubby corner should match the socket marker. Look at the chip from the top and the side to make sure that the pins that you can see are on top of their matching holes. (Refer to the figure in Step 3 to see how this alignment works.)

6. Okay, take a deep breath and relax, and then use your fingers to gently push down on the edges of the chip. Apply even pressure to the top of the CPU. After some initial resistance, the chip should settle into the socket. Press evenly on the CPU until the pins aren't visible from the side.

7. Lower the ZIF lever on the side of the socket. Push the lever down to lock the ZIF socket so that the CPU chip is held in place.

Never, never, *never* try to force a CPU into a motherboard. If it doesn't feel like it's correctly seated and all the pins fit, back off and check your motherboard manual to make sure that the chip is aligned correctly. If the CPU isn't correctly aligned and you try to force it into the socket, you'll bend some of the pins (which can be fixed, but only by an experienced technician). In the worst case, you'll break a pin. If this happens, you may as well bury the chip in your backyard and get another CPU.

Installing Your Fan and Heatsink

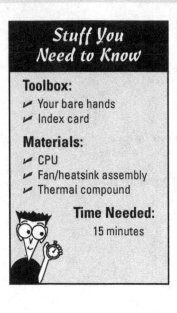

Stuff You Need to Know

Toolbox:
- Your bare hands
- Index card

Materials:
- CPU
- Fan/heatsink assembly
- Thermal compound

Time Needed:
15 minutes

All processors made these days need fans on top or on the side to keep the chip cool. The fan is clamped to the top of the chip, usually with an intervening layer of conductive glue — thermal compound — to help transfer heat. This fan will have a separate power cable that you need to connect, so refer to your CPU and motherboard documentation to find the fan connector.

I recommend using a fan and heatsink combination, so I include a heatsink in this procedure. If you're using a CPU fan that's powerful enough to keep your processor cool, you can clamp the fan to the PC in Step 4 instead.

1. Don't handle anything until you touch a metal surface first to ground yourself.

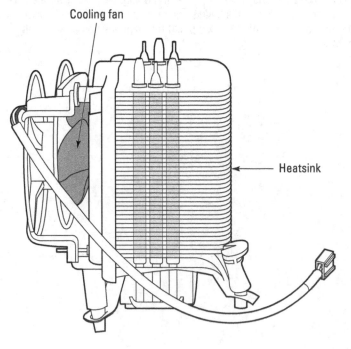

Cooling fan

Heatsink

2. Unpack the fan/heatsink assembly. Most processors you buy in a retail box include a fan and heatsink. If your processor didn't come with these parts, you can buy them separately at most larger electronics stores, or through an online retailer like Newegg.com.

3. Apply an even coat of thermal compound to the top of the CPU using a paper index card. Don't apply too much compound: Just make sure the chip is covered with a thin coat.

Make certain that none of the compound falls on the motherboard or around the CPU.

4. Align the fan/heatsink assembly on top of the processor and snap it in place. Because heatsinks vary in how they attach to the motherboard, check the documentation that came with your components to see how the assembly fits.

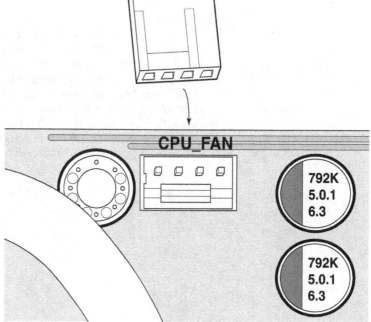

5. Plug the fan's power cable into the motherboard's CPU fan connector. It's generally located close to the CPU socket.

Installing Your RAM

Stuff You Need to Know

Toolbox:

✔ Your bare hands

Materials:

✔ RAM modules
✔ Motherboard

Time Needed:

5 minutes

Ready to add one or more RAM modules to your motherboard? Adding RAM is a simple task — much less daunting for most first-time techs than installing a CPU — and this procedure shouldn't take long.

Make sure that you handle your RAM modules by the edges to minimize any contact with the chips, and don't forget that the modules have a keyed slot in the connector that prevents them from being installed the wrong way.

1. Touch something metal to banish the static monster.
   You know the drill!

2. Locate the memory slots, which you can generally find at one corner of the motherboard, close to the CPU itself. If Picasso designed your motherboard, check the manual, which should include a schematic drawing to help you find the memory slots. You should also find instructions on which bank of slots to fill first. Always make sure that you add the memory in the order specified by the manual. (The banks are usually marked on the motherboard itself, just to avoid confusion.) In general, most people fill bank 0 first, and then bank 1, and so on.

3. Position the motherboard so that the memory slots are facing you. The slots should look like those shown in the figure. The clever little locking mechanism uses friction to lock the module firmly in place. Notice that the notches cut into the connectors at the bottom of the module match the spacers in the memory sockets; you can't install DDR chips the wrong way. The notch is an example of good thinking on someone's part.

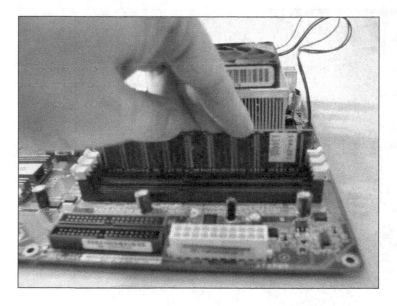

4. Align the metal teeth at the bottom of the module with the socket, and then push down lightly to seat the chip, as shown in the figure. As the module moves into place, make sure that the two levers at each side of the socket move toward the center, until that clever little locking mechanism clicks into place. That's it! When correctly installed, the module should sit vertically on the motherboard, and the two levers should be flush against the sides of the module.

Fire That Puppy Up!

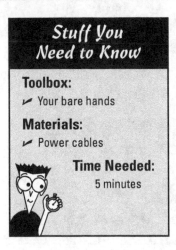

Stuff You Need to Know

Toolbox:
- Your bare hands

Materials:
- Power cables

Time Needed:
5 minutes

Time to test your work and see how well you did. Although your computer doesn't even have a monitor or keyboard connected yet, you can still check out your assembly so far. You finally get to press that Power button!

1. Plug the power cord that came with your computer case into the matching connector on the power supply! Go ahead and push this one in pretty firmly. You don't want it to wiggle free.

2. Plug the power cable into your friendly wall socket.

3. Push the power switch on the front or back of your case. *If* you connected your cables to the motherboard correctly, and *if* your switches are hooked up correctly (both of which are covered in detail in Chapter 3), and *if* your CPU and RAM chips are installed correctly, the following should happen:

✔ **The power light should be lit.**

Troubleshooting: If the power light doesn't go on and the fan on your power supply is turning, reverse the connector attached to the power light pins on the motherboard. For all the information on motherboard connections, refer to Chapter 3.

✔ **The fan on the CPU should be spinning.**

Troubleshooting: If the fan isn't spinning, check to make sure that you plugged in the cable from the fan to your power supply.

4. Decode the beeps. Your computer might blurt out a series of beeps. Don't worry — it's merely trying to tell you that it can't find a video adapter, a keyboard, and other such components. (You install and attach those elements in later chapters.) In fact, the beeps are your friends, and you can use them later in the assembly process to help you diagnose problems. For example, if the machine emits one long beep followed by two short beeps, you have a video problem. If your PC sounds eight or more long, continuous beeps, it's telling you that it's encountering a memory problem. Your motherboard manual should list these audio status codes. That's about all the testing you can do at this stage. After your chassis passes all these tests, you're ready to add more components to your computer. See Table 4-2.

Table 4-2	Beep Code Descriptions
Number of Beeps	*What Your PC Is Telling You*
Single short beep	Normal boot
Repeating short beeps	Problem with power supply or motherboard
Repeating long beeps	Problem with RAM modules
One long, two short beeps	Problem with video card
No beep	Problem with power supply, CPU installation, or PC speaker

Chapter 5

Installing Your Ports, Mouse, and Keyboard

Tasks performed in this chapter

✔ Installing a port adapter card

✔ Hooking up built-in ports

✔ Connecting a keyboard

✔ Installing a non-USB mouse

Both your mouse and keyboard connect to your computer through special connectors plugged into *ports* on the front or back of the case. Your computer also needs a port for sending information to your printer as well as a port for sending and receiving data through an external modem. Although some of these ports have changed over the years, others are virtually unchanged since the arrival of the first PC.

If you bought a new motherboard, it should have several of these ports built in already. For example, all motherboards have a built-in keyboard connector. However, less expensive (or older "antique") motherboards might require you to buy an adapter card if you need to add less common ports (like a FireWire or an eSATA port) to your computer.

Because you installed an ATX motherboard into an ATX case (see Chapter 3), your ports are already set! However, if your motherboard came with built-in ports but without connectors, you still need to attach the port connectors to the motherboard and then add the ports to your case. So don't skip this entire chapter; instead, jump to the "Connecting Built-In Ports" section.

Pursuing Your Port Preferences

Prepare to be amazed by the variety of ports that you can add to your computer! Your computer definitely needs the first three or four ports mentioned in the following list (and illustrated in Figure 5-1) although the rest are optional ports that handle the special hardware that power users just love.

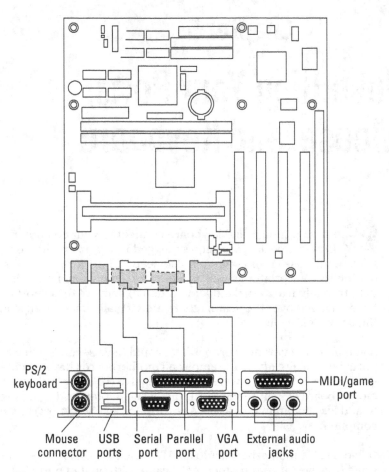

PS/2 keyboard

MIDI/game port

Mouse connector USB ports Serial port Parallel port VGA port External audio jacks

Figure 5-1: Most ATX motherboards sport these ports.

✔ **Keyboard port:** Keyboard ports come in two varieties:

- One type fits the IBM PS/2 connector that's shown in Figure 5-2.

- An older type of keyboard port is larger than the PS/2 connector.

All motherboards made in the past few years have a keyboard port that accepts the smaller PS/2 plug. If you want to use a keyboard that has a good feel to it but uses the older-style, round connector (usually called an AT connector), you can pick up a converter that enables you to plug the older keyboard into a PS/2-style port.

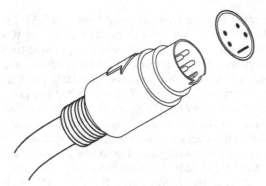

Figure 5-2: The IBM PS/2 standard keyboard connector.

 ✔ **USB port:** This high-speed port is the universal method for attaching all sorts of peripherals (such as digital cameras and external modems) to your computer. A single USB port can accommodate as many as 127 *daisy-chained* (that is, connected) devices — probably even enough for Bill Gates. USB 2.0 ports move data at speeds as fast as a blistering 480 Mbps. Plus, any peripheral that you plug into a USB port is automatically recognized by Windows XP and Windows Vista (as it should be), and you can remove that same device without rebooting your computer. Figure 5-3 illustrates the USB ports and connectors on both the PC and peripheral ends.

 USB reigns as king for connecting scanners, joysticks, controllers, digital cameras, printers, and even some mice and keyboards. If you're shopping for a new motherboard, make *sure* that it comes with USB 2.0 ports, and you can kiss port confusion goodbye!

✔ **PS/2 mouse port:** Although most pointing devices have switched to USB connectors, most motherboards still offer a dedicated mouse port, which frees up your USB ports for other things.

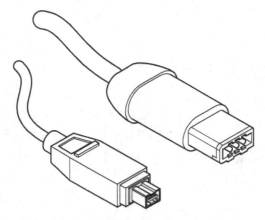

Figure 5-3: The USB connectors that conquered the world.

✔ **FireWire port:** Otherwise known as your friendly neighborhood IEEE-1394 high-performance serial bus, a *FireWire* port transfers data as fast as 400 Mbps, which has made it a popular choice for connecting expensive toys that generate lots of data, such as digital camcorders, videoconferencing cameras, super-fast scanners, and color laser printers. Like USB, FireWire is automatically recognized by Windows Vista and Windows XP; it supports as many as 63 devices connected together on a single FireWire port. (Although the USB 2.0 port could surpass FireWire in a speed race, FireWire allows your computer to control digital devices as well, so it's likely to hang around. A new FireWire 800 standard has appeared on a few high-end PCs and can pump an unbelievable 800 Mbps to external devices, but these super-fast connectors aren't likely to be as popular in the PC world as USB 2.0 for some time to come.)

If you're planning on editing digital video or participating in videoconferencing, consider adding a FireWire port to your PC. Virtually all PC cases now offer built-in USB ports on the front — but even if your case didn't come equipped with them, you can get a FireWire and USB port panel that takes the place of a drive bay cover on the front of your PC (Figure 5-4). As you might imagine, having these ports on the front of your computer (instead of hiding out in back) is a great convenience when connecting digital cameras, digital video (DV) camcorders, and external hard drives.

✔ **eSATA port:** Interested in adding very fast external hard drives? Adding an eSATA adapter card to your PC will allow you to run external eSATA drives in a RAID array for the very fastest data access. (Chapter 14 describes RAID arrays in more detail.) You can see what the plug looks like in Figure 5-5.

✔ **Parallel printer port:** For the last decade, the parallel port's primary purpose was to provide a connection for your printer. Today's hardware, however, is almost exclusively connected through a USB or FireWire port. Most motherboards still sport a parallel port, and if you need it, look for a rectangular port with two rows of pins (or holes) on the back of your PC.

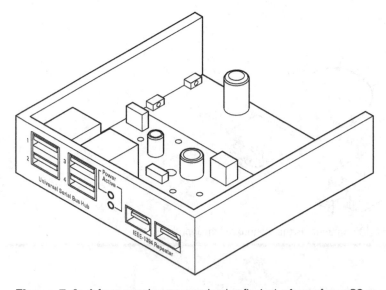

Figure 5-4: A front-panel port expander that fits in the front of your PC case.

- ✔ **Serial port:** Serial ports are primarily reserved for some exotic types of joysticks and game controllers. A serial port is commonly called a *COM port* (short for *com*munications *port*). Most motherboards offer two serial ports (but can have more than two), and each of these ports is typically assigned one of four standard COM port designations — COM1, COM2, and so on — which identifies that particular port to the computer.

  By the way, a *male* connector has pins, and a *female* connector has holes for those pins. (Go figure.)

- ✔ **Game port:** If you plan to add a sound card to your computer, the card might also have a game port for your joystick or gamepad. (Of course, you can decide to opt for a USB game controller although many gamers get very attached to their expensive older flight joysticks, steering wheels, and throttles.)

- ✔ **MIDI port:** You use this type of specialized port for connecting MIDI-capable musical instruments to your computer. MIDI (Musical Instrument Digital Interface) ports are usually added along with your sound card. (You find out more about sound cards and MIDI in Chapter 10.) Again, you can also get a USB-to-MIDI port adapter if you own a MIDI instrument.

- ✔ **Infrared port:** If you have a laptop computer or handheld device with an infrared port, you might want to consider adding one to your new computer. An *infrared port* lets you transfer data and files between two computers without the need to string cables between the two machines. An infrared port comes in handy if you travel often and like to keep your data synchronized between your laptop and desktop systems, or if you're using a remote control with your PC in conjunction with a TV tuner card. Infrared ports are typically installed on an adapter card, with some sort of external infrared sensor (which looks something like the infamous "red eye" from your TV's remote control).

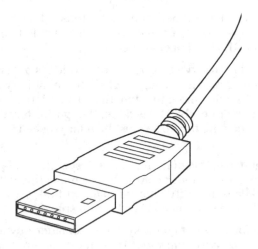

Figure 5-5: An eSATA plug.

Label your ports, and you will rejoice later.™

Put that label maker that you got for Christmas to good use. Even though you might remember *now* which port is which, I heartily recommend that you create labels for your ports after you install them. If you label your ports (or at least copy the port layout on the back of your PC on paper), you eliminate any identification problems in the future.

Of Keyboards and Mice

"Grandpa, in your day, did they really have only one kind of mouse and one kind of keyboard?" Things have *really* changed, and you can now choose from a dizzying array of pointing devices and keyboards (and even combinations of both).

The mouse has mutated

If you're at a loss about which pointing device is best for you, here are some guidelines to steer you in the right direction:

- ✔ **Standard mouse:** The basic mouse is still around; it comes in two-button and three-button varieties. Some mice even carry smaller buttons on the sides! If you choose a mouse that has sprouted more than two buttons, you might be able to program the additional buttons. (For example, the software that came with my trackball enables me to program the middle button to double-click.) A mouse is still a good choice for a traditional pointing device although it's harder to use for delicate work and requires lots of desk space.

  All fashionable mice now sport a wheel between the buttons, which enables you to scroll Web pages and documents up and down (and even left and right) by turning the wheel with your finger — nice!

- ✔ **Wireless mouse:** This type of mouse doesn't trail cords, which is a desirable feature for many computer owners. Going wireless also enables you to control a presentation with much more freedom than a standard mouse. Be prepared to feed this monster new batteries often, though (or buy a rechargeable model), and check the box to see just how far you can stray without losing the signal.

- ✔ **Trackball:** As shown in Figure 5-6, this pointing device resembles an upside-down mouse: Rather than move the housing around, you move the ball with your finger or thumb. Trackballs are a little harder to use at first; they stay in one place, however, so they require much less desktop space.

  If you decide on a trackball for your computer systems, consider buying my favorite pointing device: an *optical trackball.* They never require adjustment or cleaning, and they have fewer moving parts than standard trackballs or mice. These trackballs use balls covered with a pattern of dots, and optical sensors in the body of the trackball "read" these dots to determine movement.

✔ **Drawing tablet:** A *drawing tablet* (see Figure 5-7) is designed specifically for computer art and drafting. It allows freehand drawing on the tablet, which then appears onscreen. Depending on the size of the tablet, you can even use a ruler or stencil, but don't use a regular pen or pencil, please! (Use only the stylus that comes with the tablet.) The drawing tablet can also double as a regular pointing device when you're not drawing.

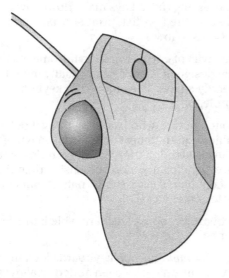

Figure 5-6: A typical trackball.

Figure 5-7: Okay, so a drawing tablet looks a little strange, but it works!

The key to keyboards

One keyboard is *not* just like another! For example, if you've been given an older 84-key keyboard, I suggest hanging it up in the barn as a good luck charm along with the horseshoes. You can easily recognize these keyboards because they don't have a separate set of cursor control keys or a separate numeric keypad. If you're using any version of Windows, you need at least a standard 101-key keyboard.

More expensive keyboards have additional features that can make your life at the computer considerably easier. For example:

- ✔ **Extra keys:** Windows XP and Vista both support extra keys. In fact, one key even looks like the Windows logo. Pressing these keys make drop-down menus appear within programs, display the task list, print special characters, and much more. (That crazy Gates fellow!)

- ✔ **Ergo, ergonomics:** Recognizing the evils of carpal tunnel syndrome, many keyboards today are ergonomically designed. This design usually includes a wrist rest and a more human-friendly shape. The ergonomic keyboard shown in Figure 5-8 is a good example.

- ✔ **Detached connectivity:** For the couch potato who has everything. Look, Ma! No wires! A *wireless* keyboard enables you to lounge on your futon while composing that Great American Novel. Just don't forget the batteries, and remember that these keyboards are significantly more expensive than their wired brethren. (My tech editor recommends also using a pair of binoculars if your futon is more than three or four feet away!)

  If you decide to use a wireless keyboard or mouse, rechargeable batteries are the smart power user's investment.

- ✔ **Multifunction buttons:** Many computer *multifunction* keyboards look more like your car's dashboard these days. Buttons have been added to allow you to check your e-mail, visit certain Web sites, and connect to the Internet.

Figure 5-8: Catch the wave! An ergonomic keyboard helps reduce wrist strain.

If you plan to use a desktop case or a huge 21-inch monitor with your finished PC, I recommend that you consider allotting some space for a *keyboard shelf,* which looks like a drawer that fits under your computer. The shelf slides out to give you access to the keyboard. After you finish typing, you can simply push the shelf back inside the unit. This device saves desk space, and it puts your keyboard at the proper typing position.

If you're buying a new keyboard, always try it out before you pull out your credit card. Because keyboards are all made differently, they have a different typing and comfort "feel" to them. People can be finicky about their keyboards, and typing a long document on a bad keyboard is roughly equivalent to poking a soggy sponge or a hard rock repeatedly with your fingers.

Check It Once, and Check It Twice!

After you complete the tasks in this chapter and your PC is sporting all of its ports, you really have no way to test them. All is not lost, though. You can test your keyboard right now. Just push the power switch on your computer case.

If you connected your keyboard to the port on your motherboard correctly, all three keyboard lights should flash — the Num Lock, Caps Lock, and Scroll Lock indicators. If these indicators light up, your keyboard is correctly installed. If these lights don't illuminate, remove the keyboard connector from the keyboard port and try plugging it in again. If you still have no luck, try another keyboard to make sure that the port is working, and then check your motherboard manual to make sure that you're connecting the keyboard to the keyboard port.

The port is the same size and shape as your mouse port; look for a keyboard icon next to the correct port.

And For Colossus, I Pick...

All of the ports I use are already integrated into the motherboard I chose back in Chapter 3, so I don't need a port adapter card for my new PC. However, input devices I *do* need!

I heartily recommend my favorite keyboard and mouse combination for you (and hereby add them to Colossus):

- **Logitech USB+PS/2 Wired Trackman Wheel:** I've been using a Logitech Trackman ever since they first appeared on the market, and an old-fashioned mouse feels . . . well . . . old-fashioned compared to the comfort, ergonomics, and efficiency of a trackball! This new model is cordless, so I can move it around my desk as needed. I especially like the Trackman because of the fine control it gives me while editing images.

- **Logitech G11 USB Standard Gaming Keyboard:** Yep, the gaming side of me wins again — this illuminated keyboard has 18 programmable keys for assigning macros, and illuminated keys for those late-night gaming marathons. The one-touch controls for media playback work great with iTunes under Windows, too.

Installing a Port Adapter Card

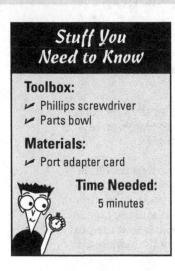

Stuff You Need to Know

Toolbox:
- Phillips screwdriver
- Parts bowl

Materials:
- Port adapter card

Time Needed:
5 minutes

If your motherboard doesn't have built-in USB 2.0, FireWire, or eSATA ports, it's time to add your port adapter card. These cards typically have at least two of the same ports on back side of the card itself, and some allow you to add cables that take up another slot on the back of your case to add even more ports. Check the manual that came with your port adapter card to determine what connectors are actually on your card and which must be added separately.

Your adapter card manual should also fill you in on any *dual inline packaging* (DIP) switch or jumper settings that have to be configured. I discuss both DIP switches and jumpers in Chapter 3. Now is a good time to move any required jumpers, before your card is mashed between several other cards and you have to be a contortionist like the Great Zambini to reach it. I do have good news about most port adapter cards: The factory default settings are usually just what you need although it never hurts to check first.

To install your port adapter card, follow these instructions:

1. Don't handle anything until you touch a metal surface. Have you been shuffling your feet through that deep, plush carpeting all day? Dissipate yourself of excess electrostatic energy. I'm talking Static City!

2. Haul your open case on top of your work surface. Do not plug it in yet.

3. Locate an adapter card slot of the proper length at the back of your case.

I cover the different types of adapter slots in Chapter 4, but here's a refresher just in case: Peripheral Component Interconnect (PCI) cards use the short slots, and 16-bit industry standard architecture (ISA) cards are twice as long. Because USB 2.0 and FireWire port adapter cards are PCI, you need a PCI slot. Also, make sure that any notches cut into the connectors on your card match any spacers within the slot. These spacers help ensure that you don't try to stick a 16-bit card into a PCI slot. Found an empty slot of the right length? Good! Move along to the next step.

4. Take your trusty screwdriver and remove the screw and the metal slot cover at the back of the case. Stick both these parts in your parts box. You might need this slot cover later to close your case if you decide to remove an adapter card. If you haven't installed any slot covers yet, just skip this step. (Some folks add them as soon as the motherboard is in the case; others wait until all the cards have been installed. It's up to you — I show you how to install the covers in Chapter 3.)

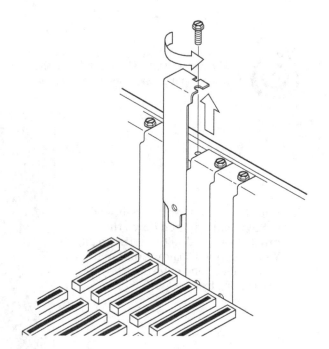

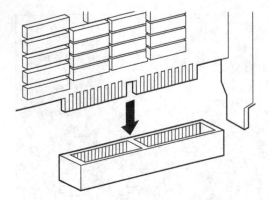

5. Pick up the adapter card by the top corners and then line up the connector on the bottom of the card with the slot on the motherboard. The card's metal bracket should align with the open space created when you removed the slot cover. If the adapter card has extra connectors that aren't positioned above the slot, you're trying to fit the wrong type of card into the wrong slot. Look for a slot that has matching connectors and notches.

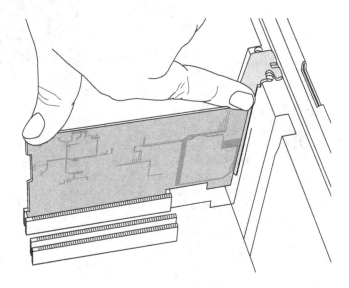

6. Houston, are we go for launch? If so, apply even pressure to the top of the card and push it down into the slot on the motherboard.

Although you won't hear a click, you should be able to tell when the card is firmly seated. The bracket should be resting tightly against the case.

7. Add the screw that you removed in Step 4 and tighten down the bracket — but don't overtighten it. Your computer is now equipped with at least one external USB, eSATA, or FireWire port.

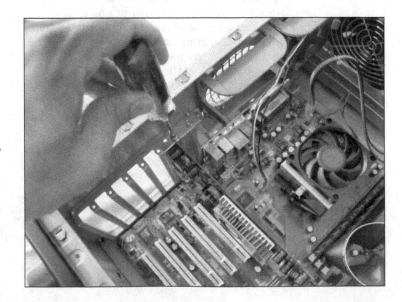

Connecting Built-In Ports

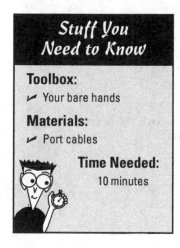

Stuff You Need to Know

Toolbox:
- Your bare hands

Materials:
- Port cables

Time Needed:
10 minutes

If your computer uses a standard ATX motherboard and case (which I discuss in Chapter 3), your ports are already connected at the back of the case. (If you recall, they stick out the back of the PC through that funky cutout.) Therefore, you can skip this section with a smile (unless your case includes front-mounted ports that you need to connect).

If you need to attach *external* ports to the front or back of your case so you can connect them to your motherboard, you're in the right place. External ports for the back of your case should look something like metal slot covers, sporting one or two ports on the outside and separate ribbon cables (or twisted wires) for each port. External ports for the front of your case are usually built into the case already, complete with cables for connecting to your motherboard.

External ports are not the same as the ATX-standard ports that are permanently attached to your motherboard — they need to be connected manually.

To install external ports, follow these steps:

1. Don't handle anything until you touch a metal surface. Put down that slick, plastic, handheld video game; you might be carrying static now. (Chapter 2 includes more on grounding, and why it's so important.)

2. If you're connecting an external port on the front of your case, skip to Step 5. If you're installing an external port on the back of your case, remove the screw and the metal slot cover at the back of the case and save both in your parts box.

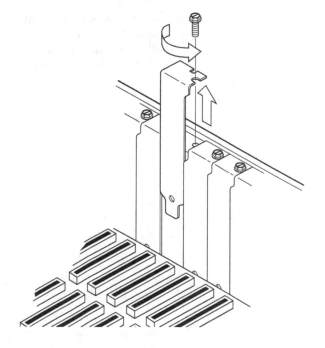

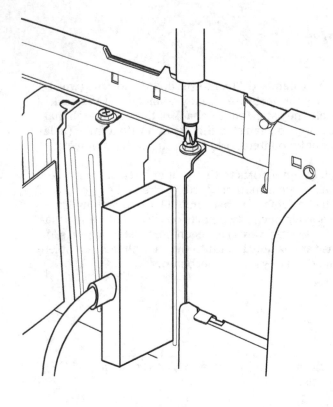

3. Insert the slot cover with the ports into the vacant slot.

4. Add the screw that you removed in Step 2 and tighten the bracket.

5. Check your motherboard manual and find the connectors for the external ports. These connectors are similar to the motherboard connectors for your reset button.

6. Attach the cables to the connectors on your motherboard as instructed by your motherboard's manual. Pin 1 on the motherboard connector should align with the marked wire on the cable; this marking is usually a red stripe or red lettering.

Installing a Keyboard

As I mention earlier in this chapter, computers use one of two types of keyboard connectors. The steps that you follow are determined by your motherboard and what it provides.

Connecting the keyboard is as easy as plugging in the cable through the case and into the keyboard port. To install your keyboard, follow these instructions:

1. Locate the keyboard port on the back of your case. If you have an older keyboard, the port should be as thick as a permanent marker. If you have a PS/2 keyboard port, it should be about the thickness of a pencil eraser. If your keyboard connector is the same size as the keyboard port, rejoice and continue. If the connector is the wrong size, grumble, visit a local computer shop, and ask for an adapter to make an older keyboard fit a PS/2 keyboard port (or the other way around).

2. Place the tip of the keyboard connector into the port and rotate it slowly while applying light pressure. The connector should fit into the port only one way, so you should be able to feel when the pins line up. If your connector has a little arrow or a flat area on the outside, that indicator usually points up (although not every motherboard has the decency to define "up" the same way). Figure 5-2 (earlier in this chapter) illustrates how this arrow alignment works.

3. When the keyboard connector is correctly aligned, push it in firmly.

Installing a Non-USB Mouse (Or Other Pointing Thing)

Stuff You Need to Know

Toolbox:

✔ Your bare hands

Materials:

✔ A non-USB mouse or pointing device

Time Needed:
2 minutes

If you invested in a USB mouse, you already know the drill: Just plug it in. However, if you've grown attached to an older non-USB mouse — my goodness, that sounds somewhat racy — you'll be happy to know that virtually all of today's motherboards still offer a PS/2 mouse port.

Follow these steps to install the mouse:

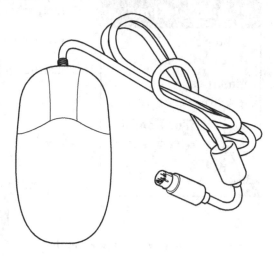

1. Locate the port on the back of your case.

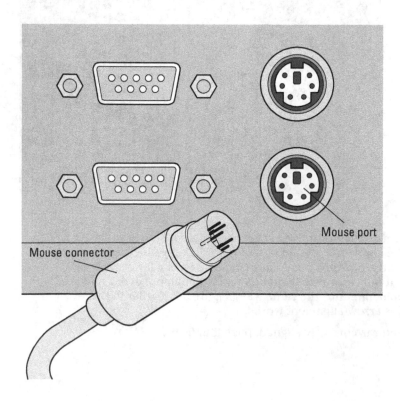

Mouse port

Mouse connector

2. Place the tip of the connector into the port and rotate it slowly while applying light pressure. The connector should fit into the port only one way, so you should be able to feel when the pins line up. If your connector has a little arrow or a flat area on the outside, that marker usually points up (although the direction that "up" takes seems to vary in the eyes of some engineers).

3. After the connector is correctly aligned, push it in firmly.

Chapter 6

Adding Video Hardware

Tasks performed in this chapter

✔ Installing your video adapter card

✔ Hooking up your monitor

✔ Testing your work

While you're building your computer, you'll be dazzled by more features, functions, acronyms, and assorted hoo-hah surrounding your video display than just about any other component of your computer system. Computer components such as your floppy drive and your keyboard have remained largely unchanged since the 486-class computers of old, but today's multimedia applications and operating systems demand monitors and video cards that deliver photographic-quality color and sharp detail. PCs running Windows Vista need extra graphics horsepower from a video card to support all the fancy eye candy and special effects. Game players and multimedia techno-jocks will also spend their dollars freely for advanced 3-D graphics and good-quality digital video.

In this chapter, I help you understand the buzzwords and acronyms that surround the technology behind all those video features so that you can make an intelligent decision on what to buy. I give you the inside information about your video subsystem, which has two parts: the video adapter card that fits inside your computer and the monitor that displays the images. You find out how to select the features that you need and how to install your video components.

The Video Card Explained

Your video card plays a very important role in your computer: It sends the visual output produced by a program to your monitor, which displays the output onscreen. That visual output could be alphanumeric characters that form words; high-resolution graphics, such as a photograph taken with your digital camera; or even the realistic 3-D shape of a monster in your favorite PC action game.

Get set because in this section, I take you on a whirlwind tour designed to help you find the video card that's exactly right for your applications.

Full speed ahead with accelerated graphics

Today's standard PC video adapter includes enhancements that allow your PC's CPU to concentrate on running programs and performing calculations: The video card actually handles most of the graphics work. With the arrival of the accelerated graphics card, operating systems like Windows Vista can include a truly dazzling look!

If you're building an inexpensive, low-end PC, you can save money by choosing a motherboard with *integrated* (built-in) video hardware. An integrated video card offers mediocre performance at best when compared with a separate PCI-Express video card, but you might find the integrated solution a money-saver if games aren't high on your list.

Accelerated cards have a separate processor onboard (called a GPU, for *graphics processing unit*) to handle complex graphics functions, such as drawing 3-D objects and displaying menus (which means that your CPU doesn't need to worry about these tasks). When you're shopping for a fast video card, keep these guidelines in mind:

✔ **Choose PCI-Express.** You get the best performance from a PCI-Express video card. Sticking a fast video card in a standard Peripheral Component Interconnect (PCI) slot is a little like forcing a thoroughbred horse to pull a plow: It will do the job, but you're holding it back. Only the PCI-Express bus type provides the super-fast throughput that your new video card needs to work its magic. Chapter 3 includes more information on selecting a motherboard with support for PCI-Express adapter cards.

Older AGP video cards are rapidly disappearing as the PCI-Express bus has become the standard, so stay clear of AGP at this point.

✔ **Go for memory.** Look for the most onboard RAM that you can afford. Most cards feature anywhere from 128MB to 1GB. More is better, natch. (Read more about this in the upcoming section, "Thanks for the memory.")

✔ **More colors and higher resolutions.** The deeper the color depth and the higher the resolution, the better. Find out more about these features in the next section.

✔ **Compare speed.** Compare the speeds that most video card manufacturers provide benchmark for speed of their accelerated cards. As an example, the manufacturer of my video card measures its card's speed by using the 3DMark Vantage utility from Futuremark (`www.futuremark.com`), which is a well-known benchmark program for graphics hardware under Windows.

For example, my NVIDIA GeForce 8400 GS video card turns in a respectable 4000+ rating, but today's top-rated cards can turn in double that figure! (And adding multiple video cards to your PC in SLI mode can result in truly astronomical benchmark figures — more on SLI mode in Chapter 14.) Some video card manufacturers also list the frame rate that a card can achieve while running a popular game, such as Half-Life 2. The higher the frame rate, the better the performance, which makes it a good figure to use while comparing video cards.

Strive for a minimum GPU speed (called the *core clock* in technospeak) for a mid-range PC of about 500 MHz, with the high-end gaming cards turning in over 750 MHz.

✔ **Verify driver support.** Make sure that your new card is fully supported with drivers for Windows XP and Windows Vista, OpenGL, and DirectX versions 9 and 10. (The last three in that list are the high-performance graphics subsystems that gamers use when playing today's most demanding 3-D games under Windows.) With the right software drivers, just about any operating system can benefit from the same accelerated video adapter. You'll find the drivers a card supports on the side of the box, or in the specifications section of a product review if you're shopping online. (I've also done a little digging on video card manufacturer Web sites to find out what operating systems and subsystems a certain card will support.)

If you're looking for a specific software driver, I heartily recommend DriverZone.com, at www.driverzone.com, which is a comprehensive Web site that provides links for just about every manufacturer and every type of computer component that I've ever seen.

Will 3-D video transform my entire existence?

You might have seen 3-D computer graphics on television or in the movies, but what good is a 3-D video card if you're not running an expensive graphics program? Computer gamers will tell you that there's no better piece of hardware to improve 3-D games, such as Age of Conan. With a 3-D video card, objects in these games look so realistic that you can practically reach out and touch them, and these games will run much faster, too. And if you're going to work in a beefy graphics program — say, Adobe Photoshop, Flash, or Illustrator — this hardware spec is a must-have.

A 3-D video card handles the complex math necessary to produce 3-D images (just like an accelerated video card does for Windows), thus enabling your CPU to focus on handling the program. The most popular 3-D video cards use hardware *chipsets* (the integrated circuits that control your hardware, like the BIOS chip on your motherboard) from the following two top manufacturers:

✔ **NVIDIA:** NVIDIA (www.nvidia.com) is known in the 3-D world for its GeForce chipset. At the time of this writing, the GeForce GTX 200–series chipset is on the most powerful 3-D video cards available.

✔ **ATI:** ATI (http://ati.amd.com/products/index.html) continues to update its Radeon GPU chipset (currently the Radeon HD 4800 series) to compete head-to-head with GeForce, so it's also a 3-D video card to compare.

For reviews and benchmarks of the latest video cards (along with comparisons between the newest NVIDIA and ATI chipsets), visit Tom's Hardware at www.tomshardware.com.

Thanks for the memory

Your computer's motherboard isn't the only part of your computer that has its own RAM. Your video card needs memory as well. In essence, your video adapter uses RAM to store colors and pixel values. The more RAM on your video card, the more colors you can display and the higher the video resolution you can use. I recommend using a minimum of 128MB of video memory for a PC running an office suite (think MS Office) and Internet applications, or a minimum of 256MB if you're running graphics-intensive games and applications on a 3-D video card. (See the preceding section for more on 3-D video cards.)

Color depth

You hear techno-nerds talk about color depth all the time, especially when they argue about the Web. *Color depth* refers to the number of colors in an image. Popular color depths are 256 colors, 64 thousand colors, and 16 million colors. (Today's video cards easily support 16 million or more colors.) Most graphics on the Web use a color depth of 256 colors because the lower the color depth, the less time it takes to download the image to a Web browser. Most people who create Web pages like to use 16 million color graphics because those graphics look better. Today, the popularity of broadband Internet access allows Webmasters to strut their stuff with more confidence.

Resolution

Extra video RAM lets your monitor display images at a higher resolution. To explain resolution, I need to introduce you to a single dot on your monitor: the *pixel.* The display on your monitor is built from thousands of pixels arranged in lines, each pixel displaying a certain color. Your video system's resolution is expressed in the number of pixels displayed horizontally and also the number of lines displayed vertically. For example, a resolution of 1024 x 768 means that the monitor displays 1024 pixels horizontally across the screen and 768 pixels vertically.

At lower resolutions, graphics look big and chunky, with ragged edges and blocky shapes. Any resolution lower than 800 x 600 is pretty much unusable these days. You can see how using a high, medium, or low resolution can really change how something looks onscreen in Figure 6-1.

Figure 6-1: High, medium, and low resolution.

Look out! Digital video from the planet MPEG!

Yep, video cards are just chock-full of acronyms, and this one is a real winner: MPEG stands for *Moving Pictures Expert Group.* (Now that's a piece of trivia you can toss around to your friends, right?) At least the name suggests something of value — MPEG is one of the most popular formats for digital video on your computer.

If you plan to use your computer extensively to edit digital video, make sure that your video card has *hardware MPEG support*, which can encode (and decode) MPEG digital video all by itself without bogging down your CPU.

At higher resolutions — such as 1024 x 768, 1152 x 864 (my favorite), 1280 x 1024, 1600 x 1200, or even higher — you can fit more images, data, icons, and information on your screen at one time. With such a higher resolution (especially with today's 19-inch and larger monitors), you can work on an entire brochure in your desktop-publishing program without zooming out. Or you can fit more of your favorite Web page on the screen without scrolling. Details look better, too, and you can work more efficiently.

But wait — it couldn't be that easy, could it? Nope, you're right: There's a trade-off between resolution and the readability of the fonts and graphics on your screen. For example, I simply can't work for long with a resolution of 1600 x 1200: my older (read that *wiser* and *more mature*) eyes end up producing a whopper of a headache trying to read text while I'm writing.

Note that LCD (or *flat-panel*) monitors typically favor one resolution, which the manufacturer usually specifies as the *native* resolution. If you switch an LCD monitor to a resolution other than the native resolution, the screen is likely to look fuzzy or out of focus.

What's the best display resolution? Only you can tell: The decision is completely personal, like choosing that keyboard that feels "just right." After installing your video card, try a wide range of resolutions to see what suits you best. But remember, every monitor has a maximum resolution it can display, so keep your experimentation within the limits of your hardware!

What's the bill, and what else do I need?

By this time, you might be shrugging your shoulders in disgust, thinking that you'll probably have to pay a thousand bucks for a good-quality video adapter with a top 3-D chipset, at least 256MB of RAM, and hardware MPEG decoding. Perhaps you'll have to take a second mortgage on the house?

Fear not, good citizen! A good-quality, 3-D gaming card with the NVIDIA GeForce 8600 GTS chipset and 256MB of memory, for example, has all these features and even a few more — and you can pick one up at a local computer store for well under $75. (Other comparable cards are around the same price.) Not a bad price for a power user part, eh?

Knowing about a few other features can help you determine which video card to buy. Along with the 3-D features that I mention earlier in this chapter, here's a short checklist of features that add value to any video card:

✔ **Support:** Before buying a video card, check the company's Web site. Here are some questions to ask: How often does the manufacturer update its drivers for the card that you're considering? Does it offer tech support over the Web, or will you end up getting put on hold, waiting for the next available customer service rep?

✔ **DVI output:** Oh, joy — yet another strange abbreviation created by engineers to confuse normal humankind. In this case, the seemingly random collection of letters stands for *digital visual interface* (often called *digital video interface* as well), which refers to a relatively new port that connects your video card to many new, flat-panel LCD monitors. A DVI port (which looks nothing like a standard VGA port) provides the fastest transfer of video data (hence the best performance) and the highest-quality digital video signal (compared with the tired analog signal offered by a standard VGA port). As long as your current monitor uses a standard VGA connection, you don't need a DVI port . . . but there's always the future, right? See the difference between the two ports in Figure 6-2.

✔ **Bundled software and Windows utilities:** Most video adapters available today include bundled software. The software usually highlights the top features of the video card. For example, a 3-D video card typically includes one or two games that take advantage of the card's 3-D hardware. Other favorites are multimedia encyclopedias and educational multimedia software for kids, as well as a software DVD player program. The best cards have utilities that add functionality to Windows, such as enabling you to quickly change the resolution of your desktop. Look for the software bundle that best fits your needs.

✔ **TV output:** If you create business presentations or broadcast-quality animation on your computer, the easiest way to display your work on your television (or transfer it to videotape) is to buy a video adapter that can display output from your computer on a TV or camcorder as well as on a monitor.

A video card with *TV output* is not the same thing as a *TV card.* Don't expect to be able to watch TV just because your video card has TV output. For that, you need a TV card, which is an adapter with a built-in TV tuner that enables you to watch TV in a little window on your monitor. It's just the thing for sports fanatics and those who refuse to miss their soaps.

✔ **Video panning:** If you have the necessary RAM, some cards enable you to *pan* (move) across your screen around a huge image or document, rather like how a movie camera pans to keep an actor in view while he or she moves from one part of the set to the other. This feature lets you view the whole image or document even if it's so big that it doesn't all fit on one screen. If you're going to edit large graphics in Photoshop or perhaps edit large documents or brochures in a desktop-publishing package, video panning might be a valuable feature for you.

✔ **Dual display:** A card with this feature can support two monitors at once, placed side by side. Both Windows XP and Vista allow you to use the two monitors as one super-large desktop, or you can display two different desktops at the same time. *Sweet!* See the magic in Figure 6-3. (Of course, you'll have to spring for a second monitor — such is the techno-wizard's lifestyle.) Typically, the card will offer both a VGA and DVI port (see Figure 6-2), and you connect each port (with a converter, if necessary) to a separate monitor. Although Windows provides basic controls for dual display, most video cards on the market today come with software that does a far better job, allowing fine adjustments that allow you to perfectly synchronize the edges of both displays.

✔ **DPMS support:** A video card with display power management signaling (DPMS) support can shut down your monitor to save energy in case you leave your computer unattended for a preset amount of time. (This feature requires a DPMS-enabled monitor, which I cover later in this chapter.)

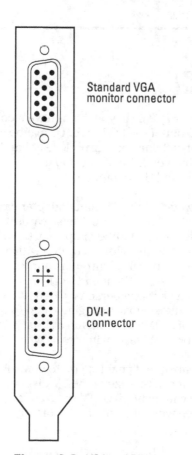

Standard VGA
monitor connector

DVI-I
connector

Figure 6-2: VGA and DIV ports.

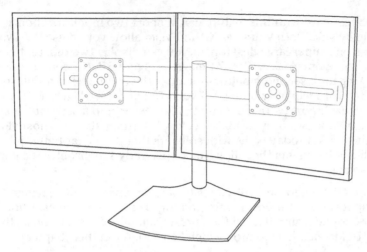

Figure 6-3: Dual monitor displays are a must for some tasks.

Hey, I Can Get TV on My PC!

Do you love your PC? I mean, really, *really* love your PC? If so, you might have a comfortable reclining chair in case you fall asleep in front of the keyboard. Or maybe one of those little refrigerators to keep your source of caffeine and sugar close at hand. (Considering a late-night burrito? I recommend that you keep the portable microwave a healthy distance away from both you and the computer.)

The ultimate in PC mouse-potato technology, however, is the TV tuner adapter card. Install one of these tuner cards, and you can watch TV on your PC. These cards carry full-featured TV tuners. Instead of using a separate TV tube or speakers, though, the display is shown on your monitor. Because the audio is routed with a cable from the TV card to your sound card, you hear the audio through your PC speaker system. Some TV tuner cards, such as the AVerTV Combo PCI-E, from AVerMedia Technologies, Inc. (www.aver.com), can act as a personal video recorder as well. Sweetness, and all for $100. (See the sidebar "Bringing video to your PC" for more details.) You need a minimum of 512MB of RAM and at least a set of stereo speakers, and I recommend a monitor of at least 19 inches as well.

Most tuner cards provide an onscreen remote control that enables you to control the volume, change the channel or station, and choose the size of the TV display. If you're running another program on your PC, you can display the TV program as a picture-in-picture window or toggle it to full screen when it's time for that really important cartoon.

Bringing video to your PC

You can use TV tuner cards for more than just watching TV or listening to the radio on your PC. Most tuner cards also enable you to capture incoming video or audio to your hard drive, making captured video a cheap source of multimedia material for your next project. If you want to watch or capture a home movie that's still stuck on a VHS tape, you can also plug your VCR into most tuner cards.

Warning: Capturing copyrighted video or audio and distributing it yourself is illegal.

Depending on the TV tuner card, you might also get bundled software that enables you to take individual still images from the incoming video. It's the perfect way to get a good image of Uncle Milton from that family reunion video — amateur video editors, rejoice!

Time to Meet Your Bus Slots

While you have your case open and you can see everything clearly, take a moment to determine what type of bus slots you have. *Bus slots* are the connectors on your motherboard that accept adapter cards. (And note that the type of slots has nothing to do with the processor, memory, and motherboard's bus speed.) If you add internal adapter cards to your computer, they fit into these bus slots — becoming, in effect, an extension of the motherboard itself. For example, plugging a video card into the appropriate bus slot can provide you with better performance and more features than the integrated card built into your motherboard. If you're confused about which types of slots you have, check your motherboard manual.

Most motherboards that you buy today have a mixture of the following slots:

- ✔ **An accelerated graphics port (AGP) slot (4x or 8x) or a PCI-Express x16 slot reserved for a video card.** These cards are generally longer than the standard 32-bit PCI card.

- ✔ **Four or five Peripheral Component Interconnect (PCI) slots for 32-bit PCI adapter cards.** (Typically, this includes sound cards and the like although a number of 32-bit video cards on the market don't use the PCI-E slot.)

This information becomes really important really quickly because you need to buy the proper type of adapter card for many other parts in your computer. If the card doesn't match your available slots, you can't use it! These slots are a series of long, parallel connectors on your motherboard, and most motherboards come with anywhere from five to seven slots. Your motherboard manual will detail how many slots you have, and which kind they are.

If you're rapidly becoming tired of the word *slot,* here's good news: You're finished with it, at least for this chapter!

Staking Out Your Visual Territory

Luckily, choosing a suitable monitor is easier than your video adapter although it's still just as important in providing you with the best possible display. In this section, I discuss the selling points of a good monitor.

 Like a keyboard, a monitor is something that you really need to try in person. You need to *see* the monitor and its display with your own eyes before you buy it. Often, the only difference between two monitors with similar prices is that one simply looks better to you.

I recommend visiting at least one or two computer stores to take a look at the monitors they offer. Before you decide to buy, write down the brand name and model number of the monitor and see whether you can buy it online or through mail order for less. (With the brand name and model number, you can easily use Pricewatch at www.pricewatch.com to locate the best prices across the entire Internet.)

Deciphering monitor sizes and shapes (and choosing the one for you)

You can buy a monitor in several different sizes, starting at around 17 inches. (All monitors are measured diagonally, just like a TV.) You can easily find larger monitors, up to 22 inches and even larger. The extra screen real estate is especially useful for those doing desktop-publishing or computer-aided drafting.

So which is the right size for you? Think of buying a car. A 17-inch monitor is like a '71 Volkswagen Beetle, and a 22-inch monitor is like a Cadillac sports sedan. They both do the same job — driving you where you want to go — but one is faster, bigger, and more fun to drive (as well as much more expensive). You can stretch out in the Caddy, and it has all the latest controls and a gaggle of automatic functions that keep everything in sync. It's the same with a 22-inch monitor.

In general, the larger the monitor, the easier it is on your eyes, especially if you'll be chained in front of your computer for hours at a time. At the same resolution, a 19-inch monitor displays the same images as a 17-inch, but the image is physically bigger and the details stand out more clearly. When you increase the resolution of your desktop (to 1280 x 1024 or so), the monitor size becomes more important because the smaller monitor needs to shrink everything to fit the entire desktop on its screen.

Many of today's flat-panel LCD monitors are advertised as *widescreen*: That is, they're longer in the horizontal dimension, just like a typical HD-TV, allowing you to watch DVD movies in widescreen format. Even if you don't watch DVD movies, however, widescreen displays are supported in Windows Vista, giving you more screen real estate for all of your programs. (I like to leave Microsoft Word open next to my Internet Explorer window, all of which fits on my widescreen display.) Today's 3-D games also support widescreen display, giving you a larger view of your alien worlds.

Ever heard the teaser, "So, exactly how big is a 17-inch TV?" Computer monitors suffer from the same head-scratching conundrum. Here the deal: You have to weigh the diagonal width of the monitor case against the total viewing area. These are two very different things. Here's an example. Two monitors are advertised as 17 inches, but one has an actual viewing area of 15.9 inches, and the other has a viewing area of 16.1 inches. (*Remember:* Viewing area measures the diagonal size of the screen.) As you might expect, the second monitor displays more than the first. The first monitor probably looks the same size, but you'll probably be paying for more plastic case. When you're shopping for a monitor, it's worth paying a few dollars more for the monitor with a larger actual viewing area.

For general home use, a 17-inch monitor is fine. If you prefer viewing larger text and graphics, plan to do graphics-intensive work for several hours at a time, or are a hard-core gamer, I would point you toward at a 19-inch monitor at the minimum.

Remember that the best judge of a monitor's display is your own eye, so *use* it!™

Select a monitor by shopping at your local computer stores; then buy it online to save money.

What else makes a great monitor?

When you're familiar with the major features of a good monitor, you're almost ready to go shopping. In this section, I list a number of extra features to look for while selecting the flat-panel display that works best for you.

Flat-panel color displays are a dream come true. LCD monitors use the same liquid-crystal technology as laptop computer screens (not like those old clunker flat-panel CRT screens), so they require only 15–20 percent of the physical depth of a CRT monitor. This size difference can save you a ton of desktop space because your monitor's footprint just went from Bigfoot to Betty Boop. See the svelte in Figure 6-4.

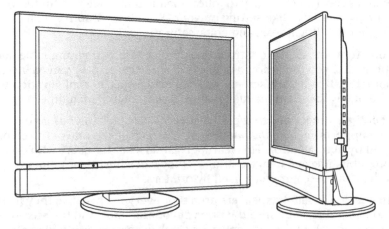

Figure 6-4: LCD minotors: lithe, lean, and thin.

Here's why folks love them so. With a flat-panel monitor, you get a truly flat, edge-to-edge display with no distortion but gorgeous color. Flat-panel screens also give off very little heat and use much less electricity. And, unlike a tube-based CRT monitor, a flat-panel display emits virtually no radiation, so it's easier (and safer) on your eyes, and you can spend longer periods of time in front of your computer without discomfort. Once available only in 15- and 17-inch models, larger 19-, 21-, and 22-inch flat-panel displays are becoming affordable now that the price of the technology has dropped.

Make sure you note the *response time* (given in milliseconds, such as 5 ms, 8 ms, or 12 ms). The lower the response time, the better a flat-panel monitor will be for gaming and digital video. If you're a gamer or you're into digital video, I strongly recommend an LCD monitor with an 8 ms response time or lower.

Keep in mind that these features can appear on a good 17-inch display as well as on an expensive 22-inch model:

- **Antiglare coating:** As a general rule, whatever you create or do on your computer should shine — *not* the monitor itself! An antiglare screen can be a big help in an office that is brightly lit or has many windows.

- **Energy Star/DPMS–compliant:** All motherboards sold these days have the Energy Star power management system built in. You can configure an Energy Star motherboard to power down the computer while you're off getting doughnuts. If your monitor is Energy Star–compliant, your computer can shut the monitor down, too. When you return, press a key or move your mouse to wake up your computer, and then congratulate yourself on saving both your money and your environment.

Some video cards can also perform this power-down function for your monitor; see whether your card's manual mentions that it's Energy Star/VESA DPMS–compatible. If so, follow its instructions for enabling the power-saving features. (VESA is the Video Electronics Standards Association.)

- **Digital controls:** Techno-nerds like me favor precise digital controls with an onscreen display (OSD) of easy-to-follow menus that make fine-tuning your monitor's picture more like setting up your DVD player. Controls can include contrast, brightness, and color saturation.

Most monitors with digital controls also offer separate programmable configurations that you can store in memory. If a particular program changes the characteristics of your screen, you can load a special configuration to take care of it rather than manually adjust your monitor each time.

- **Color configuration:** Does that pink really look like pink to you? If your monitor supports *color configuration,* you can change the hue of the colors displayed by your monitor. This feature is a real killer for users who do desktop publishing and image editing — they can adjust their colors to match the Pantone color chart used by printers.

- **Built-in speakers:** Built-in speakers aren't for everyone because they usually add a considerable amount to the price of your monitor, and the stereo separation from speakers that are only a few inches apart is pretty dismal. (Remember that the sound card has jacks that enable you to add your own external speakers, which typically sell for less than $30 per pair. For more information, see Chapter 10.) However, if you're looking for convenience and you want to save desktop space, you can investigate a monitor with built-in speakers.

✔ **Work ergonomics and comfort:** Take it from someone who spends hours a day writing at the keyboard: Elevating your monitor correctly is important. You should be able to sit down at your keyboard and type naturally, with your monitor at eye level and at least two feet distant from your eyes. With a properly positioned monitor, you should be able to work without undue strain on your neck or your eyes. Many displays take this a step further, with stands that tilt forward and backward, or adjust up and down.

If you need extra height on your monitor and the stand doesn't adjust upward, consider purchasing a shelf unit, which allows you to store your keyboard beneath the monitor. Using a shelf allows you to elevate your monitor.

✔ **Warranty:** Because you can use a typical LCD monitor with just about any PC that you might build or buy in the foreseeable future, pony up extra for a longer warranty. Most top monitors these days have a three- to five-year warranty; economy models typically offer only a one-year warranty.

And for Colossus, I Pick . . .

Have I mentioned I'm a gamer? Big-time. Therefore, Colossus will need some real horsepower for a video card, and I'm going to need a widescreen flat-panel LCD monitor for my DVD movies.

My graphics picks are

✔ **EVGA GeForce 9800 GX2:** This monster card carries 1GB of onboard memory, has a 600 MHz core clock, and supports SLI mode (which I discuss in more detail in Chapter 14). It has two DVI connectors, so I can run dual DVI flat-panel monitors easily in the future. The EVGA card also supports DirectX 10 and Windows Vista with ease.

✔ **ViewSonic 20-inch Widescreen LCD:** Note that this monitor is not shown on the companion DVD, but this would be my pick for its maximum resolution of 1680 x 1050, tilting base, OSD controls, and both VGA and DVI connectors.

Installing Your Video Card

In this section, I show you how to add your video adapter card to your chassis. Your video adapter card will have at least one DVI port on the side of the card itself, and most cards still include a VGA port as well. (You see what these ports look like in Figure 6-2, earlier in the chapter.) And as I mention earlier in the chapter, most of today's video cards allow you to run two monitors using both of these ports in conjunction.

If your motherboard includes integrated video hardware and you decided to use it, you won't need to install a separate card, and your DVI and/or VGA port is already installed at the rear of your PC's case. Instead, head directly to the section, "Connecting Your Monitor" later in this chapter.

1. If your computer chassis is plugged in, unplug it. And let me guess: You've been making balloon animals to amuse your kids? If so, your skin is now one big conductor for static electricity, and that static could damage your video card. Touch a metal surface before you handle your video card (or anything else on your computer).

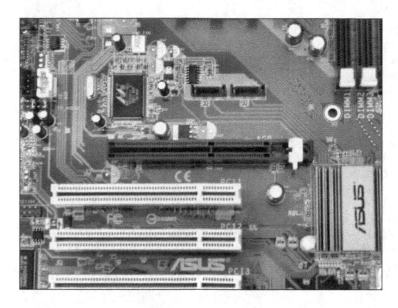

2. Locate a PCI-Express adapter card slot of the proper length at the back of your computer case. You should be able to easily locate the single PCI-Express slot. (It's usually in the middle of the motherboard, and is molded in a different color from your other PCI slots. Consult your motherboard manual if you're uncertain of its location.)

If you have a 32-bit PCI video card, use one of the shorter PCI adapter card slots. (Need help identifying what type of card slots you have? Chapter 4 illustrates these slots.)

3. When you locate the slot, take your favorite screwdriver and remove the screw and the metal slot cover at the back of the case. Stick both parts in your spare-parts box.

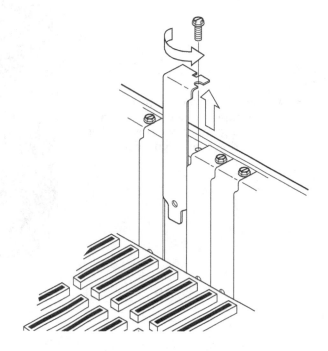

4. Pick up your video adapter card by the top corners. Line up the connector on the bottom of the card with the slot on the motherboard. All the connectors and any notches on the video card should line up with the slot; the card's metal bracket should align with the open space created when you removed the slot cover.

If the adapter card has extra connectors that aren't positioned above the slot, you're trying to fit a "square peg into a round hole"! Look for a slot that has matching connectors and notches. Refer to your motherboard manual if you need help locating the proper slot.

5. When everything lines up as it should, apply even pressure to the top of the card and push it down into the slot on the motherboard. Although you won't hear a click, you should be able to tell when the card is firmly seated, and the bracket should rest tightly against the case.

Never apply undue force. The card should pop in easily!

6. Add the screw to the corresponding hole in the bracket and tighten down the bracket, but don't overtighten it.

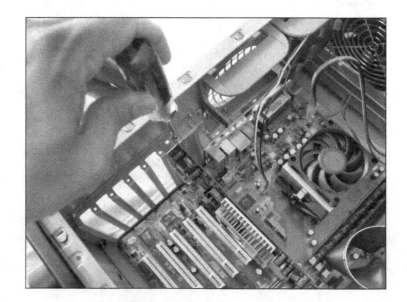

Installing Your TV Tuner Card

Decided to add a TV tuner card to your PC? I understand completely, seeing as how viewing football is an integral part of any computer user's task load! (Luckily, you can hide the video window when your significant other approaches.) A TV tuner card will work fine with either a separate sound card or audio hardware that's integrated into your PC's motherboard, and any monitor should work fine for standard-resolution analog and digital TV broadcasts.

Note that you will need to have a cable long enough to reach from your external antenna, cable box, or satellite box to the corresponding input connector on your TV tuner card.

If your new TV tuner card supports HD, you'll probably get the best possible results from a widescreen monitor.

1. If your computer chassis is plugged in, unplug it. As always, touch a metal surface before you install your card to discharge any static electricity.

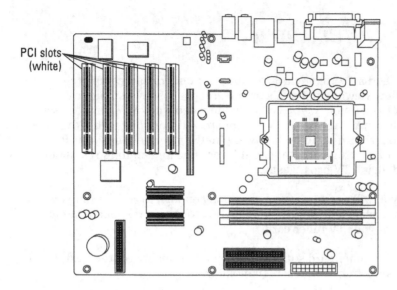

PCI slots
(white)

2. Select an open PCI adapter card slot for your TV tuner card. (For more information on PCI cards and PCI bus slots, see Chapter 4.)

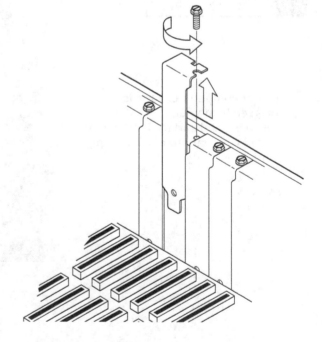

3. Remove the screw and the metal slot cover adjacent to the selected slot, and add the screw and slot cover into your parts bowl.

4. Line up the connector on the TV tuner card with the slot on the motherboard. The card's metal bracket should align with the open space that remains when you removed the slot cover.

5. Apply even pressure to the top of the card and push it down into the slot. If the card is all the way in, the bracket should be resting tightly against the case.

6. Add the screw from your parts bowl and tighten down the bracket.

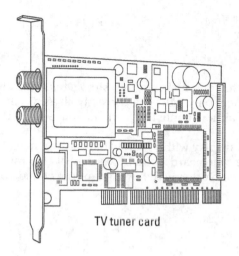

TV tuner card

7. Connect the cable from your external antenna, cable box, or satellite
box to the corresponding input
connector on the TV tuner card.

8. Connect the patch cable from the
audio output/line out jack on your
TV tuner card to the audio
input/line in jack on your sound
card. (Note that some TV tuner
cards work directly through the
operating system with your sound
card, and may not require an external patch cable.)

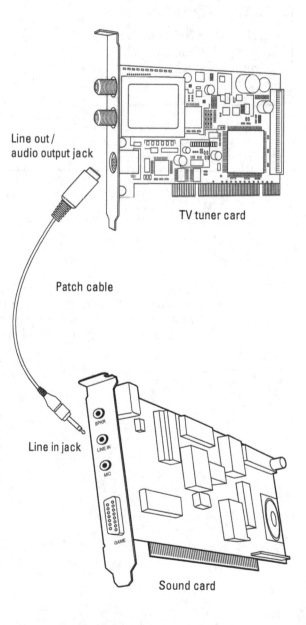

Line out /
audio output jack

TV tuner card

Patch cable

Line in jack

Sound card

Connecting Your Monitor

Stuff You Need to Know

Toolbox:
- Your bare hands

Materials:
- Power cable
- DVI (or VGA) cable

Time Needed:
5 minutes

Connecting your monitor to your computer is a simple task. Luckily, the DVI video port and cable connect only if they're correctly aligned. The same is true for a VGA connector, although most PC owners now use the DVI port.

If you're using a flat-panel display with a VGA cable and you need to connect to a DVI port on your video card, drop by your local electronics store and pick up a VGA-to-DVI converter, which will adapt the connector to fit your cable.

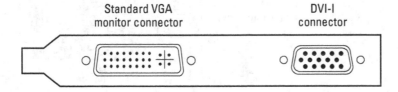

Standard VGA monitor connector   DVI-I connector

1. Locate the DVI video port on the back of your case. (If you're using the VGA port, look for the 15-pin port shown in at the top of the card in the figure.)

2. Align the connector on the end of the monitor cable with the video port. Note that the DVI connector and port are designed to fit together in only one way!

3. When the connector is aligned correctly with the video port, push the connector in firmly. You should hear a click as the DVI connector seats. Some connectors still use screw knobs. If you have one of these, tighten the connector by turning the knobs on the connector clockwise.

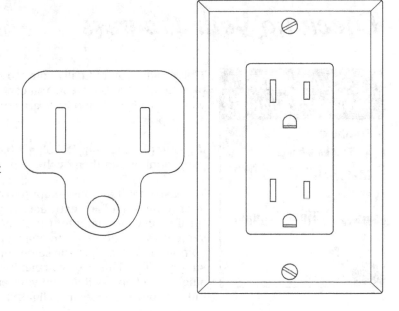

4. Plug the three-prong power cord that came with your monitor into the matching connector on the back of your monitor's case. Push the plug in firmly to make sure that it doesn't pop out.

5. Plug the monitor's power cable into your friendly local wall socket. If your wall socket accepts only two prongs — indicating that it isn't grounded — I would heartily recommend that you relocate your computer to a socket that *is* grounded instead of sticking an adapter plug on the cable.

Checking Your Progress

Stuff You Need to Know

Toolbox:
- Your bare hands

Materials:
- None

Time Needed:
5 minutes

That's right. You're finally going to see something on the screen after completing this chapter's test. You can also visually check to make sure that your CPU and RAM modules are correctly recognized by your motherboard at this point.

If you unplugged your PC, plug it back in now. Push the power switch on your monitor and then push the power switch on your case.

To make sure that your computer recognizes all your stuff correctly, turn on your monitor and any external peripherals (such as your printer) before turning on your computer (or at the same time). The easiest and most convenient way to do this is to connect all the power cables from your various computer devices into the same surge protector or uninterruptible power supply (UPS). This way, you can turn the entire system on or off with a single flip of one switch, and your entire system is also protected against indirect power surges from lightning strikes or alien encounters.

Check for the following activity to make sure you installed your video adapter and connected your monitor correctly:

1. You should see a message on your screen, which identifies either the video adapter or the motherboard. It doesn't matter which you see. The important thing is that your monitor is *displaying* the message! If your monitor doesn't display any text, check the installation of your video card and then make sure that the monitor cable is firmly connected and that you plugged in your monitor. Also, make sure that you set both the contrast and brightness on your monitor to medium.

2. After a few seconds, you should see your computer displaying motherboard information, including the type of CPU you installed and the amount of RAM on your motherboard. Watch to make sure that no error messages are displayed. If your computer returns an error message about your system memory or RAM, go to Chapter 4 and check your RAM to make sure that you installed it correctly. You might also need to consult your motherboard's manual to make certain you chose the right bank in which to add RAM. If your computer locks up, press and hold the Power button until the PC shuts off; then return to Chapter 4 and double-check your CPU installation.

3. At this point in the boot process, your computer tries to find a hard drive or floppy drive (if you installed a floppy drive) and then promptly gets upset when it doesn't find them. Poor thing. Your computer will probably beep once or twice and then sulk in frustration. Chapter 4 includes a table of what these beep codes mean.

TIP

No beep? Check your PC's internal speaker to make sure that it's properly connected, as described in Chapter 3.

4. Turn off your computer, pet the case affectionately, and reassure your half-assembled chassis that you will be adding a hard drive in Chapter 7. If your machine completes this test, you successfully added your video adapter and monitor to your system, and your RAM and CPU are properly installed. **Good going!**

Chapter 7

Installing Your Hard Drive and Other Storage Devices

Tasks performed in this chapter

- ✔ Connecting your controller card

- ✔ Installing your hard drive and floppy drive

- ✔ Configuring your PC for your new hard drive and floppy drive

- ✔ Formatting your hard drive

Ah, the quest for storage. Whose domicile ever has enough closets and room for all your stuff? (Even Bill Gates probably needs another closet.) Likewise, your new computer needs a warehouse to permanently store all those programs and all that data that you'll be using. And for that, you need a hard drive.

Of course, you could simply run a trusty Web browser on another PC, jump to your favorite online hardware mega-super-colossal-mall, and buy the first hard drive that you see. If you're looking for the best value, however, you should take your time and consider your options. To make an informed choice while you're shopping (and to make the installation easier), you need to know which hard drive features and specifications are most important.

Although you can consider a hard drive to be the main memory "closet" of your computer, it isn't the only magnetic storage device that your computer can use. In this chapter, I also introduce you to alternative data storage options such as

- ✔ Floppy disk drives

- ✔ External USB hard drives

- ✔ Removable cartridge hard drives

- ✔ 4GB universal serial bus (USB) Flash drives no bigger than a key chain

You can also store data by writing it to CD or DVD by using laser light — hence the moniker *optical drive* — but I cover that in Chapter 9.

Choosing Betwixt Hard Drive Technologies

If you've started looking at ads or online for hard drives, you're probably drowning in techno-babble and funny numbers and odd acronyms. Is it EIDE or E-I-E-I-O? Little Miss Muffet SATA on a tuffet? (Okay, that last one was a stretch, but I couldn't help it.)

To help you select a hard drive that's suitable for your system, get ready because the acronyms and jargon are going to flow fast and free through this section. You'll find out more about what types of hard drives will fit in your computer, and the advantages and disadvantages of each breed of hard drive. Then you use this information to determine which type of hard drive is appropriate for your needs.

Luckily, virtually all of today's PCs use only two types of internal hard drive technology: EIDE and SATA. Let the alphabet soup begin — and don't forget the Glossary if you need help decoding those acronyms.

Enhanced IDE (EIDE) hard drives

An *enhanced IDE* (commonly known as *EIDE*) hard drive is the successor to the IDE (or integrated drive electronics) throne. The *enhanced* part of the name simply means that these drives are smaller, run faster, and have more storage capacity. As you can guess from its name, an IDE drive carries onboard most of the electronics that were located on a hard drive controller card. Enhanced IDE is the single-most popular hard drive technology, and this type of drive is used in just about every PC manufactured today. Most EIDE adapter cards can control a maximum of four EIDE devices (including hard drives and DVD recorders).

By the way, EIDE drives are also called PATA (that's short for *parallel ATA*) devices. This gets important in the next section, as you'll see.

Figure 7-1 illustrates the business end of a modern EIDE drive. Note the appearance and position of the power connector, the ribbon cable connector, and the master/ slave jumper set. (*Note:* You need to be familiar with all three components when you install your hard drive.) These components might be in different spots on your particular hard drive, but they're there somewhere. Check your hard drive documentation for their exact location.

A *jumper* is a tiny metal-and-plastic part that can connect two or more pins to configure a device. On an EIDE hard drive, the master/slave jumper is particularly important: The setting that you choose for this jumper determines whether the drive is the *primary* (master) drive or the *secondary* (slave) drive in a PC with two hard drives. If you have only one drive, you should select master drive — if you have two EIDE drives on the same cable, one drive should be set to master, and the other drive should be set to slave. Your hard drive jumper diagram (which usually appears printed on top of the drive) provides the settings for the master/slave jumper, and you'll find more about jumpers in Chapter 3.

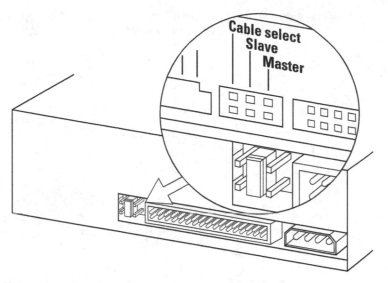

Figure 7-1: The EIDE hard drive is the workhorse of today's PCs.

Serial ATA hard drives

For most PC owners, an EIDE (PATA) drive is probably the best choice. If you're willing to spend a few dollars more, though, you can join the ranks of the SATA faithful. (SATA is shorthand for *serial ATA*, as opposed to *parallel ATA* for EIDE drives.) The SATA interface delivers data back and forth between your PC and your hard drive significantly faster than EIDE/PATA — about 20 MBps faster — and this faster data transfer rate means that programs load faster and documents get saved faster, too. Also, the SATA cable itself is smaller (which allows for better airflow inside your PC's chassis), about half an inch wide.

SATA devices also require a different power connector, which uses 15 pins. You'll never mix up a SATA power cable with a standard EIDE/PATA power cable, which has only 4 pins. In fact, many SATA hard drives include one of each type of power plug (like you see in Figure 7-2), just in case you're using an older power supply that doesn't have a SATA plug. If your SATA device doesn't have a legacy 4-pin power plug, you'll have to pick up a converter at your local computer store. One end of the converter connects to the 4-pin plug from your power supply, and the other fits your SATA drive.

Besides the simplified cable connections and the performance boost, SATA drives have one huge advantage: no master/slave jumper! (For more on master/slave, see the preceding section.) A SATA drive is designated as primary or secondary according to the cable connection you make on the motherboard, so there are no jumpers to set. (Remember, today's motherboards are typically equipped with two SATA connectors and two EIDE/PATA connectors. For each type of interface, one connector is called the *primary,* and one is called the *secondary.*)

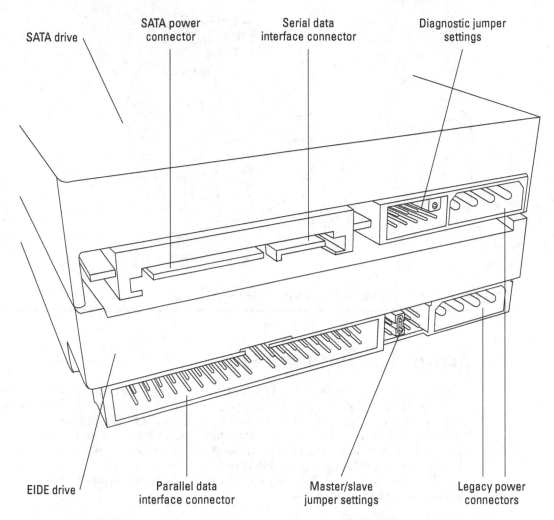

SATA drive

SATA power connector

Serial data interface connector

Diagnostic jumper settings

EIDE drive

Parallel data interface connector

Master/slave jumper settings

Legacy power connectors

Figure 7-2: Comparing the connectors and cables of an EIDE/PATA drive and a SATA drive.

Comparing EIDE and SATA hard drives

"Okay," you say, "SATA wins, right?" Wrong, believe it or not. EIDE/PATA is still the hard drive of choice for three important reasons:

- ✔ **Less expensive:** EIDE drives and adapter cards are typically less expensive than SATA hardware, which makes EIDE more popular with computer manufacturers.

- ✔ **No significant performance difference:** Not every computer application sees a dramatic performance increase from faster SATA hardware. For example, your word processor doesn't perform any better with a SATA drive than with an EIDE drive because hard drive access isn't important while you're typing.

> ✔ **More popular with hardware manufacturers:** At the time of this writing, most CD/DVD recorders and internal tape drives still use EIDE connections. And as long as the common denominator is still EIDE/PATA instead of SATA, EIDE will remain King of the Hill!

What do I recommend? I agree that SATA is indeed superior to EIDE hardware, and it's slowly but surely replacing EIDE as a standard. You'll notice that Colossus (my super machine I build in this book) uses only SATA drives, so you can tell what I'd pick!

On the plus side, you can mix SATA and EIDE hardware in the same computer. If you find that you need an EIDE device after your computer is up and running with a SATA drive, you can add it. The majority of motherboards on the market today offer both onboard EIDE and SATA controllers.

More stuff about hard drives

What specifications does a smart shopper look for in an EIDE drive? Here are a few:

> ✔ **Storage capacity:** No big mystery here. The more storage capacity, the more data you can store on a drive. Modern EIDE drives hold anywhere from 80GB to 1TB. (*TB* is short for *terabyte.* A lot!) Hard drive capacities are always increasing over time.

On average, most home computers running Windows Vista need at least 60GB of hard drive space. For an office computer, the size of your hard drive is more dependent on what type of programs you run; some office software suites take up an entire gigabyte of space all by themselves. My recommendation? Buy a drive so large that you can't imagine ever running out of space. (Believe me, my friend, you'll fill it up!) I would suggest a drive of *at least* 120GB, which will set you back less than $80. Remember, that's a bare minimum; gamers, digital photographers, and digital video connoisseurs will want far more room.

> ✔ **Access time:** A drive's *access time* (sometimes called *seek time*) is a measurement of how fast the drive can read and write data. The lower the number, the faster the drive. This time is measured in milliseconds (ms), and it's usually listed next to the drive in advertisements. Naturally, the faster the drive, the more expensive it is. (Just once, I'd like the best of something to be the cheapest.)

Today's fastest EIDE drives have access times of around 7 ms although any speed less than 10 ms should be fast enough for all but the most demanding needs. If you're a power user, stick with a drive less than 10 ms. Super-fast SATA drives often deliver access times around 5 ms.

> ✔ **rpm:** At last, an abbreviation that most of us understand! Yes, indeed, this is your old friend, *revolutions per minute,* and it measures the speed at which the platters within your hard drive are moving. (The *platters* are the spinning discs in your hard drive that store data magnetically.) In general, the faster the rpm, the faster the drive can retrieve data. Before you strap a tachometer onto your drive, however, you should know that rpm is not as accurate as *access time* in predicting a drive's performance. I recommend a drive with a minimum of 7,200 rpm. (My Western Digital Raptor SATA drive spins at 10,000 rpm, and Windows feels like a Ferrari.)

✔ **Size:** Most drives are 3½ inches, which means that they fit in a standard 3½-inch bay. (Most PC cases have one of these bays left open: It's reserved for an additional drive. However, these bays can be covered as well, without an outside opening — perfect for a hard drive's nest.) If you have an available standard half-height 5¼-inch bay in your case, you need a drive cage kit to enable the 3½-inch drive to fit. A *drive cage* is simply a metal square that holds the smaller 3½-inch drive inside; in turn, the cage is fastened to the computer chassis as if it were a 5¼-inch device.

✔ **Cache:** A hard drive's *cache* (sometimes called a *buffer*) holds data that's used frequently (or will soon be needed) by your central processing unit (CPU). With a disk cache, the hard drive itself doesn't have to re-read that data. As you might guess, the larger the cache, the better (and usually the more expensive) the drive. I recommend a drive with at least an 8MB cache.

✔ **Warranty:** A hard drive is one of the few parts in your computer that is both complex and has moving parts of its own. A typical hard drive has a reliable lifetime of about six years or so under normal use. The standard industry warranty for hard drives is three years although you can find drives with warranties as long as five years.

The Ancient Floppy Still Lives

Despite all the well-known drawbacks to floppies — too fragile, too slow, and their tiny storage capacity — floppy drives are still found on many PCs because of the universal nature of 3½-inch floppy disks. Because they've been around for so long and because everyone's so accustomed to them, some computer manufacturers still produce PCs with a floppy drive.

Of course, better forms of removable media have been developed — for example, the USB flash drive, which I mention later in this chapter. Unfortunately, important data still resides on 3½-inch floppies around the world. (On unreliable, potentially unstable floppies. Makes you shudder thinking about it, eh?)

There isn't much in the way of features to look for when you're buying a floppy disk drive. Color is pretty much it, and you can easily buy a black floppy drive to match that smashing ebony case you bought for your new system.

So, just in case you absolutely have to have one, I show you how to install a floppy drive later in this chapter. However, if you can possibly avoid using this less-than-adequate and less-than-desirable storage device, do so.

Don't Forget Your Controller Card

Many motherboards sold these days feature more than just integrated serial ports and parallel ports. All modern motherboards already have at least a built-in EIDE hard drive and floppy drive controller. A *controller* directs the flow of data to and from your hard drives, floppy drives, and any additional devices.

Here are three other features that you should consider for your motherboard's built-in controller:

✔ **SATA support:** Motherboard manufacturers are rapidly adopting the SATA standard, but you can still buy a motherboard that doesn't include SATA support. If you're itching to push the performance of your PC to the limit, make sure your new motherboard has the SATA connectors you need.

✔ **RAID support:** Great, another acronym. This one stands for *Redundant Array of Independent Disks*. In plain speech, a RAID is a combination of two or more hard drives linked together by your motherboard's onboard controller. RAID can be configured to boost the transfer speed for the files on the array's hard drives or to provide *redundant* (backup) copies of those files in case one of the hard drives fails. Either way, most home PC owners should probably steer clear of RAID. Just make sure you back up your data. (Heck, even a RAID needs to be backed up regularly.)

✔ **Cache:** A controller memory cache stores data that's used often or that your CPU will probably require very soon. It improves performance because the CPU can retrieve the data from the memory cache, which is much faster than re-reading it from the drive. Don't spend any extra on a caching controller, however, unless you're a power user intent on cutting-edge gaming or professional-quality video editing (or you plan to use your computer as a network server or something equally taxing). A "Cunningham Edition" home PC (from Chapter 2) or a simple office PC really doesn't need such high-speed disk access.

Hey, You Just Removed Your Media!

In this section, I tell you about an old friend that enables you to take up to 8GB of data and run with it — or mail it, or toss it to a co-worker, or even lock it in a safety deposit box. I'm talking about the popular USB Flash drives, which store data without moving parts, batteries, or a power cord. I also highlight the nifty update on the Iomega Zip drive system, the Iomega REV drive.

Do you really need removable storage, or are you just fascinated by toys?

To be honest, you don't absolutely need a removable storage drive unless your primary application fits one of these criteria:

✔ **File size:** If you plan to send or receive files that can't be efficiently sent over the Internet (perhaps because the files are just too big), you'd benefit from a removable media solution.

✔ **Security/portability:** If security is an issue and you want to protect your data, the best way to do so is to take your data with you or lock it up so that others have no access to it. Flash drives make taking your important data with you easy.

✔ **Archiving:** If you want to store information without filling up your hard drive, a flash drive can act as a warehouse for archiving data.

The Flash drive: Small but spacious

Today's USB flash drives are just downright nifty. (Yep, I actually used the word *nifty* seeing as how *neat* just didn't cover my excitement.) Prices have dropped on these drives to a pittance, yet they still beat archaic floppies and Zip drives in a number of different ways:

- ✔ Flash drives transfer data much faster than floppies.

- ✔ Flash drives are compatible with both PCs running Windows and Macs running Mac OS X, so they make great drives for transferring stuff with your buddy in the next dorm room.

- ✔ Finally (and probably most importantly), USB flash drives are easy to use and don't require any techno-wizard knowledge to master!

The REV has landed

If you want a removable media drive with anywhere from 35 to 120GB of capacity and a wealth of connection options, you're asking for the Iomega REV drive. REV cartridge drives are available with USB external connections and with internal EIDE and SATA drives. Street prices range around $380 for the internal versions (and around $75 per 120GB cartridge). The REV cartridge is essentially a hard drive subsystem, with the platters enclosed and protected. When you load the cartridge into the REV drive, you end up with a complete hard drive, ready to use. These cartridges are sturdy enough to mail or ship across town or around the world — but remember, the person on the receiving end will need their own REV drive to read that cartridge!

The average access time for the REV drive is close to that of a traditional hard drive — much faster than a CD or DVD disc — so it's a good choice for retrieving digital video and sound files for your multimedia projects. You can also use the REV drive as a fast backup unit for selected directories on your hard drive; a simple backup application is included with the drive.

And for Colossus, 1 Pick . . .

Slower hard drives are a major bottleneck for a high-performance PC, so Colossus deserves to read and write data as fast as possible! I'm opting for two drives because as a gamer and video editor, I need the elbow room!

As of this writing, my storage solution for Colossus is

- ✔ **Two Western Digital VelociRaptor 300GB SATA drives (WD3000GLFS):** 10,000 RPM and a 16MB cache add up to super-fast data reads and writes, and the small form factor means it fits easily into an internal drive bay. Programs and documents load faster, and Windows runs like the lithe animal it should!

Connecting Your Drive Controller

A hard drive is an expensive doorstop unless you connect it to your motherboard. In this task, I show you how to connect that all-important EIDE or SATA cable. Remember that your EIDE or SATA controller is built into your motherboard — congratulate yourself.

1. If your computer chassis is plugged in, unplug it. Oh, my goodness! You've been struck by lightning! Now is *not* the time to install a computer component. In case you can't wait, however, touch a metal surface before you handle anything. This action discharges any static electricity that your body might be carrying.

2. Check your motherboard manual for the location of two connectors.

✔ One connector attaches one end of the hard drive cable to the motherboard (either EIDE or SATA).

✔ The other connector attaches one end of the cable from your floppy drive to the motherboard.

3. Attach the cables that came with your controller or motherboard to these connectors, as shown in your manual. Make sure that you connect the correct cable to each connector. If you're going to add a floppy drive, note that the floppy drive cable usually has a twist in it toward the end that connects to the drive.

For any flat-ribbon cable connector that you attach to an EIDE drive or your motherboard, pin 1 on the male connector must always match the hole for pin 1 on the female connector. In almost every case, pin 1 on the male connector is the pin in the upper-left corner of the connector. "Okay," you say, "but how can I tell which side of the ribbon cable is wire 1?" No problem! Every ribbon cable has one wire that's painted red or somehow marked with a design (or lettering, perhaps). That wire is wire 1, which should always connect to pin 1.

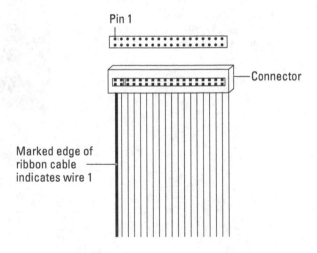

Pin 1

Connector

Marked edge of ribbon cable indicates wire 1

Installing an EIDE Hard Drive

Stuff You Need to Know

Toolbox:
- Phillips screwdriver
- Parts bowl

Materials:
- Internal hard drive
- Data cable
- Screws

Time Needed:
15 minutes

The steps in this procedure describe the installation of a single EIDE hard drive configured as *single drive, master unit* (which is the default already set by most hard drive manufacturers). If the jumpers aren't set correctly, move them to the correct positions for *single drive, master unit*. If you're installing two devices (or a second device on a PC that already has one EIDE hard drive), your EIDE hard drive must be set as *multiple drives, master unit,* and the other device should be set as *multiple drives, slave unit.*

1. If your computer chassis is plugged in, unplug it. Just finished combing your hair? Now that you look marvelous, touch a metal surface before you handle your drive. This action discharges any static electricity that you might have picked up.

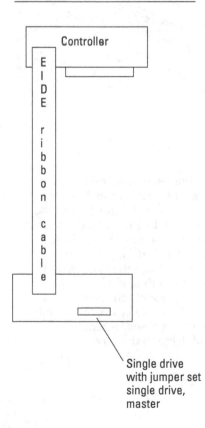

Single-drive EIDE System

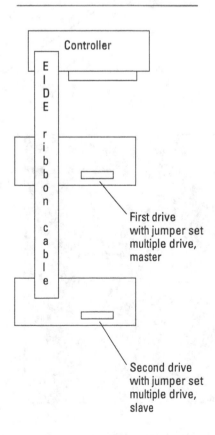

Two-drive EIDE System

2. If you're installing only one drive, check the jumper settings on your hard drive to make sure that they're set for *single drive, master unit.* As I mention at the beginning of this task, this setting is the default factory setting for most drives although it never hurts to be sure.

3. Select an open drive bay for your hard drive. Depending on the size of your drive, it might fit in a 3½-inch bay, or you might have to use a 5¼-inch half-height bay. If you want to fit a 3½-inch drive into a 5¼-inch half-height bay, you need a *drive cage kit,* which contains rails that fit on the side of the hard drive, bringing its total width to 5¼ inches.

4. If your drive needs a cage kit, attach it by using the screws that came with your drive to attach the cage rails onto both sides of your drive. If the drive is the same size as the open bay, you don't need a cage kit, and you can simply skip to Step 6.

5. Slide the drive into the selected bay from the front of the case. The end with the connectors should go in first, and the electronic stuff should be on the bottom.

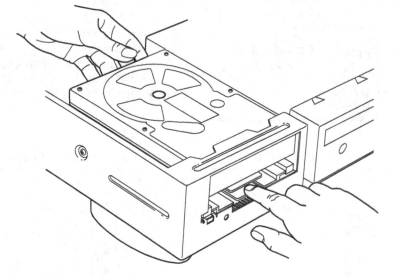

6. Carefully slide the hard drive back and forth in the drive bay until the screw holes in the side of the bay line up with the screw holes on the side of the drive. Unsheath your mighty screwdriver and use the screws that came with the drive (or your cage kit) to attach the drive to the side of the bay. You generally use four screws to secure the hard drive to the bay.

7. Connect one of the power cables from your power supply to the power connector on the hard drive. This connector fits only one way. Press it in firmly to make certain that it doesn't pull out.

8. Connect the ribbon cable coming from your motherboard's built-in controller to the back of the hard drive.

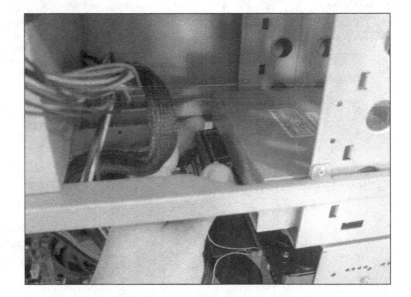

The wire with the markings is wire 1. If you're unsure which pin on the drive's connector is pin 1, check your drive's manual. The connector should fit snugly, so after it's correctly aligned, press it all the way on. Many drive and cable manufacturers now block one hole and one pin on the two connectors (a trick called *keying*) so that the cable fits only one way! Good job! You just proved that you don't have to be an electrician to install a hard drive.

Installing a SATA Hard Drive

Stuff You Need to Know

Toolbox:
- Phillips screwdriver
- Parts bowl

Materials:
- Internal hard drive
- Data cable
- Screws

Time Needed:
15 minutes

Okay, so installing a SATA drive is even easier than adding an EIDE drive! No jumpers to set, and both the power and data cables fit only one way.

In fact, the first six steps of this process are exactly the same as the previous procedure, "Installing an EIDE Hard Drive," so I won't repeat them here. Just follow those first six steps and then come back here.

After you attach the drive to the bay, follow these two additional steps:

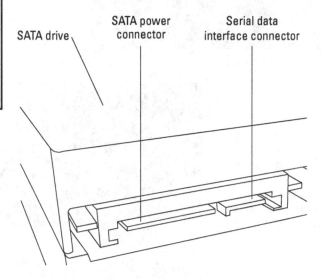

SATA drive — SATA power connector — Serial data interface connector

7. Connect one of the SATA power cables from your power supply to the power connector on the hard drive.

8. Connect the SATA cable coming from the controller card (or your motherboard if it has a built-in SATA controller) to the back of the hard drive. When you're all done, don't forget to dance the jumperless SATA Superiority Dance!

REMEMBER

Your SATA hard drive might have a legacy 4-pin power connector. If not (and your power supply doesn't have SATA connectors available), run to your local computer store and pick up a 4-to-15 pin (EIDE-to-SATA) power converter. Luckily, most of the PC power supplies on the market now either provide SATA power cables or include one or two SATA power converters.

Installing Your 3½-inch Floppy Disk Drive

Stuff You Need to Know

Toolbox:
- Phillips screwdriver
- Parts bowl

Materials:
- Internal floppy drive
- Data cable
- Screws

Time Needed:
15 minutes

If you decide to add a floppy drive to your system — perhaps to handle any antique floppies you receive from your Aunt Mildred — these steps will lead you through the procedure.

1. If your computer chassis is plugged in, unplug it. Now that you're done dusting the furniture and building up static, touch a metal surface before you install your floppy drive. This action discharges any nasty static electricity that you might be carrying.

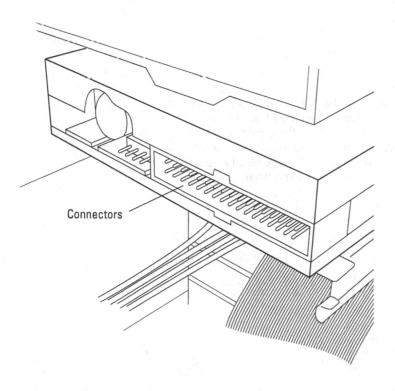

Connectors

2. Select an open drive bay for your floppy drive. All cases come with at least one 3½-inch bay especially for your floppy drive, so use that one. If your 3½-inch drive bay sits vertically so that it's sideways in the case, never fear. You weren't sold a mutant case. Floppy drives work both horizontally *and* vertically. Smile knowingly to yourself and continue the installation.

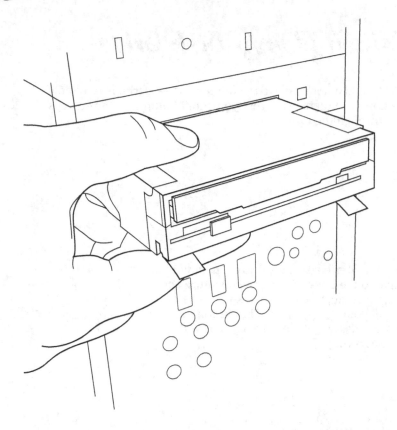

3. Slide the drive into the selected bay from the front of the case. (The end with the connectors should go in first.) If you're installing the drive horizontally, the button that ejects the disk should be on the bottom; if you're installing the drive vertically, it doesn't matter which way it faces.

4. Slide the floppy drive back and forth in the drive bay until the screw holes in the side of the bay line up with those on the side of the floppy drive. Use the screws that came with the floppy drive to attach the drive to the side of the bay. You generally use two screws to secure the floppy drive to the bay.

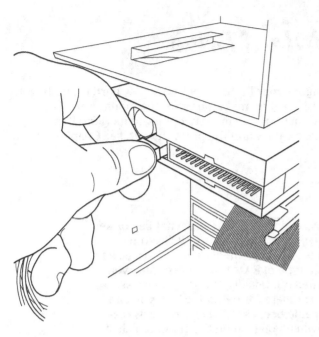

5. Connect one of the power cables from your power supply to the power connector on the floppy drive. To avoid mistakes, this connector fits only one way. Push it in as far as possible.

6. Connect the ribbon cable coming from your motherboard's built-in controller to the back of the drive. If you're installing this floppy drive as your drive A: (the standard configuration for PCs), use the last connector on the cable (the one after the twist in the cable). This connector goes on only one way and should fit snugly. When the connector is aligned correctly, press it all the way on.

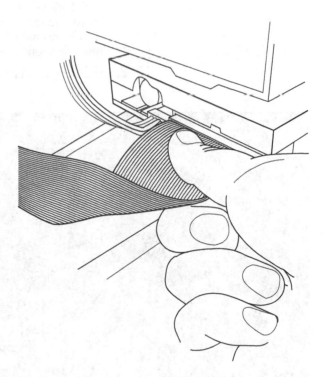

Configuring Your PC and Hard Drive

Stuff You Need to Know

Toolbox:
- Your bare hands

Materials:
- Notepad

Time Needed:
5 minutes

In this section, you configure your PC to accept your new hard drive. To get started with your hard drive setup, make sure that the monitor and keyboard are connected and that your computer is plugged in. (For all the details on connecting these cables and the ports they fit, see Chapter 5.)

1. Check your motherboard manual and see what key or key combination displays your computer's CMOS setup screen. CMOS stands for *complementary metal-oxide semiconductor,* which is a type of RAM that stores data even after your PC is turned off. Usually, the key you press to display this screen is Delete (or perhaps F1). If you can't find the key, don't panic because all motherboards display the setup key when you turn on the computer. Just watch closely and be prepared to press the key. If it goes by too quickly, just power off; then turn it on again and watch carefully. It might take you a few tries, but you'll find the proper key(s) to press.

2. Push the power switch on your case.

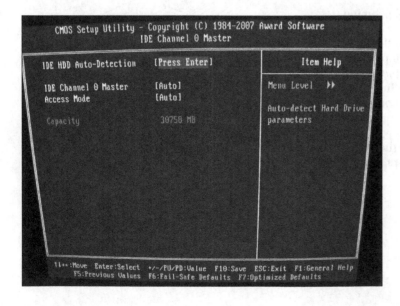

3. When you see the screen prompt to enter your setup screen, press the indicated key. Although the screen that appears varies with every motherboard, you should see a menu with at least one entry for `EIDE HDD Auto Detect`, `SATA HDD Auto Detect`, `Hard Drive Auto Detection`, or something similar. Use your cursor keys to select that function and follow the onscreen instructions. Your motherboard should identify your hard drive's characteristics automatically.

4. After you enter the hard drive settings, select the standard settings screen and set your drive A: as a `3@@bf1/2-inch 1.44MB floppy drive`. (If you didn't install a floppy drive earlier, you can leave drive A: set to None or Off.) On this same screen, set the computer's internal clock with the current date and time.

5. Make sure to save the values you entered, and then exit the setup screen. Usually, you see a separate menu item to `Save values and exit`. Your computer should now reboot. Your PC can now recognize its hard drive and floppy drive. For your floppy drive, that's all that's necessary. Your hard drive, however, must now be formatted before your computer can access it.

Formatting Your Hard Drive

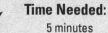

At this point, your new computer knows that it has a hard drive (and maybe a floppy drive) and the specifications of that drive. However, the hard drive isn't partitioned or formatted, so when you reboot your PC, it can't access the hard drive. Thus, you can't load that fancy operating system you've been hankering to use. In nontechnoid terms, *partitioning* means to divide your hard drive into one or more drives, designated by letters. You must create at least one partition to store data on your drive. After you create one or more partitions, it's time to *format* those partitions, which prepares them to hold data by creating areas to store information on the magnetic surface of the platters (as well as creating a directory that stores the location of all the files that you save to your hard drive).

1. After you exit the setup screen in the last step of the preceding task, your PC will automatically reboot. Then, after what seems like an agonizing wait, your computer beeps and informs you that there's been a hard drive failure. Panicking is not allowed nor encouraged.

2. If your hard drive manufacturer provided a formatting utility disk, insert the disk and continue the boot process by pressing the indicated key. The floppy drive should spring to life, and eventually the drive manufacturer's partitioning and formatting program appears.

3. If you didn't receive a formatting utility disk (or you didn't install a floppy drive), your hard drive can be automatically partitioned and formatted by the Windows XP or Windows Vista Setup programs. After you install your optical drive, boot your system by using a Windows XP or Vista installation disc and then follow the instructions that appear. The Windows XP/Vista Setup programs can automatically prepare your hard drive before Windows is installed! (Pretty snazzy, yes? Hoo-ah, Redmond!)

Chapter 8

Choosing and Installing an Operating System

Tasks performed in this chapter

✔ Installing Windows Vista

✔ Installing Ubuntu Linux

No matter what type of computer you build, you can't enjoy that hardware without an operating system (OS). An OS controls all your programs, providing the foundation for all the work you do. As I'm sure you know, Microsoft Windows Vista is the current operating system of choice for PCs around the world, but a significant minority of PC owners have instead opted for the security and advanced features of Linux.

So how do you determine which operating system is right for you? In this chapter, I show you the good points and bad points of both Vista and Linux: Is Vista fast enough? Stable enough? Does Linux support the applications that you want? Most important, what makes life on the computer easier for you?

Become Your Own Consultant!

If you're wondering whether to just not run the OS most everyone else runs, well, you're not alone. True, today's common PC operating system of choice is Windows Vista, and it does a great job for most of the PCs around the world. But what if your needs fall outside that box? Or you just plain don't like it? That's why you need to become your own consultant to choose the right operating system for your needs and druthers. (Heck, if you want to make things as authentic as possible, you can even charge yourself a tremendous amount of money. Just don't try claiming it on your taxes.)

Consider these points when choosing between Vista and Linux:

✔ **Cost:** Yep, I put this first for a reason. Most flavors of Linux can be obtained for free although you can buy commercial packages as well (such as Red Hat Enterprise and Mandriva). Microsoft, on the other hand, doesn't give Vista away. (Heck, I wouldn't either, after all the work done by those folks in Redmond!)

✔ **Speed:** If you're looking for the fastest operating system, score one point for Linux, which allows you to customize your interface *shell* (the actual controls and special effects you see onscreen).

No matter what your decision, if speed is all-important to you, make sure that you install a 64-bit version of the operating system you choose. (Vista comes in two flavors — 32-bit and 64-bit — but virtually all Linux-based operating systems are 64-bit.) 64-bit systems can use more memory and provide faster hard drive access, along with faster data transfer betwixt your hardware components.

✔ **Stability:** Maybe stability is a major factor to you. If your applications need to keep running day after day, solid as a rock, consider Linux. Me, I choose Linux as a more stable platform than Windows Vista. A PC running Linux is somewhat less likely to lock up (or, as computer types like to say, *crash*). *Downside:* You generally don't have tech support to call on with a Linux installation. And if you love to experiment with new software and features, don't forget that any significant change you make to your Linux system might introduce instability!

✔ **Legacy applications:** Will your new computer be running older programs, like games that are a number of years old? Vista is more likely to run these programs, so it gets the nod here.

✔ **Hardware auto-configuration:** If you want your operating system to automatically configure new hardware whenever possible, Windows Vista is the winner. Microsoft spends a whole heck of a lot of time creating *drivers* (programs written to allow hardware devices to communicate with Windows) and requiring hardware manufacturers to provide them. (To its credit, Linux is becoming more hardware-friendly as time goes on.)

✔ **Cutting-edge technology:** Vista just can't keep up with the constantly evolving Linux varieties available today, so if you're looking for the latest in features (like multiple-CPU multitasking, which is supported by some motherboards), I'd choose Linux. (It's no accident that Linux was the first generally available 64-bit operating system.)

✔ **Software compatibility:** If you're looking for the operating system offering the most applications and software, Windows Vista is your choice. However, Linux PCs can run emulators for many Windows-only programs. (An *emulator* is a program that allows one operating system to run programs written for another operating system.) However, running software under a Vista emulator will be slower than running that same program under Vista. Go figure.

✔ **Hardware support:** As you might expect, most hardware is designed for Vista, and getting every hardware device you buy to run under Linux will likely take significantly amount more work.

✔ **Security:** If your new computer is to be used as a Web server or an FTP server, the platform to watch is Linux, which includes the low-level security features needed for an Internet server. In fact, the Internet was built on a backbone of Unix computers, and most machines carrying the Internet's digital traffic still use Linux or Unix.

✔ **Networking:** If your new computer needs to run on an office network, give the nod to Windows Vista, which offers the industry standard, built-in networking capabilities with automatic configuration. Linux PCs can also network although they require more work.

The Straight Talk on Vista

There's no doubt about it: Windows Vista is now the top dog at Microsoft. Like Windows XP before it, Windows Vista is universally supported and runs both 32-bit and 64-bit software (depending on the version you buy). So what improvements have been added by the Microsoft crew to Windows Vista over Windows XP? The major change is in the addition of a new "look-and-feel" (developer-speak for the appearance of your desktop; see Figure 8-1), along with a new Windows Explorer design and improved visual special effects. Of course, Vista also includes updated drivers, including the best support for recent hardware components and devices, such as your MP3 player and digital camera.

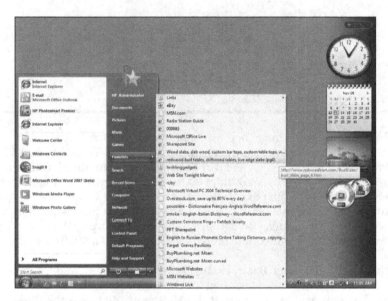

Figure 8-1: The Windows Vista desktop.

If you're accustomed to Windows XP and are stubborn, you can turn off certain parts of the new interface in favor of what's dubbed the Classic look as shown in Figure 8-2.

Even novices find Windows Vista easy to learn. Online help is plentiful and easy to access — including the capability to retrieve the latest help from the Internet — and tech support is available online and by voice.

Conveniences abound within Windows Vista. For example, its automatic hardware-detection feature makes adding a new modem, printer, or scanner to your system much easier. Just plug in the new device or install it within your computer's case, reboot, and Windows Vista will likely recognize the device automatically. Windows Vista also includes new applications for spyware detection, digital video, image editing, a slew of new games, as well as new versions of Internet Explorer and Windows Mail. Gamers will find a new version of DirectX — and DirectX 10 is a must-have for today's most advanced 3-D games.

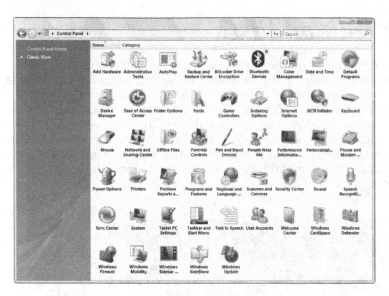

Figure 8-2: You can make Vista look like "Classic" XP.

The downside? Vista demands a huge increase in hardware performance over Windows XP. All that eye candy needs horsepower to look good! To build a fast Vista PC, you'll need the latest (and most expensive) hardware you can afford. (*Incoming warning:* If your video card is over a year old, you may find that you can't use all the graphic goodness within Vista.) Just like its ancestors, Windows Vista is also a drive hog: Expect it to gobble up at least 50GB of your hard drive for a full installation, and that figure rises exponentially when you add programs and features. (Whatever happened to the days when you could comfortably fit everything on a 40MB drive?)

Vista comes in four editions: Home Basic, Home Premium, Business, and Ultimate. Most home PC owners should consider opting for the Home Premium or the Ultimate version. You can read more online at the Microsoft site to see the difference between the four, but I'm sure you can guess that each version gets progressively more pricey.

I think this is a good time to mention my book *PCs All-in-One Desk Reference For Dummies,* 4th Edition (Wiley). If you need a complete introduction to Windows Vista, you'll find it there, along with coverage of all of today's hottest PC technologies, such as wireless networking, digital cameras, DVD recording, and the Microsoft Office 2007 suite. This is truly the one book that takes a snapshot of the entire PC world, and I'm particularly proud of it!

Linux: It's Not Just for Techno-nerds!

You can't discuss Linux without mentioning its roots: the commercial Unix operating system. Unix has a long history as an unbreakable and robust multitasking platform dating back before a mouse was even imagined. In their pure form, both Linux and Unix are character-based like DOS, and their command language has inspired many a college computer student to change majors within minutes of first exposure. However, both Linux and Unix can take advantage of graphical shells that can transform them into graphical operating systems that rival Vista in sheer beauty. Linux has airtight security features, and it's a highly efficient operating system that takes advantage of 64-bit processors, CPUs with multiple cores, and even motherboards that support multiple CPUs.

Linux is such a hot topic these days because as a direct competitor of Windows Vista, Linux is basically a rewrite of Unix created by programmers from around the world, working almost exclusively on the Internet to share code, specifications, and ideas. Linux is copyrighted, but it's free of charge for personal use. (That's one of the reasons for its success right there!) It runs virtually all Unix software, and emulators that run most popular DOS and Windows programs are available for it. Linux can talk shop with most of the popular Windows and Apple Mac OS X networking protocols.

And Linux is an Internet nut's dream. Like Vista, it provides built-in support for TCP/IP (the communications protocol used on the Internet) and Ethernet networking (see Chapter 12 for networking details), so it's no surprise that many Internet service providers and small businesses choose Linux to power their Internet servers. Linux handles FTP, Internet e-mail, and the Web with ease.

With a graphical shell, Linux suddenly blooms into a beautiful butterfly — figuratively, anyway — featuring a design similar to Windows Vista. Unlike with Windows, though, you can literally choose your own interface. A rapidly growing number of shells are available, each handling appearance and functionality differently (with variations both subtle and outrageous). For example, your icons can rotate, your windows can shimmer in and out of existence, and menus can be rearranged at will. In my opinion, the most popular Linux graphical user interface (GUI) — named X — is practically as easy to use as Windows Vista. See Figure 8-3.

Linux has also proved popular because of its broad support and development among programmers. New hardware support is added constantly, and new technologies are often implemented within a few months. Programmers are constantly writing applications and utilities that run under Linux. In fact, the full source code package for the entire Linux operating system is available for the asking. (On the Web, you can download the source from the Linux Kernel Archives, at `www.kernel.org`.)

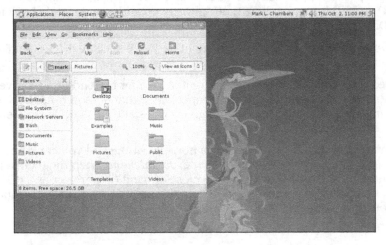

Figure 8-3: The Linux desktop.

Even with the appearance of mainstream applications, however, I can't say that Linux has reached the home market like Vista has. Although new user-friendly commercial versions of Linux (such as Red Hat Enterprise and Mandriva) now ship with simpler installation programs as well as automated setup and configuration utilities, the character-based behemoth that is Linux still hides underneath. If you're going to use the full power of Linux — for example, by setting up an Apache Web server or an e-mail listserver, or by building your own network around Linux — prepare to buy a shelf full of reference manuals. As a C programmer once told me, "It's not impossible to become a Linux guru, but you're going to gain weight with all that reading!"

Linux is definitely not for the computer novice, but if you've had experience with networking and server editions of Windows — or if you've ever used Unix — it's certainly not impossible to figure out how to use it. Add to that factor the nonexistent price tag for most flavors of Linux, the reduced system requirements, the arrival of new GUIs and commercial programs, performance that beats Vista, and the constant development, and you can see why Linux is giving the Windows Empire stiff competition.

Before You Install Your Operating System

Because operating systems are installed differently, I can't give you one comprehensive procedure that you should follow before installing Vista or a flavor of Linux. However, here's a checklist of preparations that should make your installation run more smoothly, no matter which platform you choose:

✔ **Back up your hard drive.** If you're by some chance using a hard drive that's had an operating system installed on it before, back up any data and any documents that you'd hate to lose.

✔ **Read the installation instructions.** Sure, your new operating system is designed to be installed by a kindergarten kid who's half asleep, but that doesn't excuse you from at least scanning the installation instructions.

✔ **Read the README file.** If something is important enough to include in a README file on the distribution discs, it might affect your installation. Pop that CD or DVD into a machine that's already up and running and check for a README.

✔ **Keep your driver disks handy.** You might need the specific drivers that came with your parts for your new operating system.

✔ **Impose on a friend.** If you have a computer guru for a friend or a relative, enlist an expert's help if you need it, especially if that person runs the same operating system that you're installing. Brownies and steak dinners often work well as bribes.

✔ **Yell for the cavalry.** If something goes horribly wrong and you can't find anything about it in the installation guide, *do not panic!* Keep the tech support number for the operating system close at hand (if there is one); it should be located in the manual or the additional literature that accompanied your operating system.

✔ **Make a spec list.** Jot down any serial or license numbers, the type of computer you have, and the parts you've installed. That way, if you have to call for tech support, you're prepared.

   ✔ **Be patient.** Tech support representatives for major software developers answer literally hundreds of calls per day, and you'll probably have to wait for at least five minutes before you speak to a human voice.

Keeping your computer castle secure

If you need to prevent access to your computer while you get a cup of java or a can of caffeine-laden soda, use a Windows or Linux screen saver with the password option turned on. If you need tighter security, use an encryption utility.

Another surefire security measure is to use a *boot password,* which prevents your computer from running unless you enter the correct password. Most motherboards can be configured to require a boot password through the BIOS menu.

Finally, you might decide to invest in one of the newest PC security technologies: a portable fingerprint scanner, which can replace passwords and protect both your PC's files and access to the Internet or your local network. Most fingerprint scanners connect to your PC through a universal serial bus (USB) port and retail for less than $100.

For example, the APC Biometric Biopod (www.apc.com) is an affordable USB device that you can use to secure your PC's passwords. To unlock a user account or deactivate your screen saver, just place your fingertip on the Biopod metal sensor, and you're automatically logged in (just as if you had manually typed your password). The Biopod software takes care of all your passwords with a manager utility.

I've used the Biopod under Windows XP for some time now, and I can personally attest that it's easy to use, accurate, and easy to configure. In fact, if you travel with a laptop, you'll find the Biopod is effective portable security to prevent unauthorized access

to your stuff. (Naturally, it won't prevent someone from walking off with your laptop, but that's why you brought a security cable.) Because the Biopod is a USB device, it can easily be moved from computer to computer as you need it.

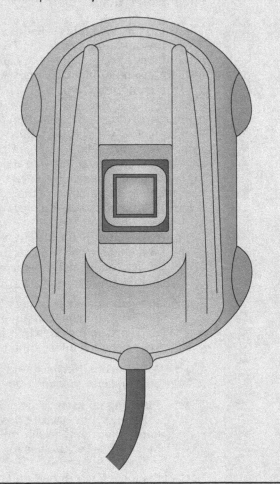

Even People Like You and Me Need Internet Security

Stories abound on the Internet, TV, and the movies about the lack of Internet security. Although it's unlikely, someone could intercept your electronic mail or discover personal information about you. You can take certain security measures, such as ordering products online only if your Web browser and the Web site can create a secure connection or using an encryption utility to encode the text within your e-mail messages. These procedures create a level of security for most Web surfers and casual Internet users.

However, large corporations make use of powerful firewall software to carry their Internet protection a step further. A *firewall* is a program or hardware device that constantly monitors the company's Internet connection to prevent unauthorized access to the company's Web server (or, even worse, the company's network itself). Firewalls are typically complicated beasts that cost hundreds (or even thousands) of dollars. A company without a firewall is a potential target for an attack by a computer hacker. Wouldn't it be nice if anyone could install a firewall, just to be safe?

Thanks to the good folks in Redmond, the Vista Firewall is on from the moment you install the operating system (and that includes Vista Service Pack 1). However, this is bare-bones protection — you can't easily modify or customize the Windows firewall, for example, and there's not much feedback on what attempts, if any, have been made to compromise your PC.

If you're like me — on the Internet for hours at a time visiting Web sites and downloading files — you can use a third-party software firewall instead. For example, Symantec's Norton Internet Security 2008 ($60; www.symantec.com) is an inexpensive firewall for protecting your machine while you're online. In fact, I recommend it for anyone who goes online, even the casual Internet user with a dial-up modem connection. Here's a quick list of the possible security violations that Norton Internet Security 2008 can monitor and prevent:

- ✔ **Guarding the cookie jar:** Norton alerts you to a site's use of Web cookies and enables you to block them. A *cookie* is a file that contains personal data about you, usually from a form that you filled out online. Cookies are often stored automatically on your hard drive without your knowledge.

- ✔ **Protecting your programs:** The Norton Firewall monitors and controls which programs on your computer are allowed Internet access so that an unauthorized program written by a hacker can't automatically connect and transfer your personal information across the Internet without your knowledge.

- ✔ **Ad filtering:** Norton filters those irritating and bandwidth-hogging banner ads. Because you don't download them, you surf the Web faster.

- ✔ **Phishing no more:** Norton Internet Security 2008 takes care of *phishing* expeditions by hackers posing as bona-fide companies who want you to enter your personal information on a bogus Web site. Norton identifies and blocks these scam sites for you.

Norton Personal Firewall runs under both Windows XP and Vista. For more information on this program, visit the Symantec Web site (www.symantec.com).

Installing Windows Vista

Stuff You Need to Know

Toolbox:

- Your bare hands

Materials:

- Vista install disc

Time Needed:

30 minutes

Decided to jump on the Vista bandwagon? I'll be honest: The majority of my PCs are happily running one flavor of Windows or another, so you've no reason to feel ashamed! Vista certainly offers the most comprehensive support and the best software compatibility available for a PC operating system — not to mention the familiar landmarks that make PC owners comfortable, like the Start button.

In this task, I show you how to install the 32-bit Ultimate version of Windows Vista, using the standard installation DVD. I assume that you haven't installed an operating system yet, and that your hard drive is unformatted. (Before a hard drive can be used, it must be formatted and partitioned, which prepares the drive for data storage.)

1. Load the Vista install disc into your DVD drive and reboot your PC. After a number of files are loaded, the Install Windows screen appears. This is a wizard application that leads you step by step through the process, so breathe easy.

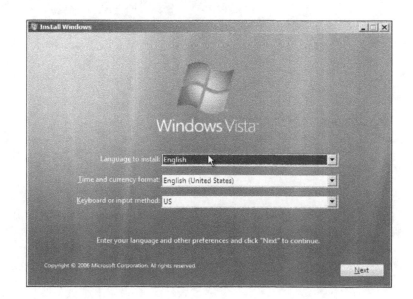

2. Click the drop-down list boxes to select your installation language, time and currency format, and keyboard type. Click Next to continue.

3. Click the Install Now button.

4. Type your Vista product key into the Product Key text box. (You'll find this important number on the DVD envelope, or packaged with your Windows documentation.) Then make sure that the Automatically Activate Windows When I'm Online check box is enabled. Click Next to continue.

5. Ah, the legalese. Read the license terms, and click the I Accept the License Terms check box to enable it. Then click Next.

6. Because you're installing Vista on a brand-new hard drive, click the Custom (Advanced) button.

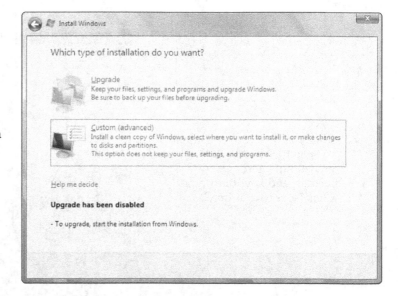

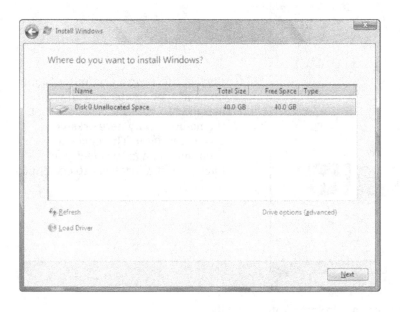

7. Click the target hard drive from the "Where Do You Want to Install Windows?" list to select it and then click Next. Vista formats the drive you select, creates a single data partition, and assigns the entire capacity as your Windows Vista boot drive. A *boot drive* is the hard drive where Windows is installed — Vista loads from this drive each time you turn on your PC.

If Vista doesn't recognize your hard drive, you probably need to load an updated driver for your motherboard. Load the driver disc that came with your motherboard into your DVD drive (or use a copy that you've downloaded to a USB Flash drive using another PC) and click Load Driver. After you load the driver, click Refresh to display the list of hard drives again. Then go back to select the target hard drive in the list, and click Next.

8. The Install program copies files to your hard drive and displays a progress list to let you know how much time remains.

9. After rebooting, Vista prompts you for an account username and password. You know the drill: Click in each text box and type. (You have to enter your password twice to verify it.) Click a thumbnail image to select an account picture, and then click Next to continue.

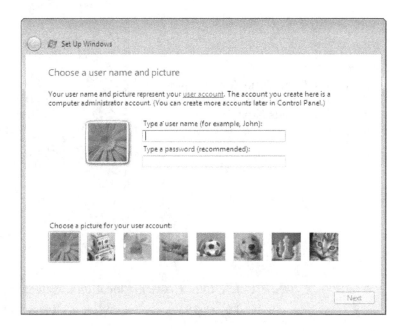

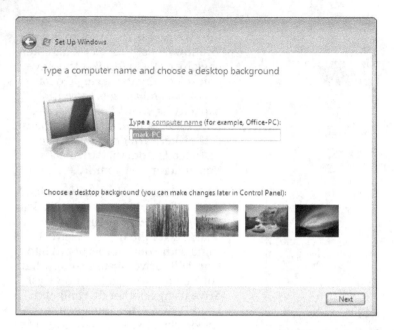

10. Click in the Type a Computer Name box and type the name you want assigned to your PC. This also sets the name for any networks you connect to later. Then click a thumbnail image to select your background. Click Next to continue.

11. On the Help Protect Windows Automatically screen, opt for Use Recommended Settings to Automatically Install Updates to Vista.

12. Click the Time Zone drop-down list box to select your location. Then click Next.

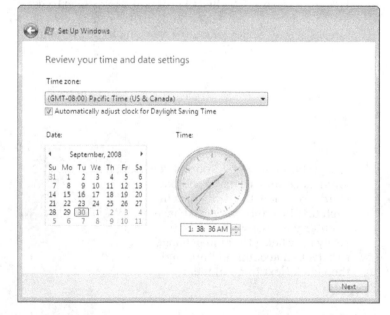

13. Click the Home location to select your level of network security.

14. Click Start to run Windows Vista. Enjoy!

Installing Ubuntu Linux

Stuff You Need to Know

Toolbox:
- Your bare hands

Materials:
- Ubuntu install disc

Time Needed:
1 hour (including downloading time over a broadband connection)

I'll use my favorite free open-source Linux flavor to demonstrate how to install Linux on your PC. Ubuntu Linux, available free for the downloading at www.ubuntu.com, is a great choice for a home PC. Ubuntu comes already configured to handle most audio and visual media, and the shell will be familiar and easy to learn for anyone who's experienced with Windows XP or Vista. You'll even find a capable Web browser and several Office-compatible applications to produce spreadsheets and word processing documents.

Professional support is available for a price, but I've found that the Ubuntu user community is accepting, patient, and knowledgeable (the Big Three requirements of user community support). You often get answers to questions posted on the site's forums within an hour! You can also download free documentation to help with the more complex features of Ubuntu.

You can create your own Ubuntu install disc by downloading the ISO CD-ROM image from the Ubuntu Web site (using another PC, of course) and burning it yourself with a CD/DVD recording application (like Roxio Creator 2009). Image files hold the contents of a disc as a file, and can be used to re-create that disc by recording it. This is a good choice if you have a broadband connection available — the disc image is over 700MB — and a DVD-burning application at the ready. Alternatively, you can order a free copy to be sent to you on CD. For a nominal charge, you can also order the DVD edition, which offers a number of support programs along with the installation files.

For this installation, I assume that you haven't installed an operating system yet and that your hard drive is unformatted.

1. Load the Ubuntu install disc into your DVD drive and reboot your PC. The Ubuntu Installation screen appears. This is a wizard, so just follow the screens.

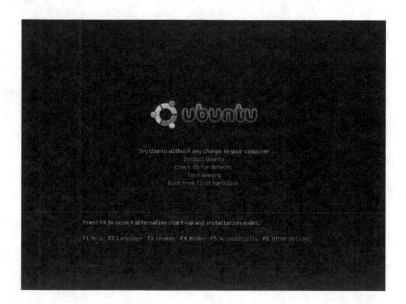

2. Press the down-arrow key to highlight the Install Ubuntu menu item; then press Enter.

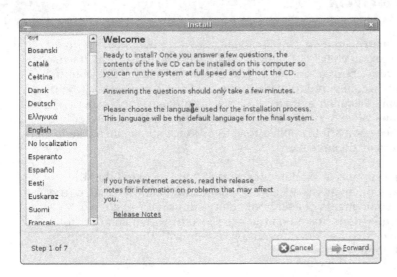

3. After the kernel loads, you see the Ubuntu Install Welcome dialog. Click Forward to continue.

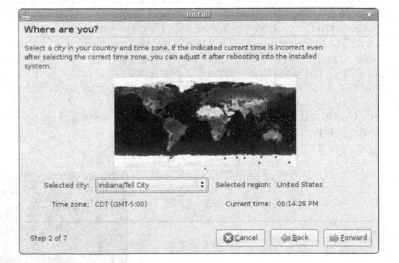

4. Click the area of the world map closest to your location to set your time zone and then click Forward.

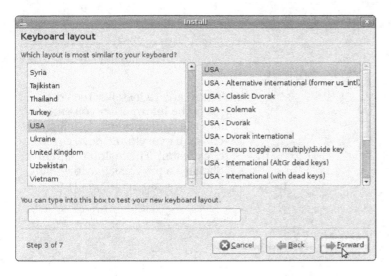

5. Click to choose your keyboard layout — by default, USA QWERTY — and click Forward.

6. The Install program partition screen appears, allowing you to choose a Guided or Manual partitioning process. Select the Guided option to select it and then click the hard drive you want to use. (This formats the entire target drive for use with Ubuntu.) Click Forward to continue.

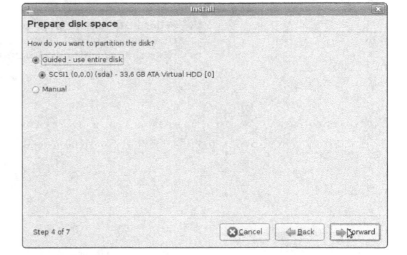

7. Enter the information required for each field within the Who Are You? screen and type your administrator account information. (Note that you have to type your password twice in the adjoining text boxes to verify the spelling.) Click Forward to continue.

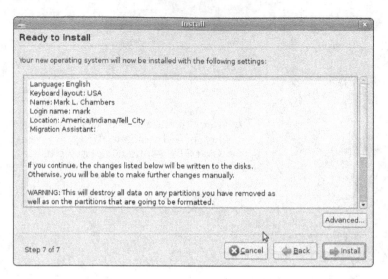

8. The Ready to Install screen displays the information you entered and the configuration settings you chose. If everything looks correct, click Install. The Install program displays a progress bar to let you know how much time remains.

9. When installation completes, you're prompted to reboot your PC. Click Restart now, and enjoy Ubuntu!

Part III
Adding the Fun Stuff

The 5th Wave   By Rich Tennant

"Yeah, I installed a PCI bus slot in my new chair.
What of it?"

In this part . . .

You add all the fancy bells and whistles that any multi-media computer needs these days, such as a DVD recorder, a surround sound card that plays MP3 music, and a DSL/cable connection for the Internet. Get ready to blast the toughest game invaders, surf the Web, or listen to audio CDs while you work on a spreadsheet!

Chapter 9

Installing an Optical Drive

Tasks performed in this chapter

✔ Installing a DVD drive

✔ Testing your work

It's becoming hard to remember the days of old. I'm speaking of prehistoric times, before computers had DVD-ROM drives. (As frightening as it sounds, most young folks don't remember a computer *without* one!) You already know that a modern PC requires at least a DVD-ROM drive for installing software and games, and many programs are available only on DVD. In fact, today's technology enables you to record your own data DVDs, data CDs, and audio CDs; or watch DVD movies with Dolby Digital Surround Sound that you recorded yourself! Owners of high-definition (HD) TVs might instead opt for a Blu-ray drive or recorder, with larger data capacity and the ability to watch today's Blu-ray movies.

In this chapter, I explore all the CD, DVD, and Blu-ray hardware that's available, and I also discuss the features that help you determine which drive is right for your new computer. After you install your drive and the software that it requires, you're ready to access the world of multimedia — and don't forget to take a few minutes to explain to the younger generation the historical relevance of floppy disks.

You need a minimum of a DVD-ROM or DVD recorder on your new PC. Without one, you'll be up a creek when it comes to installing programs, watching movies, and storing data for backups or sharing with others.

Discovering the Details about DVD and Blu-Ray

Ready for a long, highly technical discussion of bits and bytes, reflected laser light, and variable speed motors?

If so, you're reading the wrong book! The good thing about optical technology is that you don't *have* to know anything about the man behind the magic curtain. Most drives are built in the same manner, are used in the same way, and perform equally well. However, a number of extra features often help determine the price of your optical drive, and this section helps you "decode" all the options while you're shopping.

CD and DVD drives can be *internal* (installed inside your PC's case) or external. I prefer internal drives over external drives because internal hardware costs less and takes up less space on your desk (and doesn't have to be properly handled like an external drive). (See the upcoming section "Choosing an Internal or an External DVD Drive" for a comparison of external and internal optical drives.)

A number of computer applications can benefit from a DVD or Blu-ray recorder. In fact, they'd sit up and beg for one if only they could speak. If your primary application appears on this list or you're interested in any of the following applications, you should consider a DVD recorder rather than a simple read-only DVD-ROM drive:

- **Creating audio CDs:** If you're an audiophile with a ton of hard-to-find vinyl albums (or a stack of irreplaceable cassettes or tape reels gathering dust in a corner of your home), you can transfer those musical treasures to compact disc. Today's higher-end recording programs enable you to rearrange tracks in any order, print a cover for the disc's jewel box with a list of the track names, and even remove some of the crackle, pop, and hiss associated with older media.

- **Archival storage:** How would you like to remove those three-year-old tax records, spreadsheets, and word processing documents from your hard drive and free up all that space — without losing a single byte of that data in case you need it in the future? If you use recordable DVDs to archive your data, you can be assured that those old files will be available for years to come and can be read on any DVD-ROM drive. Plus, you can run programs and read data files directly from the disc, so you don't have to restore anything.

  How long does a recorded disc last? Although companies cite many different figures, the average shelf life of a recorded DVD or Blu-ray disc is usually stated as somewhere around 100 years. (I'm betting it's much longer, but only if you take proper care of your discs and store them in a cool environment.)

- **Moving data:** Do you have a presentation or slide show to perform on a business trip? A recorded disc is a perfect way to carry gigabytes of data with you wherever you go without worrying about magnetism or X-rays in airports (two dreaded enemies of magnetic media, such as floppies and backup tapes). With the universal acceptance of CD and DVD, it's now a safe bet that the computer at your destination will be able to read your disc.

- **Digital photo albums:** If you have a recorder and a digital camera (or a scanner that can digitize regular photographs), you have everything you need to create your own custom photo albums on a disc. You can display these photo albums on any computer with a corresponding optical drive.

- **Movies, movies, movies:** If you love your DV camcorder, you can burn that digital video onto a DVD and create your own DVD movies. Today's software allows you to add your own menus, animated backgrounds, and slide shows of digital photographs to your DVD movie. (Wait 'til Grandma sees the kids on her DVD player, complete with menus she can operate with her DVD remote control . . . she'll be so busy watching your movies, she'll burn her apple pie!)

Caring for your discs

Contrary to popular opinion, optical discs are not indestructible. Here's a quick checklist of the most common archenemies of any compact disc. Avoid them all, and you'll never lose a byte of data (or a single musical note)!

✔ **Heat:** Keep those discs cool! The same hot car seat that claimed your favorite cassettes (or those videos from the rental store) could render them unreadable.

✔ **Dust:** Like any audio CD player, a few specks of dust can cause a CD or DVD drive to skip to skip to skip. (You get the idea.)

✔ **Liquids:** Anything from water to grape juice to prussic acid can mess up a disc. If you're lucky, you might be able to remove a liquid stain with a little isopropyl alcohol.

✔ **Fingers:** Oily fingerprints can lead to dirty discs, and your drive will occasionally refuse to read them. Handle your discs by the edges or use your finger as a spindle by sticking it through the hole in the center of the disc.

✔ **Sharp objects:** A surface scratch on the reflective side of a CD or DVD can deflect the laser light, which leads to lost data. If you're handling a recordable disc, make certain that you don't scratch the gold or silver layer on the top side of the disc. And stay away from ballpoint pens when labeling your discs; use a permanent (nonsmudging) felt-tip marker instead.

All that said, we are but human and might get gunk on our discs anyway. If you already have an expensive, hi-tech compact disc cleaning apparatus, you can use it on your computer CDs and DVDs as well. However, I really don't think that these James Bond contrivances are necessary. Compact discs were designed to be easy to clean. I recommend a lint-free *photographer's lens cloth* for dusting the bottom of your CDs (and, if necessary, a bit of isopropyl alcohol disc-cleaning solution).

To clean the bottom surface of a CD or DVD, wipe from the center spindle hole straight toward the outside of the disc. Never wipe a compact disc or DVD in a circular motion because that can scratch the surface and result in lost data.

What You Need to Know about Optical Recorders

Optical recording is just plain neat. With CD-R (short for *compact disc-recordable*) technology, you can record (or, in techno-wizard parlance, *burn*) your own commercial-quality audio CDs with as much as 74 minutes of music or save as much as 700MB of computer data. Plus, you can play these discs on any standard drive. Need more space? A DVD recorder can pack that golden 4.7GB that I mention earlier onto a single disc, and most DVD recorders can create movie discs that you can use in your TV's DVD player. At the top end of the capacity heap is the 25GB or 50GB offered by a Blu-ray burner.

A DVD recorder for well under $50 is easy to find, and a spindle of 100 recordable DVDs will set you back less than $30. Two types of record-once DVDs are available: DVD-R and DVD+R. As you can guess, these two formats are not compatible, and you must buy the right type of disc for the recorder that you choose. (If you invested in a multiformat DVD recorder, you can write 'em both — but note that DVD+R recording speeds are generally faster than DVD-R recording speeds on the same drive.)

If you're interested in the maximum amount of storage from your DVD and Blu-ray recordable discs, consider buying *dual-layer media* (also abbreviated DL). If your recorder supports DVD-DL, you can pack over 9GB of data on a single disc. Blu-ray dual-layer discs can store up to 50GB each.

In case you're wondering, when you aren't using a DVD recorder to create DVDs, it doubles as a standard DVD-ROM read-only drive, so you need to buy only one drive. Of course, a DVD drive can also read and burn CDs. A Blu-ray recorder can handle all three types of discs.

The great disc speed myth

If you're shopping for an optical drive, you're going to be pelted with numbers: 16X, 24X, and 48X, for example. Those numbers aren't size figures for NBA basketball shoes — the number in front of the *X* indicates how fast the DVD or Blu-ray drive can transfer data (its *transfer rate*). By transferring, I'm talking about either reading data from a disc or writing data to the disc from your hard drive.

Original single-speed CD-ROM drives could read data from the disc at about 150 kilobytes per second (Kbps); the *X* figure indicates a multiple of that original speed. For example, an *8X* drive (usually read as *eight speed* by CD-ROM racing enthusiasts) can read data eight times faster than the original single-speed drives. DVD and Blu-ray X figures work the same way: The higher the X, the faster the transfer rate, based on the speed of the original single-speed drives.

Okay, so where does the "myth" come in? Well, most of today's games and applications don't need the whopping-fast transfer rate of a 16X DVD-ROM drive. Because the typical game or application is still likely to recommend a 2X or 4X drive, the biggest benefit of these is that they give techno-weenies a chance to brag about their speedy drives. (Coincidentally, this is the reason why most retail computers still come with 4X DVD drives. Those manufacturers know the fact behind the myth as well as you do!)

Don't get me wrong. High-speed drives are nice in certain situations. For example, a 16X DVD-ROM drive installs one of those huge 8GB productivity applications or 3-D games to your hard drive much faster than a 4X drive, so a fast drive can save you time. If your primary application revolves around digital video or you have the spending money and simply hate waiting, a fast optical drive is probably a better choice.

When it comes to burning, however, your speed will vary greatly from the figure quoted on the box because factors — such as the amount of memory in your PC and speed at which your hard drive reads data (or even how fragmented your hard drive is) — can affect the speed at which your recorder can pound ones and zeros into the surface of a blank disc. Generally, of course, the same rule holds true, and the higher the recording X number, the better. Just don't expect that speed all the time.

Other read-only disc drive features to covet

In actual operation, you can find but a few differences between an expensive, name-brand DVD or Blu-Ray read-only drive and a cheaper drive of the same speed from a smaller manufacturer. Both drives read and transfer at about the same speed, and both can be controlled from within your applications. (For example, you can eject a disc from your audio CD program with either drive.)

So which features really make a difference? Here's a checklist that helps you separate the wheat from the chaff when you're shopping for a DVD or Blu-Ray drive:

✔ **Access time:** If you're not careful, you can easily confuse a drive's *access time* with its *transfer rate* (measured as the X factor, as I discuss in the section "The great DVD speed myth," earlier in this chapter). *Access time* is the actual time required for your optical drive to locate a specific file on the disc. Older drives have access times of about 150 milliseconds (ms), and today's CD and DVD drives average an access time of around 100 ms for reading CDs, 150 ms for reading DVDs, and 180 ms for reading Blu-Ray discs.

In Chapter 7, I discuss how access time is important when choosing a hard drive. Most hard drives have access times of around 5 to 11 ms (much faster than the typical 80 ms for an optical drive), which is another reason why hard drives are still the champions of the multimedia world. Besides, reading and writing everyday data (such as a letter to Aunt Mildred or that Great American Novel) is much easier with a hard drive.

✔ **Audio controls:** Most disc drives these days include a headphone jack and volume control. Some external drives come with everything necessary for dual use as an audio CD player and a computer CD or DVD drive: separate channel connectors for your stereo and even a full collection of control buttons, such as skip track, pause, and play.

✔ **Cache:** Just like a hard drive, a DVD or Blu-Ray drive uses a special set of onboard random access memory (RAM) modules to hold data that your computer needs often . . . or will probably need soon. The larger this cache (also called a *data buffer*), the fewer interruptions you experience in the transfer of data. If you plan to use a DVD drive for watching digital video, consider a drive with at least 4MB of cache RAM.

✔ **Support:** Does your drive's manufacturer offer tech support through the Web, or will you end up spending your two bits calling long-distance for support over the telephone?

If your optical drive ever swallows your disc and won't eject it, it's time to straighten a paper clip. Locate the emergency manual eject hole — it's an unmarked hole under the tray (about the diameter of a piece of wire). See exactly where it's located in Figure 9-1. Stick the end of the paper clip into the manual eject hole and push firmly; the tray should pop out of the drive.

What really goes on in my optical drive?

Okay, if you absolutely *must* know, your DVD drive uses a laser to read a long series of tiny pits in the surface of a disc. (Ready for a totally useless fact? If you unraveled all the pits in a typical CD-ROM, they would stretch over three miles!) These pits represent *digital data* — a string of zeros and ones — that your computer can recognize as program data or music. In fact, your computer's DVD drive is internally similar to a regular audio CD player.

This is how the laser reads these microscopic pits: The laser light is directly reflected from the smooth areas of the disc *(lands),* and the pits scatter the light and do not reflect it. A lens in your DVD drive picks up the reflected light, and can therefore tell the difference between pits and lands. The reflective surface on a disc is a thin layer of metal, which gives the disc a shiny appearance.

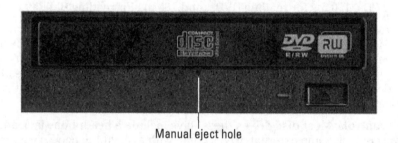

Manual eject hole

Figure 9-1: If a disc gets stuck, use the emergency eject method.

Doin' the LightScribe thing

Are you old enough to remember laser-etched vinyl record albums? (My favorite was Styx's *Paradise Theater.*) These albums played normally on your turntable, but carried cool-looking labels and borders around the edge of the album that were etched into the vinyl using a laser. About right now, you should be saying, "Hey, my DVD recorder uses a laser too! I wonder . . ."

Before you try and patent the idea, let me tell you about *LightScribe* drives and media. If your CD or DVD recorder supports this new technology and you record a CD or

DVD using the proper media, you can flip over that new disc you just burned and use your drive's laser to burn a silkscreen-quality label onto the top of the media! No printer or paper labels needed. The laser-etched label looks awesome and will make you the envy of all your techno-friends at your next party.

One downside (you knew there'd be at least one): A spindle of 50 LightScribe blank DVD+R discs is more than $50 at the time of this writing, so they're several times as expensive as their less flashy brethren.

What You Need to Know about DVD and Blu-ray

Unless you don't own a TV, you've probably already heard about *DVD,* which is short for *digital video disc.* (Some folks say that the abbreviation stands for *digital versatile disc.* Although it's probably an urban legend, I've heard that a computer novice recently asked a computer salesman for a PC with a *digital voodoo disc.*) The current generation of DVDs holds anywhere from 4.7GB to 9.4GB.

Although DVD drives work the same as those antique CD drives, they use a different type of laser, and the pits carrying the encoded data on the surface of the disc are smaller and packed more tightly. The denser the data, the more data a single disc can hold, as shown in Figure 9-2.

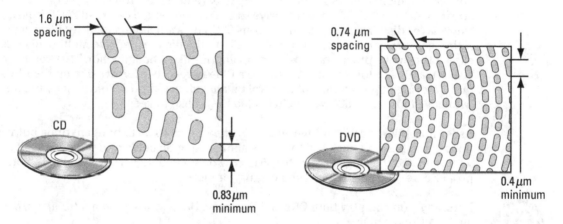

Figure 9-2: DVD technology packs more of your data into the same space than a CD-ROM does.

"Why on earth do I need that kind of space?" you might ask. Three reasons: quality, storage capability, and durability.

You can think and thank Hollywood. Today's digital video takes up gigabytes of space. A typical Hollywood movie fits nicely on a single DVD (unless it's high-definition video).

> ### The war is over now
>
> So you're wondering what happened to HD-DVD? That was the high-definition/high-capacity optical format that directly competed with Blu-ray. Like the War to End All Wars — namely, Betamax versus VHS — both formats were similar, but one eventually had to win out. Whether the advantage was in marketing or distribution, Blu-ray emerged from the fracas as the winner, and those folks with dedicated HD-DVD-only hardware will have to invest in a Blu-ray stand-alone player (and a Blu-ray PC drive) to keep up with Progress.
>
> Luckily, a number of "dual-format" set-top players and PC drives are on the market, so HD-DVD proponents won't need to trash all those expensive discs!

Speaking of high-definition video, the capacity required for today's best quality outstrips even the DVD. The Blu-ray drive to the rescue, which can read 25GB from a single-layer disc (and up to a humongous 50GB on a single dual-density Blu-ray disc). Although Blu-ray drives are still rare on all but the most expensive multimedia PCs, expect this new optical standard to drop in price like a boat anchor. That capacity is also attractive to folks who want to use a Blu-ray recorder for backing up their PCs, or for storing huge amounts of archival digital video. (Oh. *yes*, I have many friends who have more than 50GB of digital video they'd like to keep.)

As for durability, a DVD or Blu-ray disc is impervious to just about anything but very deep scratches and heat — no worries about magnetic fields or degraded quality with repeated viewings (which the VHS crowd remembers very well indeed). With proper care, your discs can last a century or more!

Naturally, you can play both CDs and DVDs in a Blu-ray drive. Compatibility is, once again, A Good Thing.

Choosing an Internal or an External DVD Drive

You might be wondering whether your DVD drive should reside inside your PC or you want it to be removable and easy to transport. Good thing all you need to consider is covered in this section!

Internal drives

An internal read-only DVD recorder drive (which also reads and writes CDs, naturally) should set you back about $30. Just like with hard drives, you can choose from two standard connection interfaces for your new internal drive. (Of course, the faster the speed, the higher the price.)

✔ **Enhanced Integrated Drive Electronics (EIDE):** Most optical drives today use the same EIDE technology as the most popular type of hard drive, so you can connect your DVD drive to the same controller as your hard drive. (I talk about EIDE technology in Chapter 7.) Enjoy this kind of convenience because it doesn't happen very often in the PC world.

✔ **Serial Advanced Technology Attachment (SATA):** If you're building a PC using serial ATA devices, you can add a SATA DVD drive as well. These drives are significantly faster and typically easier to install. (Serial ATA is covered like a blanket in Chapter 7.)

Which is better? EIDE drives are cheaper, but SATA drives are somewhat easier to configure. At the time of this writing, it's a toss-up, so I generally recommend that you use the interface you're already using for your hard drives.

Your new drive will typically be mounted horizontally, but some space-saving, mini-tower cases allow you to mount your optical drive vertically. This works just fine, but make sure you hold the disc in place while closing the drive door!

External drives

Because external drives have their own case (and sometimes their own power supply as well), they cost significantly more than an internal drive. For example, an external DVD recorder runs about $50 to $75. You have two interface choices for connecting an external optical drive:

✔ **USB:** Is it any wonder that the USB (universal serial bus) port is so popular these days? Here's yet another peripheral that you can connect. And, like with the other USB hardware that I discuss throughout this book, you don't have to reboot your PC when you add or remove an external USB DVD drive. Make sure, though, that you buy only USB 2.0 hardware, and *make sure* that your new PC has USB 2.0 ports available.

✔ **FireWire:** A FireWire port transfers data much faster than the older USB 1.1 standard, so these drives can usually read faster as well. (USB 2.0 drives are actually faster than first-generation FireWire drives.) If your computer doesn't have either a FireWire or a USB 2.0 port, you have to add a port adapter card. (You'll find more about FireWire and both flavors of USB in Chapter 5, and a detailed discussion of port adapter cards as well.)

As I mention earlier in this chapter, DVD drives that use the EIDE or SATA interface are internal drives. They fit in an internal, half-height drive bay in your computer case (just like a floppy or hard drive).

External disc drives can be convenient for file transfer and portability if you also have a laptop computer that has a USB or FireWire port but no internal DVD drive. You can connect an external drive to your laptop, carry the drive with you when you travel, and then simply reconnect the drive to your desktop computer when you return to your home or office.

External drives also eliminate much of the heat inside your case because the laser in the drive generates more heat than just about any other part in your computer. Naturally, external drives are more expensive because you're also paying for a separate case, power supply, and external cable.

You'll also have to handle your external drive carefully while moving it from place to place: No bumps or drops, please! (Remember that the optics inside an external drive can be jarred out of alignment.)

If you need to share an external DVD drive among more than one PC and they all have USB 2.0 ports, you're in luck! A portable USB DVD drive is the perfect fit for your needs.

And for Colossus, 1 Pick. . .

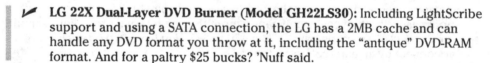

Although Blu-ray recorders are dropping in price — as of this writing, they're hovering around $250 — they're still far more expensive than a typical DVD dual-layer recorder. I don't have any Blu-ray movies to watch, and I don't need 50GB of storage on a single disc at this moment, so Colossus will just have to do with a dual-layer DVD recorder. (I do have a nice-sized collection of DVD movies.)

My optical drive pick For Colossus is:

✔ **LG 22X Dual-Layer DVD Burner (Model GH22LS30):** Including LightScribe support and using a SATA connection, the LG has a 2MB cache and can handle any DVD format you throw at it, including the "antique" DVD-RAM format. And for a paltry $25 bucks? 'Nuff said.

Installing an EIDE Optical Drive

If you already installed an EIDE (PATA) hard drive in your system, as I demonstrate in Chapter 7, you might need to unplug some connections. Your EIDE DVD drive might use the same controller and cable as your EIDE hard drive. If you like, take a permanent marker and mark the cables in their current position (with a "To Hard Drive 1" on the cable, for example) so that you can restore the existing connections quickly after you have your optical drive in place.

Note that for the most part, installing a SATA drive is exactly the same as installing an EIDE.

If your computer uses a single EIDE hard drive configured as *single drive, master unit* (the default hard drive installation that I describe in Chapter 7), you need to change the jumper settings on your hard drive so that it's set for *multiple drive, master unit.* I show you how during the process.

1. If your computer chassis is plugged in, unplug it. Now that you've taken off that heavy wool sweater, touch a metal surface before you handle your drive. This step discharges any static electricity that your body might be carrying.

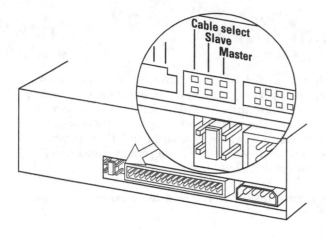

2. Check the jumper settings on your CD/DVD drive to make sure that it's set for *multiple drive, slave unit.*

3. Select an open drive bay for your optical drive. A DVD drive requires a 5¼-inch, half-height bay. (External USB and FireWire drives have their own case and don't need an internal drive bay. In fact, you don't need to follow this procedure at all if you're installing an external drive — these external drives are simple plug-and-play devices.)

4. From the front of the computer case, slide the drive into the drive bay. The end of the drive with the connectors should go in first. Usually, a label or some kind of writing on the front of your drive indicates which end is up.

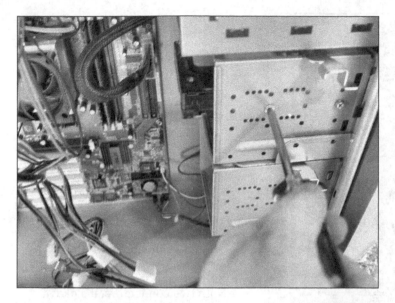

5. Attach the drive to the side of the bay. Slide the drive back and forth until the screw holes in the side of the bay line up with those on the side of the drive. Secure the drive with the screws (usually four) that came with the drive.

6. Connect one of the power cables from your power supply to the power connector on the drive. Note that the power connector fits only one way.

7. Connect the ribbon cable coming from the controller card (or your motherboard, if it has a built-in controller) to the back of the drive. A second connector should be on the ribbon cable, connecting your hard drive to your controller. That's the connector for your second EIDE device, which in this instance is your DVD drive. The wire with the markings is on the side with pin 1. If you're unsure which pin on the drive's connector is pin 1, check your drive's manual. The connector should fit snugly, so press it all the way on after you correctly align it. (If your ribbon cable didn't come with two connectors, it's okay to grumble to yourself. I do it all the time. You'll have to make a trip to your local Maze-o'-Wires electronics store and buy an EIDE cable that does have two connectors.)

Multiple drive, slave unit is the default factory setting for most EIDE optical drives although it never hurts to be sure. If the jumpers aren't set correctly, move them to the correct position. (Your drive's manual shows where the jumpers are located on your drive and how to set them.)

Testing Everything

Stuff You Need to Know

Toolbox:

↙ Your bare hands

Materials:

↙ None

Time Needed:

15 minutes

Because Windows XP and Windows Vista recognize standard optical drives without requiring you to load additional drivers, you can jump right to testing your installation.

1. After you install your drive and reboot Windows, load a computer game or application disc into your new drive and double-click the My Computer icon on your desktop (or on the Start menu).

2. Double-click the icon for your new drive to display the directory of the disc. If the disc that you loaded runs automatically, you won't even have to lift a finger because the program's installation menu will appear all by itself!

3. If something seems amiss, check these things:

   ↙ **Got power?** If your drive doesn't seem to be working, make sure that it's receiving power: Is the drive's power indicator lit, and does the tray eject when you push the button on the front of the drive? If not, shut down your PC and check the power connection to the drive to make sure that the power cable is securely attached.

   ↙ **Got power but it's still a no-go?** If the drive is receiving power but doesn't seem to be able to read a disc, you might have the cable upside down. Reverse the EIDE cable connected to the back of the drive by flipping it over and reconnecting it.

 Your new optical drive has a separate drive letter, just like your hard drive. If you installed a single hard drive, for example, your computer will probably assign drive D: to your new recorder/player.

Chapter 10

Let Your PC Rock!

Tasks performed in this chapter

✔ Installing your sound card

✔ Testing your work

Computers have evolved from room-filling silent machines to digital media warehouses. You can produce the same quality audio from games and DVD movies played on your PC as you can with the far more expensive digital audio components from a home theater system.

In this chapter, I walk you through the process of adding real, honest-to-goodness, high-quality surround sound to your PC so you can make your games and your digital music collection come alive. I discuss the speakers and subwoofer that will satisfy even the most demanding computer audiophile. No more silly beeps from that archaic internal PC speaker!

Sorting Out Sound Card Basics

As you might already know, the best way to select audio equipment is to listen with your own ears. Understandably, that presents a bit of a conundrum when choosing a sound card from a store. The secret is to know which of the computer audio buzzwords actually improves the sound that you hear. Luckily, teaching yourself the lingo of computer audio is pretty easy.

You'll find two common types of PC audio hardware available today: the PCI bus sound card and the integrated sound card (which is built-in to your motherboard). Both types of sound hardware can produce spectacular sound, and each has particular advantages over the other.

PCI bus audio

The PCI card is today's state-of-the-art sound card. (More about the PCI slot appears in Chapter 4.) Good 32-bit PCI sound hardware can deliver spectacular stereo sound effects for your games (including 3-D spatial sound, which I get into in a moment) and can record in stereo with CD quality at 44 kHz. In other words, the audio that you hear from one of these cards, which usually start around $50, can easily surpass the clarity and low noise level that you enjoy with audio CDs. Naturally, the sound card that you select for your PC will include jacks for speakers or headphones, as well as a microphone. However, it might also include a game port for your joystick or even a built-in FireWire port. Many top-of-the-line PCI cards come with a panel designed to fit in an empty slot in your PC's case, providing plugs and separate volume controls.

Don't get confused if your new sound card is listed as providing the highest-quality *24-bit sound* — it's still a 32-bit PCI card. Before you pull out your hair in frustration, let me explain. When sound card manufacturers talk about 24-bit audio, they're talking about the sound quality (or *bit rate*) that the card can produce — and not the type of card slot. 24-bit *sound quality* is top-of-the-line these days and is offered by companies such as Creative Labs (www.creativelabs.com) and its Sound Blaster X-Fi Elite Pro card. But never fear; it's still pumped out by a 32-bit PCI card. (That *32-bit* means that it uses a 32-bit bus slot on your motherboard to communicate with other PC components.)

Integrated audio

Virtually all of today's motherboards include onboard integrated audio hardware, complete with attached ports. Typically, this integrated sound hardware is a good choice for a PC dedicated to casual gaming, office applications, and Internet fun. Depending on the features of the onboard sound, you might even get some bells and whistles, such as 3-D spatial sound and Dolby DTS playback (buzzwords that I explain later in this chapter) or even a separate remote control for your software MP3 player.

Naturally, your motherboard's integrated audio hardware is not upgradeable. (Go figure.) However, your motherboard should allow you to disable the built-in audio hardware if you want to upgrade with the latest features on a PCI-bus sound adapter card.

Don't forget the software part!

Make sure that the audio hardware you choose is well supported with software and drivers written for the operating system you're using. Believe me, there's nothing more frustrating than discovering that your expensive sound card you just bought doesn't support the 64-bit versions of Windows XP or Vista.

If you're buying a new sound card or motherboard, it should include the drivers that you need and also a number of nifty software toys. These programs usually include an onscreen "stereo deck" that lets you play audio CDs, digital sound files in Windows WAV format, or MP3 files. You might also get a software-based DVD player, or a voice-recognition program that lets your computer talk to you and "read" text files aloud.

Surfing the sounds of the Web

You'll probably encounter many types of sound and music files in the multimedia world, especially if you spend lots of time on the Internet and the Web. If you have the right software or browser plug-in, your sound card should be able to play these other files, too:

✔ **WAV:** The WAV format is the Microsoft standard for recording, storing, and playing digital sound (and it's a popular format on the Web). Both Netscape Navigator and Internet Explorer can recognize and play WAV files automatically. The sound quality of WAV files can range from compact disc quality to mono sound files of telephone quality. (The lower the sound quality, the smaller the file size — and the less time that it takes to transfer over the Web.) Windows XP and Vista include simple sound-editing tools, and any sound-editing program worth installing can save and play WAV files. You'll find a hard drive's worth of WAV files at my favorite audio site, The Daily .WAV (www.dailywav.com).

✔ **AU:** You often encounter AU sound files on the Web. This sound format was developed by Sun Microsystems, and AU files are popular in the Unix and Linux worlds. Because AU files are compressed, they require less time to download. Although most sound-editing programs can play AU files, it's more important that your Web browser support them so that you can hear them directly while surfing. For example, if you connect to a Web site featuring sound files and click one of the recordings, you can hear voices speak within your browser. If you're using Mozilla Firefox or Internet Explorer, AU support is built in.

✔ **AIFF:** The AIFF format is a popular sound standard for Macintosh computers. Most sound-editing programs can import AIFF files, so you can play them if you download them to your hard drive. Like the Windows WAV format, AIFF files are CD quality, but they're usually not compressed like WAV files. Therefore, they're not all that popular on the Web because of their size.

✔ **MP3:** MP3 format music files are now the standard for digital music. Depending on their file size, MP3 files can even be far better than CD quality (and yet still be very small compared with the same music in WAV format). An entire underground of Web sites has developed to distribute dance, pop, and alternative singles in MP3 format — illegally, I might add, because many of these songs are (of course) copyrighted. You can create MP3 files on your PC, and pocket MP3 players that resemble everything from portable cassette players to ballpoint pens are all the rage these days.

✔ **WMA:** Microsoft's answer to MP3, WMA files are slightly better in quality than MP3 files and are considerably smaller. However, Bill and his gang have saddled the WMA format with extensive copy protection that severely restricts how you listen to your music (and even how often you can burn it to an audio CD). Therefore, many audiophiles steer clear of WMA. WMA is the preferred format within Windows Media Player and is supported by most portable music players (except the iPod).

✔ **AAC:** AAC was developed by Apple for use on the iTunes Store, so all the songs you purchase and download from the iTunes Store are in AAC format. AAC files are similar in quality to MP3, but they're actually slightly smaller because of better compression. As you might expect, the Apple iPod music player supports AAC songs. Unfortunately, though, most other MP3 players don't.

Why do I need 3-D for my ears?

Another feature offered by many sound cards these days — get ready for a real mouthful here — is 3-D spatial imaging. This type of sound has several applications:

- Playing audio CDs
- Playing digital audio files
- Playing sound effects within games

Sound cards with 3-D spatial imaging provide an auditorium or a concert hall effect: The music sounds as though the speakers are separated farther apart than they actually are.

Computer game players are the ones who can really take advantage of 3-D imaging. If you're playing a game that supports one of these 3-D cards, a laser bolt streaking past the right side of your ship actually comes from the right speaker. If you hear the deep, guttural growl of a dragon to your left, it would behoove you to turn your character to the left quickly (and with sword drawn)!

If you're a game player, I definitely recommend that you spend a few extra dollars for a card or motherboard that supports 3-D spatial imaging. If you're not an audiophile or you're not into computer games, this feature might not be important to you.

The software in many game programs provides a less effective form of 3-D spatial imaging that plays on standard sound cards. However, you always get better sound effects when you have a sound card with hardware that supports 3-D imaging.

"Send help! I'm surrounded by sound!"

Take 3-D spatial imaging one step further — including both sound effects *and* music — and you have surround sound, just like the super-realistic audio that you've experienced in movie theaters and with the best home stereo systems. Home DVD players usually offer Dolby Digital Surround Sound built in, and more are arriving on the market that offer THX and Dolby DTS (which deliver even higher-quality surround sound). You can join in the fun with your PC, however, if you add both a DVD drive and a sound card with Dolby Digital Surround Sound support to your computer. You can play games, watch commercial movies, and even enjoy audio discs recorded in surround sound. (For more information on DVD drives, read Chapter 9.)

You need five, six, or even seven speakers and a game, a movie, or an audio CD that's encoded for surround sound. As the line between your PC and your traditional stereo system continues to blur, however, you'll be seeing more of surround sound, and it'll be less expensive to add to your existing PC.

MP3 fanatics, pay attention!

Do you have a collection of thousands of songs in MP3 format taking up gigabytes of space on recorded CD or DVD discs or an old hard drive? You can enjoy these CD-quality sound files through your computer's sound system, or you can even record them directly to an audio CD if you have a DVD recorder. (For more information on CD recording, make a note to visit Chapter 9 when you're finished here.) MP3 files are all the rage on the Internet, and hundreds of different models of personal MP3 players are on the market. Heck, you can even invest in an MP3 car audio deck!

If you're already an MP3 fanatic and you're shopping for a sound card, I can't stress this advice enough: *Buy a card that supports high-quality MP3 encoding and digital effects!* This type of card is especially valuable when you create your own MP3 files or listen to your collection. For example, my Sound Blaster Audigy card allows me to add environmental effects to a recording to simulate a concert hall or stadium, and I can record the highest-quality MP3 files from a number of different audio sources (including analog and digital CD audio, of course).

Uhh . . . Is This Microphone On?

Your ears are not the only lucky body parts to benefit from a sound card — your mouth also gets to enjoy itself. With a microphone attached to your sound card, you can take advantage of computer applications like these:

- ✔ **Voice recording:** The simplest application for a microphone is to help you record your voice and other sounds. You can edit your recordings with a sound editor to add special effects, add these sound files to your Web page for Web surfers to enjoy, or just have a little fun with your dog. (Note that you can also record from inputs other than your microphone or sound card line-in jack. For example, you can record music in the electronic MIDI format.)

- ✔ **Voice command and dictation:** Imagine talking to your computer through a microphone to run programs, open and close windows, and even dictate into your word processor with a program such as Dragon NaturallySpeaking 10, from Nuance Communications (www.nuance.com). You can even control some computer games these days with spoken commands.

  Note: You typically have to "train" your computer to recognize your verbal patterns, and these applications are nowhere near 100 percent accurate. However, this kind of technology is constantly improving, and it's a great help to computer owners who need special accommodations and those computer owners who might not feel comfortable with the keyboard.

- ✔ **Voice e-mail:** If you have an Internet e-mail client application that allows attachments, you can record your own voice as a digital WAV file and send it along with the text. Attaching a human voice to an e-mail message still has considerable impact (especially when you haven't heard that certain voice in several weeks).

✔ **Internet telephone:** No doubt about it, Voice-over-IP (VoIP) programs are just plain neat. And if you call someone at long distance or international rates often, you can save a ton of money! An Internet telephone program turns your microphone and sound card into a telephone. Instead of talking over standard telephone lines, your voices are transmitted over the Internet as data. Therefore, the only cost that you incur is the online time from your Internet service provider (ISP). Your voice modem can also act as a speaker-phone and telephone answering service — more on this in Chapter 11.

Note: The person on the other end of the conversation must also have a computer, an Internet connection, and a copy of the same VoIP program that you're using. Some of these programs are so sophisticated that they have call screening and Internet telephone answering machines, too.

The three basic types of computer microphones are the clip-on/stick-on model, the fancier boom microphone, and the headset microphone:

✔ **Clip-on microphones:** Designed to clip onto your lapel or collar, this type of mike see Figure 10-1) is usually better for capturing your voice (unless, of course, a person is fidgeting or moving, in which case a boom mike is preferred).

✔ **Boom mikes:** This kind of mike (see Figure 10-2) sits on your desk or on top of your computer case. Boom mikes tend to pick up a little more ambient sound from around your computer.

✔ **Headset microphones:** This is kind of mike telephone operators use. They free both hands while you talk, and they're the microphone of choice when using a voice command or voice dictation system. A headset microphone usually comes with stereo headphones. (Gamers love 'em.)

If you already have a microphone with a standard jack that you use with a cassette recorder, this type of microphone should work fine with your sound card. Just make sure that it has some sort of stand to hold it upright.

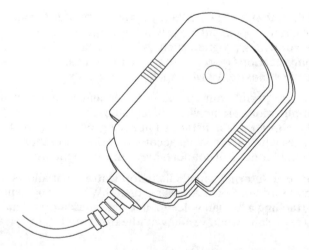

Figure 10-1: Use a lapel mike for close voice pickup.

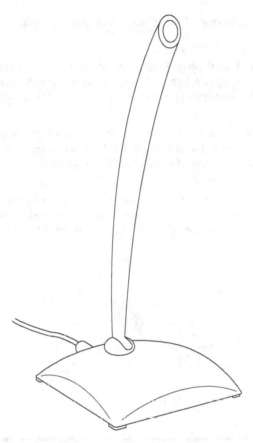

Figure 10-2: Use a desktop boom mike to pick up ambient sound.

Speaking of Speakers

No matter what kind of audio hardware you have or what you choose to listen to, you can't hear anything without a speaker. External (add-on) computer speakers are another part of your system that might vary widely with your personal preferences. For example, some computer owners are happy with a set of headphones, which helps all family members maintain their sanity (especially if the computer room is located right next to the baby's room). In fact, if you have a portable CD player or FM stereo radio, you can use the headphones that came with it with your new sound card. And don't forget the internal speaker (which I mention in Chapter 3) which is really only useful for simple beeps, but comes in handy when diagnosing problems when turning on your computer. In fact, your monitor might even have built-in speakers although they're not likely to produce top-quality sound.

On the other end of the spectrum, many computer owners are as demanding about their computer speakers as they are about their stereo speakers. For these audiophiles, only the very best audio reproduction is acceptable, especially when they're battling slobbering purple dragons from Medieval Dimension X. Your preferences in audio quality determine whether you spend $10 or $200 (or even more) on your computer's speaker system.

Speakers are connected to your system in one of three ways; compare the plugs in Figure 10-3:

✔ **Traditional analog line-out jack and plug:** Every sound card or integrated audio hardware has a line-out or speaker jack. In fact, your speakers connect to your PC exactly like the headphones on your personal CD or MP3 player.

✔ **Digital jack and plug:** Today's sophisticated stereo systems and high-end amplified speaker systems can accept a digital signal through an optical S/PDIF (Sony/Philips Digital Interconnect Format) output jack. You'll pay top-dollar for hardware that uses this jack.

✔ **Universal serial bus (USB) connector:** If you've invested in a set of digital speakers, you can usually use one of your USB ports. These speakers often don't require an AC adapter because they draw electricity directly through the USB port.

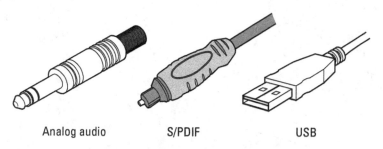

Analog audio   S/PDIF   USB

Figure 10-3: Analog, digital, and USB speaker plugs.

Unless you have a definite reason why you prefer using headphones, I strongly recommend using a set of speakers especially designed to be used with a computer. Computer speakers come in all shapes and sizes — as I mentioned earlier, some are even integrated into your computer monitor. Speakers are best placed on either side of the monitor, about a foot away from your ears.

When you shop for a set of speakers, look for these features:

✔ **Amplified power:** If you're looking for a little more power and better sound, select a speaker set that has its own built-in amplifier. The downside is that the built-in amp needs power; depending on the size of your speakers, you need to provide C or D cell batteries. *Hint:* If your speaker set comes with its own AC wall adapter or a USB connection that provides power, you don't need batteries.

✔ **Speaker controls:** If your sound card has a volume control (and you can control the volume of your speakers from within Windows), why do you need separate bass, treble, and volume controls on your speakers? I prefer using speaker controls because they're much more convenient. If you need to adjust the volume for a particular game or a Web site with audio, you can do so without opening another window, launching another program, or having to reach around to the back of your computer.

✔ **Flat-panel design:** Some people feel that flat-panel speakers are a little funny looking — they're not much thicker than a CD case — but techno-types consider them cool. Most flat-panel speakers produce the same quality of sound as a standard speaker. Although they can save space on your computer desk, they're typically a little more expensive than traditional computer speakers.

The Subwoofer: Big Dog of Computer Speakers

If you enjoy your computer games — I mean *really* enjoy your computer games — I should mention one other speaker enhancement. A computer *subwoofer* provides the deep subsonic bass punch that adds realism whether you're flying a jet or playing an old arcade classic, such as Asteroids.

You can buy a subwoofer separately or shop for a speaker system that includes one. (It's no accident that high-performance sound systems sold for home theaters include a subwoofer.) A subwoofer is about the size of a loaf of bread, and one will typically set you back around $50 to $100, depending on the power that it can handle.

Unlike the rest of a computer speaker system, a subwoofer is best placed on the floor to cut down on vibration — unless, of course, the idea of your computer desk rattling like a tin roof in a hailstorm appeals to you. (Plus, your PC will avoid dancing the Shimmy, which could in fact be bad for your PC's hard drive.)

And for Colossus, I Pick . . .

Audio quality is important to me. I'm a music lover with over 100GB of digital music, and I'm a hard-core gamer on top of that. Therefore, Colossus will need better-than-average audio hardware, and I'll disable my motherboard's integrated sound card in favor of a PCI sound card.

As of this writing, here's what goes into the hardest-working PC in show business:

✔ **Sound Blaster X-Fi XtremeGamer PCI sound card from Creative Labs:** Offering both 7.1 Surround Sound and Dolby DTS decoding, this card includes the latest 3-D positional audio standard (EAX 5.0). You also get a nifty remixer that can create a "pseudo-surround" effect for gaming, even using headphones! Audio quality is excellent, with 24-bit clarity.

✔ **X-540 5.1 PC speaker system from Logitech:** This sweet 5.1 surround speaker system includes a center channel speaker that clips to your flat-panel monitor! (Talk about audio *in your face!*) The subwoofer offers 25 watts of power, providing all the thump you're likely to need.

✔ **USB gaming headset from Logitech:** This model works equally well as a mike for podcasting and a hands-free gaming system. I appreciate the noise-canceling feature offered by this svelte, silver model.

Installing Your Sound Card

Stuff You Need to Know

Toolbox:
- ✔ Phillips screwdriver
- ✔ Parts bowl

Materials:
- ✔ Sound card

Time Needed:
5 minutes

So you bought a jiffy sound card, speaker system, and microphone for your PC, and all your audio accoutrements are unpacked and ready. You're set to sit back and enjoy anything from Mozart to Metallica!

Of course, if you'll be using your motherboard's integrated audio hardware, you won't need to install a separate card. Just head directly to the next section, "Connecting Your Speakers." I'll join you there shortly.

Keep your sound card's manual handy because you might have to perform a little jumper surgery during the testing phase.

1. If your computer chassis is plugged in, unplug it. Finished dusting your antiques? You had better touch a metal surface before you install your card to discharge any static electricity that you might have picked up before it can damage a computer component.

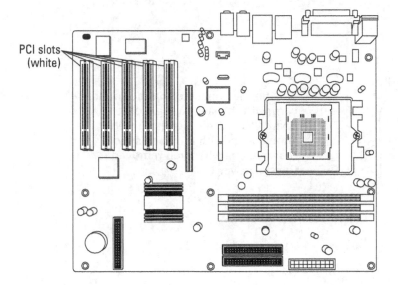

PCI slots
(white)

2. Select an open PCI adapter card slot for your sound card. (For more information on PCI cards and PCI bus slots, see Chapter 3.)

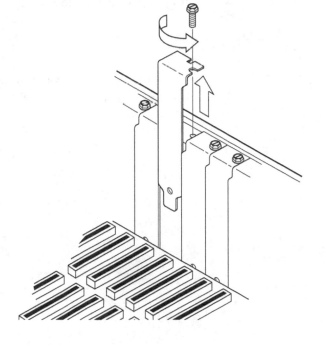

3. Remove the screw and the metal slot cover adjacent to the selected slot. Don't forget to stick the screw and slot cover into your parts bowl (or box, or can).

What's a parts bowl? You know, that covered plastic bowl, shoebox, or coffee can that holds all the small computer parts. You can't be a techno-wizard without a parts bowl.

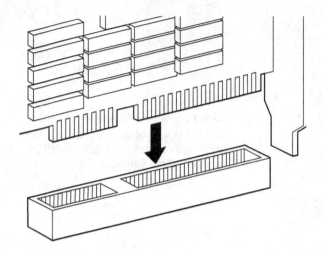

4. Line up the connector on the sound card with the slot on the mother-board. The card's metal bracket should align with the open space that remains when you removed the slot cover.

5. Apply even pressure to the top of the card and push it down into the slot. If the card is all the way in, the bracket should be resting tightly against the case.

6. Add the screw (from your parts bowl) and tighten down the bracket.

Connecting Your Speakers

Before you can test the operation of your audio hardware, you need to connect your speakers. For these steps, I use a standard analog connection from a set of external speakers to the audio hardware's speaker jack. (If your PC uses a digital connection, the steps are essentially the same — just a different port.)

If you're connecting speakers using a USB port, things are even simpler: You can skip Steps 1 and 2 in this section! Just locate an open USB port on your PC and connect the cable. (It goes in only one way, which is how everything in life should work.) With the USB cable connected, jump to Step 3.

1. Locate the speaker jack on the sound card. Usually the speaker jack is labeled Speakers or Spkr although some cards also use the stereo term Line Out. If you need help identifying which jack to use, check your sound card or motherboard manual. (Most motherboards and sound cards use a rather attractive lime-green color-coding to indicate the speaker jack.) The figure here illustrates the analog audio jacks on a typical sound card.

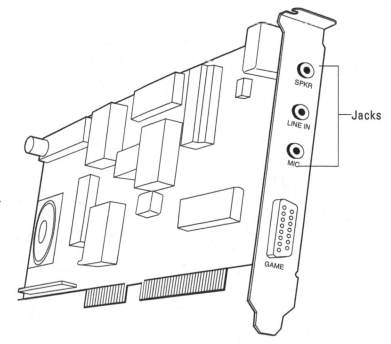

2. Insert the audio cable plug from your speakers into the sound card's speaker jack. And if your speakers are amplified, add the required batteries.

If your speaker set uses an AC adapter or power cord, plug it into a nearby wall socket and plug the connector into the power connector on one of the speakers. If your speakers use a USB connection, they might not require batteries or a separate AC adapter.

3. Set the volume controls on all parts. If your speakers are amplified, they probably have their own separate volume control. To avoid waking the neighbors and to prevent permanent hearing loss, make sure that all volume controls are set at less than the halfway point. You can always tweak the volume later. And if your speakers are amplified, turn them on.

Testing Your Sound System

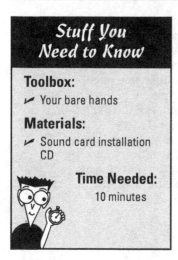
It's time to install the software required by your sound card. Afterward, you'll test it to see whether your audio hardware and speakers are working properly.

1. If you unplugged your computer, plug it back in now. Connect the monitor, mouse, and keyboard (if you haven't already done so); then push the power switch on your monitor.

2. Push the power switch on your case and allow your computer to boot. The familiar face of Windows XP or Vista should eventually appear on your screen.

3. Run the sound card installation software. Insert the installation software into your DVD drive and follow the instructions onscreen or in your sound card/ motherboard manual to install the applications and driver. The installation program will probably make changes to your system files.

4. After the software is installed,
   reboot your computer (if necessary).

5. Run the diagnostics software supplied with your sound card. Your sound card should come with a diagnostics program that lets you test its operation. Typically, these diagnostics programs play digital audio effects and MIDI music from both speakers, individually and together. For example, you might be asked whether you hear a sound effect from the left speaker, from the right speaker, and then from the "center" channel. If you can't find the diagnostics software, try installing a game that has support for your sound card to see whether the card is working correctly. (And don't forget to click the volume control in the Windows notification area at the right side of the taskbar — just to make sure that you haven't muted your PC's audio by mistake.)

Adding a Microphone

As I mention earlier in the chapter, many types of microphones are available for your PC. Follow these steps to add a microphone only after you test your installation and know that your sound card is working properly.

If you're connecting a headset microphone via a USB port, you can skip Steps 1 and 2 in this section! Just locate an open USB port on your PC and connect the cable. With the USB cable connected, jump to Step 3.

1. Locate the microphone jack on the sound card. On most cards, the microphone jack is labeled `Microphone` or `Mic` although some cards also use the stereo term `Line In`. If you need help identifying which jack to use, check your sound card manual.

2. Insert the audio cable plug from
   your microphone into the sound
   card's microphone jack.

3. If your microphone has an on/off
   switch, turn it on.

4. Adjust (or affix) your microphone.

   - **If you're using a clip-on microphone,** attach it
     to your shirt.

   - **If your microphone is meant to be mounted
     on your PC,** remove the paper backing and
     stick the holder on your case. (Make sure that
     the microphone and its cable don't obscure or
     block any switches, lights, or openings on the
     front of your computer.)

   - **If you're using a boom microphone,** place it
     to one side of your monitor.

For best operation, your microphone should be no more than one or two feet away from your chair. Of course, clip-on microphones work best attached to your person, and headset microphones will work correctly only when worn.

Chapter 11

Modems and the Call of Broadband

Tasks performed in this chapter

- Installing your internal modem

- Installing your external modem

- Sharing the Internet through software

- Adding a hardware Internet sharing device

Time to join the online crowd? If so, I recommend using a *broadband* connection — typically, a cable or digital subscriber line (DSL) link to the Internet — even if you think you don't need a high-speed Internet connection. Even if a dial-up connection is available to you — and maybe even a little less expensive — you should really consider going broadband for a host of reasons. Even if all you do on the Internet is occasionally visit a Web site, read your e-mail, or use instant messaging, you'll still find broadband essential because you'll experience "the Web without the Wait." And if you're going to spend two or three hours nightly on the 'Net, I strongly recommend that you invest the money in a high-speed connection — if it's available in your area, that is.

Broadband Internet connections represent a dream come true for telecommuters and Internet junkies. Imagine transferring data over existing telephone lines with throughput anywhere from 640 Kbps to 10 Mbps or faster. Think about smooth, real-time videoconferencing, high-resolution graphics over the Web, and the ability to enjoy today's latest online games with thousands of other players? Huzzah! You just *have* to have a broadband connection, right?

As my favorite Western star, John Wayne, used to drawl, "Hold on there, pardner." Yes, you can do all that with broadband (think *high-speed Internet,* as compared with an old-fashioned analog dial-up modem). But a high-speed broadband connection, like digital subscriber line (DSL) or a cable Internet connection, isn't available everywhere yet. So what can you use to connect if you're outside your local cable or DSL broadband service area?

In this chapter, I cover all the advantages and disadvantages of broadband, the latter including expensive hardware and higher subscription rates compared with a dial-up connection. To boot, the rate that your telephone or cable company charges for access might be outrageous.

If you think you can't get high-speed Internet access, stay right here! In this chapter, I show you how to select a modem (yup, you gotta have one) with the features that you need. Then I show you how to install the modem, either inside or outside your computer case. You might want to celebrate your new modem by sending a few faxes to your friends and co-workers — without ever touching a fax machine!

Figuring Out Whether You Need Broadband

Before you go any further in this chapter, decide whether you even need a broadband connection to the Internet for your new-built computer. For example, there's no reason to even consider the expenses involved in cable or DSL if all you plan to do is connect to the Internet for a few minutes a day to check your e-mail. Of course, you don't have to meet any certain criteria to add a broadband Internet connection to your system, but it really isn't cost effective to use it for only a few minutes per day.

Choosing cable or DSL could be a winning proposition if you fit one of these descriptions:

✔ **Internet junkie:** I'm talking heavy-duty Web surfing here — at least three or four hours daily of Internet access. If your primary activities on the Internet are Web surfing or file transfers via File Transfer Protocol (FTP), a broadband connection will be great for you. If you use the Internet for only an hour per day — or if your primary Internet applications are e-mail, newsgroups, or instant messaging, broadband is still the best choice. However, such limited use may make it easier to endure a slow 56 Kbps analog modem. (It depends on your level of patience. And whether or not you can live with the repeated disconnects that occur with an analog connection.)

✔ **Telecommuter:** If you need high-speed access to your office network from your home, DSL is a good choice. You can connect to the network at your office and log on normally, just as though you were sitting at a computer at work. (Take my word for it: If you work from a home office using your computer, broadband is a must-have. Heck, perhaps your employer will pay for it.) DSL is also a good idea for those who don't have a local cable provider.

✔ **Conferencing wizard:** A broadband connection is practically a requirement for high-quality videoconferencing, such as over a local area network (LAN) connection or over the Internet. If you've tried conferencing over an analog modem, you'll be amazed at the difference. Broadband provides the fast data-transfer rates for audio and a larger screen as well.

✔ **Multimedia lover:** Looking for the best sound from Internet radio stations? Do you crave online music downloading from services such as Apple's iTunes Store? Or perhaps you love to download those trailers for upcoming movies? Then sign up for broadband because a dial-up connection just won't cut it.

✔ **Online gamer:** Whether your game of choice is World of Warcraft or Warhammer Online, you need a broadband connection. These programs transfer such a huge amount of game data back and forth between the developer's server and your PC that gameplay suffers if you use a dial-up connection.

For many years, people wondered whether 28.8 Kbps was the fastest transfer rate that could be squeezed out of an analog modem over a typical telephone connection. (You get the gist in Figure 11-1.)

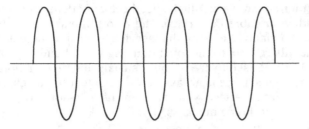

Figure 11-1: A slow, tired analog signal.

Nope. Modem manufacturers again proved the techno-types wrong. The v.90 and v.92 international standards now provide a top data-transfer rate of 56 Kbps (with compression). Will these faster dial-up speeds forestall the eventual doom of the dial-up analog connection?

The answer is "Definitely not!" If you fit the mold of the typical broadband customer that I outline previously, the advantages of DSL or cable far outweigh the money that you save with a simple analog modem connection. The nearly perfect quality of the DSL line means virtually no interference. Both cable and DSL will still be superior in raw throughput.

Analog dial-up technology just can't keep up. You'll need a nearly perfect analog v.92 connection to get anywhere near the top throughput of 56 Kbps on an analog modem, and that just doesn't happen often in the real world. (You'll more likely end up with anywhere between 36 Kbps and 43.2 Kbps throughput.) Your throughput will vary from call to call.

On the other hand, Figure 11-2 illustrates a *digital* signal, which is basically a long string of zeros and ones, or on and off states (the same digital vocabulary spoken by your computer and your audio CD player). That means no interference and approximately the same connection throughput at all times. Plus, most cable and DSL systems remain connected to the ISP (and therefore the Internet) at all times, so you need never listen to those screeching dialing-up tones again.

Figure 11-2: A spunky digital signal, full of vim and vigor.

"So, Mark, what's the difference between DSL and cable connections? And what other higher-speed connection options do I have?" I'm glad you asked!

   ✔ **Cable modems:** With a cable modem and an enhanced cable network (which must be capable of two-way communications), your cable company suddenly becomes an ISP and can supply you with a digital Internet connection of 500 Kbps or faster. Cable modem service is now available to most cable subscribers. With the nearly universal access of cable, this type of broadband connection has turned out to be the long-awaited, high-speed connection for the common person. (Unfortunately, a cable modem connection forces you to share bandwidth with all the other cable Internet subscribers in your area. Therefore, your top speed depends on the time of day and the current number of connections to your cable provider.)

Cable service has other advantages: A high-speed cable modem connection doesn't interfere with your cable TV service. And if your house is already wired for cable TV, it's a cinch to expand that service to a cable modem. Your telephone suddenly reverts to the job it had originally: handling voice (and sometimes fax) calls, blissfully free of busy signals and modem noise! Finally, your cable Internet service is always on. (If you elect to pay extra for business-class cable Internet service, you can even run a 24-hour Web server and FTP site for your home business.)

Most cable Internet providers include a cable modem as part of their service. This "black box" looks like a regular analog modem, but it connects to your coax cable on one end and to a network card installed in your computer on the other. If your computer doesn't have a network interface card installed already, your cable company will probably provide one and install it as well.

✔ **DSL:** Like cable modems, DSL was once another "could be big in just a year or so" technology. Like cable Internet access, it was about as available as sunshine in Carlsbad Caverns. Recently, however, DSL has become a power player as local telephone companies expand and improve their DSL coverage, with top speeds around 4 to 10 Mbps for received data (depending on the flavor of DSL being installed) and as much as 2 Mbps for transmitted data.

DSL uses a digital signal, and it works over the standard copper telephone line in your home, so all you need is — you guessed it — a DSL modem (which is usually supplied by your local phone company) and a network interface card for your computer. (Depending on the service that you receive, you might also need a splitter — as shown in Figure 11-3 — to separate the regular phone signal from the higher-frequency DSL signal.) Like a cable modem connection, most DSL connections are always on, so you don't have to dial your ISP, and you can use your voice telephone and place regular calls at the same time you're connected to the Internet! Most DSL connections require you to have an Ethernet network card in your PC, but some ISPs offer USB DSL modems for computers without a network port.

Whether you can obtain DSL service also depends on your distance from the telephone switch. In most areas, your home or office can't be farther than 18,000 feet from a switch or local cable loop that supports DSL, so obtaining DSL service in your mountain cabin might be nigh impossible.

✔ **Satellite Internet connections:** Satellite Internet connections are fast, but they usually require you to continue to use your analog modem connection — and most Internet junkies don't want anything to do with those "antique" 56K analog modems anymore. However, if you can spend the money, you can get a *two-way* satellite Internet connection that doesn't require a phone line or modem — and that might be the only viable alternative for that mountain cabin I keep mentioning.

Do you want a WAN?

If you've installed an Ethernet network (see Chapter 12), you can use your broadband Internet connection to create a WAN (a ridiculous sounding acronym that stands for *wide area network*). This procedure is one method of tying together more than one network; you connect the two networks through your Internet connection using a virtual private network (VPN). Suddenly your home network can become a part of your office network, enabling you to share the same files and access the same e-mail server with aplomb! Creating a WAN is no easy matter, and there are security concerns (such as hackers trying to access your network through the Internet), so I recommend seeking professional help when tying your home network to an outside network.

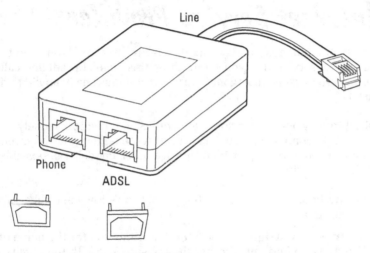

Figure 11-3: A typical DSL splitter.

Figuring Out Those Connection Charges

The biggest expense in going broadband isn't the hardware that you add to your computer, which is usually covered by your cable or DSL provider as part of your subscription. Rather, it's the installation charges and monthly access fees levied by your local carrier.

Installation charges for a broadband connection differ widely across the globe, and every local telephone and cable company has a different pricing plan. Some telephone companies make it as easy to install a DSL line as a standard analog line. They offer telephone ordering for DSL service and Web sites with helpful instructions; some will even charge a flat monthly rate. Other telephone companies offer no pre-sale help for DSL users (forget the Web site) and charge an hourly rate that will leave you pounding your head against a wall when the bill comes in. It all depends on where you live.

The important thing to remember is that you need full support from your telephone or cable company before you begin your broadband quest. Although some carriers provide "do-it-yourself" broadband installation kits for PC owners, most folks would still agree that installing a cable or DSL modem is not a fun project that you can do yourself. These connections are usually installed professionally. Therefore, I won't go into the installation of a broadband connection here. In fact, it's important to note that you can't follow the same procedure that you would use to set up a dialup Internet connection because DSL and cable Internet subscribers are effectively connecting through a local area network (LAN). They don't dial to connect to an ISP.

What's an average rate for broadband service? Installation costs an average of $25 to $50, although you might get free installation if you're on the ball. Monthly broadband ISP charges typically range from $35 to $50.

Locating an Internet Service Provider

After you decide to go broadband, you have another bridge to cross: You need to find an ISP that offers the service that you want. (From this angle, broadband callers are no different from callers using analog modems. You still must have an ISP to link you to the Internet.)

You might be limited to only one ISP for your cable or DSL connection: namely, your cable company or local telephone company. However, some larger cities offer more than one choice for your broadband provider. Here's a quick checklist of possible sources for local ISP information:

- ✔ **Your telephone book:** Like any other business, the Yellow Pages likely lists the ISPs in your area.

- ✔ **Friends, relatives, and neighbors:** Ask those around you for the name of their ISP. You can also find out whether they're satisfied with the quality of service that they receive from their ISP (and whether their connection slows down during peak hours).

- ✔ **Local computer stores:** Computer stores are always a good source of information.

- ✔ **Computer club or user groups:** You'll get a chorus of possibilities from club members.

Use the 'Net to find an ISP

Do you already have Internet access . . . perhaps at work? If so, check out ISPs.com at (you guessed it) www.isps.com. This Web site has information and links to thousands of ISPs in the United States, Canada, and around the world (so that even you readers in Djibouti or Liechtenstein can find an ISP easily). Use these resources to find out which ISPs in your area offer DSL, whether they support 56K modem connections, and what the ISP charges for broadband installation and monthly access.

A Modem Primer for Real People

I could give you the lengthy techno-nerd description of a modem. Or, for those folks with things to do, here's a simple explanation favored by those who'd rather do something else with the next 30 minutes of their lives. The word *modem* is short for *mo*dulate-*dem*odulate, which are the terms usually used for the digital-to-analog and analog-to-digital conversion processes. A modem is a device that translates *(modulates)* the *digital* language of computers (zeros and ones) into an *analog* signal (variable waves, like a human voice), which can travel over a telephone line. This analog signal doesn't sound anything like a human voice, but it can carry data. The receiving modem then translates *(demodulates)* the incoming signal from analog back to digital, which the receiving computer can then use. Figure 11-4 gives you an idea of what's happening.

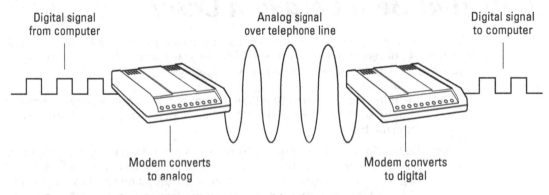

Digital signal from computer

Analog signal over telephone line

Digital signal to computer

Modem converts to analog

Modem converts to digital

Figure 11-4: Two modems strut their stuff, transferring data over a telephone line.

The whole speed thing explained

Here's the scoop: The fastest possible telephone modem available today can *theoretically* reach speeds of 56 Kbps. (That is 56,000 bits per second — keep this number in your mind when you read about broadband earlier in this chapter.)

However, let's be honest. You're more likely to encounter an African wildebeest wearing a hula skirt in your living room than to connect at a full 56 Kbps with *any* telephone modem. Your telephone line has to be crystal clear, and conditions must be perfect. In fact, I have never received a full 56 Kbps. (And, coincidentally, I've never seen a wildebeest, either, grass skirt or not.)

In essence, 56 Kbps is the fastest modem speed available, but the most that you can squeeze from a standard telephone line is a respectable 49.3 Kbps connection. This restriction is because of the conversion process between digital and analog that the modem must perform and the less-than-perfect conditions provided by an analog telephone line.

This speed limit doesn't apply to DSL or cable Internet, though, which are broadband connections. A broadband Internet connection couldn't care less about even the fastest dial-up analog modem, which it considers strictly horse-and-buggy. If you're a speed racer, aren't afraid to spend money, and want all the facts on a *really* fast connection, zip directly to "Figuring Out Whether You Need Broadband," earlier in this chapter.

If you do stick with dialup and you don't have a locally accessible Internet service provider (ISP) — meaning that you have to dial long distance to connect — bear in mind that a long-distance call to your ISP is still that: a long-distance toll call! If you do have to use a dial-up connection, make sure the access number is local to your area.

Will That Be a Card or a Case?

You can uncover plenty of pros and cons for choosing an internal or an external modem, so determining which type is right for you is generally easy. Here's a list of the clouds and their accompanying silver linings:

- ✔ **Cost:** Internal modems don't need their own case and separate power supply, so they're generally 20 to 30 percent less expensive than their external brethren.

- ✔ **Status lights:** As you can see by the example shown in Figure 11-5, external modems have lights that let you monitor how your connection is proceeding. If you know something about what the lights mean, they can be a valuable tool in figuring out whether your modem and computer are cooperating (or whether your modem has sprung a leak). Internal modems — which live inside your computer's case — have no lights, so it's hard to tell exactly what they're doing.

- ✔ **Less clutter:** If you have limited desk space, an internal modem means one less box cluttering up your computer desk.

- ✔ **Overcrowding:** If you already filled all the slots in your computer with various goodies, such as a separate TV adapter and a FireWire card, you won't have room for an internal modem. This is another reason why many technoids have external modems.

- ✔ **Ease of installation:** A USB modem is about as easy to install as your keyboard or mouse! On the other hand, installing an internal modem is just a bit more complex.

If you're installing an external modem, embrace your USB port!™

Time to face the fax

All new modems sold today have built-in fax support. In fact, even if you decide to use a broadband connection to the Internet, you might find that you still need a dialup modem to use as your dedicated fax hardware.

Just what exactly can you do with a fax/modem? Actually, just about anything that you can do with a real fax machine, and a whole lot more to boot! Naturally, you can use a fax/modem to send and receive faxes from other fax machines or other computers. You can also build a telephone directory, automatically send faxes at night, allow other fax machines to poll your computer for new documents, send broadcast faxes to multiple destinations, and design your own cover sheets, just like you can with an expensive fax machine. With a fax/modem, you can even send programs and data files to other computers with fax/modems. Remember, though, that the source document must be stored (or scanned) on your computer, and you must leave your PC on to receive faxes.

If you decide to use your new computer as a part of a home office, I strongly suggest that you have a second telephone line with a dedicated installation especially for your computer. Otherwise, anyone trying to send you a fax while you're on the phone ordering pizza is going to get an irritating busy signal. You can also use a separate telephone line for voice mail, as described in the section "Let Your Modem Speak."

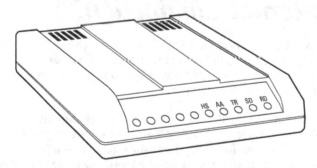

Figure 11-5: A typical external modem, complete with light show.

Let Your Modem Speak!

Have you ever called a business and tried to contact someone who was out of the office? You likely encountered *voice mail,* with which you can leave a verbal message for a specific person. If you think that this kind of technology is too expensive for your home office, think again. With today's voice modems, callers are presented with a professional telephone answering service for your business. The cost is usually only $50 or so more than a regular fax/modem.

Voice modem hardware and software provides a number of individual, personal voice mailboxes. (The number of mailboxes and the features available for each mailbox vary with the modem and the software that comes with it.) A caller can store a voice message for you by pressing keys on the telephone, which sends numeric commands to your computer. Most voice modems allow you to pick up your voice mail from a remote telephone, so you don't even need to be at your computer to check your messages.

Most voice modems also provide other amenities. For example

- ✔ **Speakerphone:** One of my favorite voice modem features, the speakerphone can be used to dial the phone and talk to someone through your PC's microphone and speakers — no telephone handset necessary! (You can read more about microphones and speakers in Chapter 10.)

- ✔ **Personalized mailbox:** If you have more than one message mailbox, your voice modem should enable you to store an individual voice greeting for each mailbox.

- ✔ **Caller ID:** If you're curious about the origin of a call, make sure that you get a voice modem with caller ID support, including an onscreen display of the caller's telephone number. (You also need to sign up for caller ID service through your telephone company.)

Why Share Your Internet Connection?

"Don't I need a separate Internet connection for each PC on my network?" Actually, you just answered your own question: The *network* you installed (Chapter 12's the spot for all things networky) allows for all sorts of data communications between PCs, including the ability to plug in to a shared connection.

I should note here that it is indeed technically possible to share a dialup Internet connection by using the software connection-sharing feature in Windows Vista. However, I don't think that you'll be satisfied with the results. (Sorry — it just doesn't provide enough horsepower to adequately handle more than one computer.) Therefore, I assume for the rest of this chapter that you're already using a digital subscriber line (DSL), a cable modem Internet connection, or a satellite connection.

Here's a list of benefits that help explain why Internet connection sharing — whether through a program or a dedicated hardware device — is so doggone popular these days:

- ✔ **It's cheap.** As long as your ISP allows you to share your broadband connection, you save a bundle over the cost of adding completely separate connections for multiple machines in your home or office. (Naturally, this is the major benefit.)

- ✔ **It's convenient.** With a shared Internet connection, other PCs on your network are easy to configure, and each one is as content as a sleeping cat. Each PC on your network operates just as though it were directly connected to the Internet, and the computers on the network can all do their own thing on the Internet simultaneously.

✔ **It offers centralized security.** With a *firewall* in place — either running on the PC (if you're sharing through software) or on the device itself (if you're sharing through hardware) — you can protect the Internet activity on all the PCs on your network at one time.

✔ **It's efficient.** Most folks I know are surprised that a shared Internet connection is so fast — even when multiple computers on the network are charging down the information superhighway at the same time.

A connection shared through a dedicated hardware device, however, is always faster than a connection shared through software.

Speaking of convenience and efficiency, I should also mention that many hardware-sharing devices also double as Ethernet switches. They allow you to build your entire home or office network around one central piece of hardware rather than use a separate switch and a PC running a software-sharing program.

Sharing through Hardware

As I mention earlier, I think that a hardware-sharing device is somewhat preferable to sharing a connection through software. For example, with a software solution

✔ At least one PC on your network must always remain turned on if anyone wants to use the Internet.

✔ You notice a significant slowdown on the sharing PC when several other PCs are using the Internet.

✔ You still need a switch or wireless base station.

With a hardware device, all the PCs on your network can concentrate on their own work, eliminating the need to leave a PC running constantly as an "Internet server." (After all, a PC that's capable of running Windows Vista at a decent clip is an expensive resource compared with an investment of $50–$125 on a hardware-sharing device.)

In this section, I familiarize you with the two different types of hardware-sharing devices.

Wired sharing devices

For PC owners who either already have a traditional wired Ethernet network — or who are considering building one — a *sharing device* (like the wired router in Figure 11-6) is the perfect solution to Internet connection sharing. Today's hardware-sharing devices provide *Dynamic Host Configuration Protocol,* or *DHCP.* DHCP allows your hardware-sharing device to automatically configure IP addresses, providing unique network addresses for each computer you've connected to the network. (If all that sounds like gibberish, by the way, you'll find more about Ethernet networks in Chapter 12.)

Figure 11-6: An Internet router.

For an idea of why hardware sharing is so popular, look at what you can buy — in one small, tidy box — online for a mere $50:

✔ **A built-in, four-port Ethernet 10/100 switch:** You can plug four PCs, to start with, directly into the router for an instant Ethernet network at either 10 Mbps or 100 Mbps speeds.

✔ **A direct-connect port for your DSL or cable modem:** The port can also be used as a WAN connection to hook the device to an existing external network.

✔ **A DHCP server:** Such a server provides near-automatic network configuration for the PCs hooked into the device.

✔ **The hardware and software controls you need to block certain Internet traffic (both coming in and going out):** You can also lock out individual PCs from Internet access.

✔ **An easy-to-use, Web-based configuration screen:** You can configure it on any PC connected to the router.

Pretty neat, eh? Remember that this device is used in tandem with your existing cable or DSL modem, which is typically included by your ISP as part of your Internet subscription (even though you might be paying more because you're renting the modem).

I should also note that you can get a similar device with all these features *and* a built-in DSL or cable modem. Because you aren't charged a monthly rental fee for a modem, you can thumb your nose at your ISP and save money in the long run. (Please avoid mentioning my name when you gleefully return your modem to your ISP.)

Wireless sharing devices

Most folks think that sharing an Internet connection over a wireless network must be harder to set up than a traditional wired network — and that it's likely to be a tremendous security risk. I'm happy to tell you that both preconceptions are wrong. Wireless connection sharing with a hardware device is as simple to set up as the wired device that I discuss in the preceding section.

We're talking a truly versatile all-in-one Internet sharing device. It's got the antenna that marks it as a wireless switch and it also sports four 10/100 Ethernet ports on the back for your old-fashioned wired network. Yep, you guessed it, this is just plain neat: It can accommodate multiple 802.11n wireless connections *and* four wired connections, all at the same time!

As you might expect, the cost on this puppy (about $125 online) is much higher than the wired-only device (see the preceding section). Another factor is the speed of the wireless connection; 802.11g devices are rapidly disappearing from the market, so costs are dropping fast on 802.11n hardware. (And yes, if you opt for a wireless-only network, you can find a cheaper wireless sharing device that doesn't include any of those silly "antique" wired ports.) Wireless adapter cards (including the USB variety) are much more expensive than standard wired adapter cards, too.

Installing an Internal Modem

Stuff You Need to Know

Toolbox:
- Phillips screwdriver
- Parts bowl

Materials:
- Modem adapter card
- Screws

Time Needed:
15 minutes

Installing an internal modem used to be compared favorably with wrestling an enraged tiger with your bare hands. Often, this observation had more to do with trying to shoehorn an internal modem into an existing computer, where several devices are already fighting over resources. Windows XP and Vista make the installation generally smooth, though.

Follow these instructions in order to install an internal modem, and you should come out unscathed on the other side.

1. If your computer chassis is plugged in, unplug it. And did you just brush the family dog? You'd better touch a metal surface before you install your card! By touching a metal surface before you touch any components, you release any static electricity that you might have picked up.

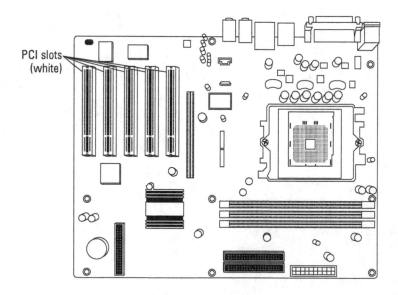

PCI slots (white)

2. Select an open PCI adapter card slot for your modem.

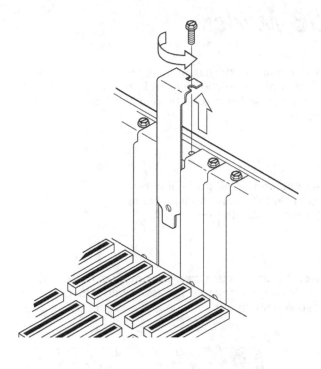

3. Remove the screw and the metal slot cover adjacent to the selected slot. Don't forget to stick both these parts in your spare parts bowl.

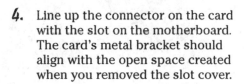

4. Line up the connector on the card with the slot on the motherboard. The card's metal bracket should align with the open space created when you removed the slot cover.

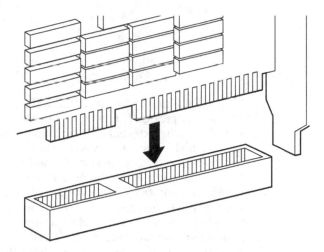

5. Apply even pressure to the top of the card and push it down into the slot. If the card is all the way in, the bracket should rest tightly against the case. Add the screw and tighten down the bracket.

6. Plug the telephone line from the wall into the proper jack on the back of your computer. If you have two jacks on the back of your modem, your modem accepts both the telephone line and a standard external telephone (so you can still call out with the telephone when the modem isn't using the line). Check your modem manual to see which jack should receive the telephone line from the wall; it's typically marked Line or has a picture of a wall telephone jack next to it. If you want to use a separate telephone, connect the cord from the telephone to the other jack (usually marked Phone).

Installing an External USB Modem

Stuff You Need to Know

Toolbox:

✓ Your bare hands

Materials:

✓ External modem
✓ Cables

Time Needed:
5 minutes

Bully for you! You decided to use an external modem, and by using a USB modem, you made the right connection choice as well! You'll be able to install this modem with no tools, so feel free to tie one hand behind your back (if you're in a daring mood).

1. Locate one of your computer's USB ports. If necessary, connect the USB cable to your modem. Some modems have USB cables that are permanently connected.

2. Connect the power cord from your modem to the wall socket. Some USB modems are powered by the USB port itself, so you might not even need a separate power cord.

3. Plug the telephone line from the wall into the proper jack on the back of the external modem. Some external modems have two jacks, which means that you can also plug in a standard telephone and still use it when the modem isn't using the line. Your modem manual should tell you which jack should receive the telephone line from the wall; it's usually marked Line or has a picture of a wall telephone jack next to it. To use a separate telephone, connect the cord from the telephone to the other jack (typically marked Phone).

Line jack   USB port

4. Turn on your external modem.

5. Align the connector on the end of the modem's USB cable with the USB port. The USB connector goes in only one way.

6. After the connector is correctly aligned, push it in firmly. Windows automatically recognizes that you added a USB modem, and you'll probably be prompted to load the installation disc from the modem manufacturer so that Windows can install the modem's drivers. After the driver software is loaded, you're ready to go. You can connect or remove your modem from your PC at any time without rebooting. *That's* convenient — and it's one of the reasons why USB devices are so doggone popular these days!

Sharing an Internet Connection through Software

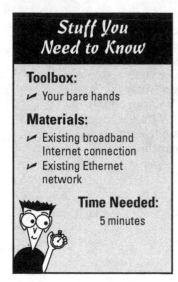

Stuff You Need to Know

Toolbox:
- Your bare hands

Materials:
- Existing broadband Internet connection
- Existing Ethernet network

Time Needed:
5 minutes

If you decide to use the built-in Internet Connection Sharing (ICS) feature of Windows Vista, first double-check to ensure that you use a working Ethernet network — emphasis on "working." Don't try to share your connection if your network isn't already running like a well-oiled machine. You need a working broadband Internet connection to one of the PCs on your network and an installed copy of Windows Vista on the PC that's connected to the Internet. (See Chapter 8 for more on installing Windows Vista.)

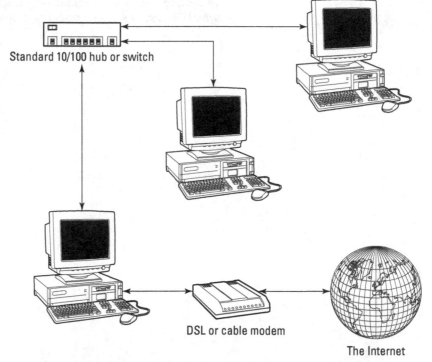

Standard 10/100 hub or switch

DSL or cable modem

The Internet

This PC also needs two network ports installed: one that leads to the network switch and a second one that leads to the cable or DSL modem. Because many flavors of network cards exist (using many different connections — like USB, PC Card, and the more traditional internal adapter card), follow the installation instructions provided by the card manufacturer to add both cards to your PC.

Everything ship-shape? Good. Follow these steps to share that existing Internet connection with the other computers on your network. Remember to verify that you're connected to the Internet. (I always open Internet Explorer and do the Google thing.)

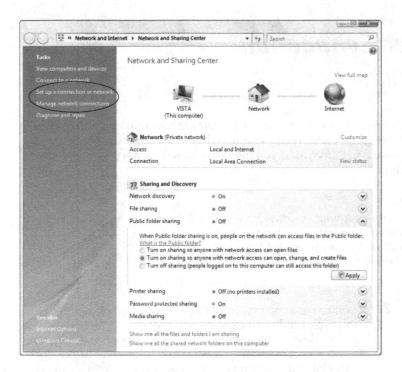

1. Choose Start⇨Control Panel⇨ Network and Internet⇨Network and Sharing Center⇨Manage Network Connections. Right-click the Internet connection you want to share, and then choose Properties. Vista displays the Properties dialog box for your Internet connection.

2. On the Sharing tab, click the Allow Other Network Users to Connect through This Computer's Internet Connection check box to enable it. Then click OK to save your changes. Windows Vista indicates that a connection is shared by adding a "couple of friends" badge under the connection icon.

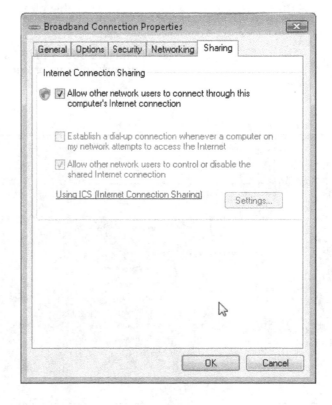

Sharing an Internet Connection through Hardware

Stuff You Need to Know

Toolbox:

✔ Your bare hands

Materials:

✔ Wired or wireless Internet sharing device
✔ Existing broadband Internet connection

Time Needed:

5 minutes

Naturally, the setup procedure for each device on the market is different — as are the configuration steps for wired and wireless devices — but here's a sample of what's in store when you take your new Internet sharing router out of the box.

1. Make sure that your Internet connection to your ISP is working: Just open your Web browser and load your favorite page.

2. If you're running a typical stand-alone network switch, you can either unplug all existing computers and put them on the new device (most come with built-in ports) or connect the WAN port from the existing switch into one of the ports on the Internet sharing device. The device manual tells you how to take care of the latter method. If you're setting up a new network, naturally, you just connect each Ethernet cable directly to the sharing device.

3. Configure one of the PCs on your new network with the default network settings provided by the device manufacturer.

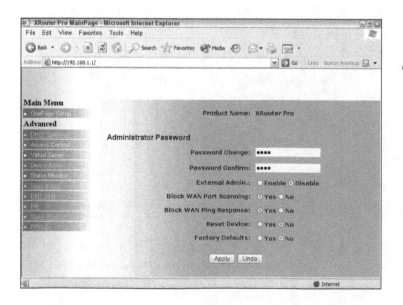

4. Run Internet Explorer on the PC you configured in Step 3 and use the Web-based configuration utility to finish configuring the device. (You can see mine in the figure here.) That's it! If you're running a typical home network or home office network, you'll likely keep the default settings for everything. Luckily, you probably don't have to use any of the optional settings, but it's good to know that they're there.

Part IV
Advanced PC Options

In this part . . .

Here I describe the power-user peripherals often found on high-performance computers. You discover more about building a simple network and using a digital scanner or digital camera. The advanced (and sometimes expensive) technology that you find in this part isn't a requirement for your average home or small-office PC, although these chapters serve as an introduction to the world of power-user computing. I even throw in a chapter on building a PC for the serious gamer.

Chapter 12

So You Want to Add a LAN?

Tasks performed in this chapter

✔ Installing a network interface card

✔ Creating a network

Among the many revolutionary concepts that have rocked PC design for more than two decades, the most important has been the desktop computer network. On a local area network (or LAN, for short), your desktop PC can share programs and data with other computers in your home or office. With the right equipment, your networked PCs can run programs and use shared hardware that resides on a central server computer. You can use a network to share a broadband digital subscriber line (DSL) or cable Internet connection, too, or play the latest games with others using the computers on your network.

Networks can be as small or as large as you like: They can link desktop computers in an entire building or an office with ten computers, or you can simply connect two or three PCs in your home to share the same printer and exchange e-mail.

Adding network support isn't for everyone. If you have access to only one computer or you have no pressing reason to add your computer to an existing network, you can stop reading here and jump to the next chapter. Within these walls (um, pages), I cover traditional wired networks as well as a number of network technologies that eschew wires altogether.

Feel like connecting? Then read on!

Adding the Network Advantage

If you use more than one PC in your home, you might want to connect them through a network. By doing so, you can share data between your computers — everything from a shared family calendar to your kid's artwork. In addition, with a network you can also look forward to the following benefits, which I call the *four Cs*: convenience, communication, cooperation, and contact.

Convenience

Imagine being able to load a document into your word processing application directly from someone else's hard drive. No running back and forth with a CD-ROM or a USB Flash drive. If your PC is connected to a network, you can transfer files, run programs, and access data on the other networked computers, just as though those programs and files resided on your local hard drive (that is, the drive that's physically in your own PC).

The convenience of a network doesn't stop with just data, though. You can also share peripherals. For example, on a network, you can share a printer, Blu-ray recorder, fax/modem, or tape drive. Sharing peripherals is a great way to cut expenses for a large family. Instead of buying a printer for each PC, everyone can share the same printer.

Communication

One of the primary uses for a small network is electronic mail. E-mail software is built into Windows XP and Windows Vista; you can include attachments such as data files, voice and video clips, or even entire programs.

Unfortunately, you can also share a virus with the outside world through a LAN connection or e-mail attachments. *Get yourself a good antivirus program,* such as Norton AntiVirus (www.symantec.com), *install it, and keep it updated!*

With an antivirus program running while you're using your computer, you're protected — just in case.™

Cooperation

For businesses of every size, the answer to office cooperation is a groupware system. A typical *groupware system,* such as Lotus Notes from IBM (www.lotus.com), includes e-mail and an electronic public *message base* (where you can leave messages of general interest, such as announcements), along with a common word processor, spreadsheet, and database program that everyone uses. Each of these common applications shares the same documents, so anyone can use and update those documents. You can also work with the same type of cooperative documents using Microsoft Office 2007.

Contact

The final benefit, contact, refers to contact with the Internet. If your computer has access to an existing network, that network might already have a fast, dedicated connection to the Internet. With a network connection on your PC, your file transfers and Web surfing will be many times faster than they would be over a modem connection. Home office types can also distribute a single Internet connection amongst the entire network gang!

Windows XP and Windows Vista allow you to share a broadband Internet connection among all the computers on your network. Or, if you like, you can allow everyone on your network to access the Internet connection by using a hardware device called an *Internet router* (also called an *Internet gateway* or *Internet sharing device*).

Do you need to connect to a network to access the Internet? Definitely not! A majority of home computer owners still connect to the Internet through a dial-up connection or one of the high-speed connections I describe in Chapter 11. Although the Internet is actually a huge network of smaller networks, you do *not* need your own network to use it.

Ethernet Networking 101

This section explains the basic terms that you need to know when discussing Ethernet networks. I show you the fundamentals of network *architecture,* which is the structure in which you string computers together. Read on to find out how to construct a basic network with the smallest investment in time and money.

You could go full-bore and network all the PCs in your entire neighborhood, but that's not what this book is about. For you home users and small-business owners, this section gives you the basics on constructing a small network of two to five computers, called *nodes* in network terms. For more detailed information on building a network, I suggest that you check out *Home Networking For Dummies,* 4th Edition, by Kathy Ivens (Wiley).

Comparing client-server and peer-to-peer networks

Desktop networks fall into one of two mysterious categories; you continually hear them mentioned if you hang around a networking techno-nerd. Rather than force any well-adjusted human being into hanging around such a social derelict, let me explain these terms up front:

✔ **Client-server:** On a network, a *client* is simply a computer that uses the network's resources. Usually, a client computer is the computer on your desk.

The other half of the name — the *server* — refers to a computer dedicated to providing a resource for the client computers on the network. For example, a *file server* provides the other computers on the network with the fastest access possible to a set of files, which reside on the server instead of the individual client computers. Other servers, such as dedicated DVD servers, printer servers, and modem servers, allow everyone on the network to use the same hardware and access the same data.

A *client-server network* is a network that includes one or more server computers, no matter what the function of the server. Although file servers and printer servers are the most common shared resources, any server transforms your network into a client-server network.

✔ **Peer-to-peer:** For once, a name that means what it says. A *peer-to-peer* network has no servers: All computers are connected to each other. (In fact, every computer is as good as its peers.) You save the cost of an expensive server computer, but it's harder for computers to share the same information. A peer-to-peer network is best for the home network where everyone simply wants to exchange e-mail and files or use a common printer. Windows XP and Windows Vista both include simple peer-to-peer networking, which is suitable for file and printer sharing.

On an Ethernet network, each computer's network card is assigned a unique identifying electronic number. Packets of data are broadcast across the entire network. The computer that matches the number collects the packet and processes it; computers that don't match the packet ignore it. If two computers attempt to broadcast packets at the same time, the entire network is basically placed on hold until the conflict passes. This on-hold delay accounts for the relative inefficiency of an Ethernet network without a switch.

Today's Ethernet networks are built much like a modern railroad switching station: Each computer sends data packets to a central switch, which routes the data to the proper receiving node. Because each node is separately connected to the switch, each computer can now send data packets at the same time, and no conflicts arise that might reduce the efficiency of your Ethernet network. The switch simply keeps up with each packet and suspends those it can't send immediately (rather like an airport control tower placing an airplane in a holding pattern). When the receiving node is ready to accept the data, the switch gives the packet "clearance to land," and the packet is allowed through the switch. Figure 12-1 illustrates an Ethernet network with a switch.

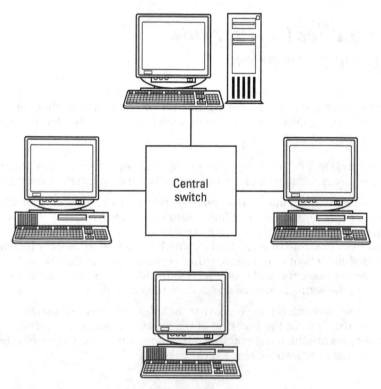

Figure 12-1: Most Ethernet networks use a central switch.

Collecting What You Need for an Ethernet Network

Naturally, you need to make sure that you have the proper hardware before you build your network. Here's a quick checklist of what you need:

✔ **Network interface cards:** You need a network interface card (NIC) for each computer that you plan to connect to your network. I discuss these cards in the next section. (If the PCs on your network use motherboards with integrated NIC hardware, you won't need separate cards, and you have my admiration.)

✔ **Cabling:** Today's Ethernet networks use *twisted-pair cable,* which resembles telephone wire. Twisted-pair cable has a connector (an RJ-45) that looks very much like a telephone jack, as you can see in Figure 12-2. With twisted-pair cabling, each computer is connected to the switch.

You *can* connect two computers using twisted-pair cable without using a switch, but three or more computers on a twisted-pair network require a switch. If you're connecting just two computers for multiplayer games, file transfers, or printer sharing, ask your local computer store for a *twisted-pair crossover cable.*

I'd show you the difference between these two cables, but they look just the same from the outside, and their connectors look the same, too. Just make sure you ask for the right type at your favorite Maze o' Wires computer store.

✔ **Software:** If you're running any flavor of Windows XP or Vista, the software that you need for a peer-to-peer network is built in. (Thanks, Microsoft!)

✔ **Switch:** A switch makes the maintenance and upgrading of your network much easier because all your network computers are connected to a single central device. As I state earlier, a switch also provides the best performance and highest efficiency for an Ethernet network — A Good Thing indeed.

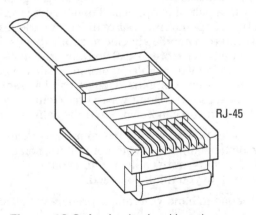

RJ-45

Figure 12-2: A twisted-pair cable and connector, ready to rock.

More stuff about network interface cards

As I mention earlier, if your motherboard has network hardware built-in, you can skip this section with a smile.

The most expensive part of an Ethernet network is the NIC required for each computer. A typical network card uses a PCI slot. Like every other adapter and part you can stick in your PC, some cards cost more than others. The following checklist tells you what important features are offered by a good network card:

✔ **Light emitting diode (LED) status lights:** The status lights on a network adapter card help determine what's gone wrong if you experience problems. For example, a green light usually indicates that the adapter is correctly receiving a broadcast signal from the cable.

✔ **Automatic or software configuration:** No one wants to bother with setting jumpers to configure a network card. The best network cards automatically configure themselves after you connect them to your network.

✔ **Full driver support:** Check the manufacturer's Web site or technical support department to make sure that the card comes with the necessary drivers for Windows XP and Vista.

More stuff about cables and connections

Installing the cables and connecting everything is the most time-consuming chore involved in setting up a traditional cabled Ethernet network. Keep these guidelines in mind when you shop for cables and connectors (and also while you crawl around under desks):

✔ **Making cables is no picnic.** I can't stress this enough, so it's Mark's Maxim time.

Unless you've created your own network cables before, buy them ready-made!™

Building your own cables from scratch is roughly akin to crafting a grand piano from a bowl of jelly — with a pair of chopsticks. I'm not going to discuss how to create cables in this chapter. A number of different varieties are available, each of which is rated to handle specific network speeds. It's much easier to walk into your computer store or call your favorite mail-order outlet and ask for a premade network cable (sometimes called a *patch cable*). Ready-made cables come in several standard lengths and already have the connectors on both ends, too. You don't waste time or money trying to learn how to cut cable, and you can be sure that the cable works.

✔ **Always buy extra cable.** No matter how well you plan your network and how closely you measure the distance between your computers, something's going to come up that demands more cable or more connectors. Buy cables at least a foot longer than you think you need.

✔ **Get help.** Enlist the aid of someone to hand you things, prepare cable, and listen to your epithets.

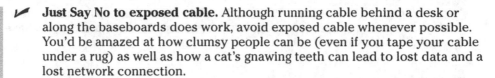

✔ **Just Say No to exposed cable.** Although running cable behind a desk or along the baseboards does work, avoid exposed cable whenever possible. You'd be amazed at how clumsy people can be (even if you tape your cable under a rug) as well as how a cat's gnawing teeth can lead to lost data and a lost network connection.

If your cable has to cross a hallway or corridor and your building uses a suspended ceiling, you might try routing the cable above the ceiling tiles. For a solid ceiling, the molding used by electricians to cover exposed cables works well.

There Are Always Exceptions!

After you become familiar with the virtues and requirements of a twisted-pair network, guess what? You can toss all that to the four winds! What if I told you that I can install a network without running a single piece of Ethernet cable or a pesky network interface card?

It's true: Thanks to the arrival of four alternative network technologies, you're no longer tied down to your grandfather's LAN, and these technologies work with any network software that uses a standard Ethernet connection. All four are compatible with Windows XP and Windows Vista, too.

However (isn't there always a *however* whenever it comes to computers?), these new networks also have their own limitations, so take a look at all four. After you finish this section, you can decide whether to stick with the tried-and-true, twisted-pair cable Ethernet network or whether to strike out on your own with a new breed of home network.

Use your telephone wiring

Alexander Graham Bell would have never conceived that his invention could carry network packets, too. (Of course, he had very little training in computer hardware.) With a home phoneline network (HomePNA for short, at www.homepna.org), your Ethernet hardware uses existing telephone wiring in your home or office to transmit network data packets. To connect a new PC to the network, you install a special network interface card (using the same general procedure as installing an Ethernet card), locate the nearest telephone jack, and (snap!) plug in a cable. The jack can be located anywhere within your home.

Unlike a dialup connection to the Internet through your modem — which rudely claims your telephone line and presents a busy signal to the world — a HomePNA network allows you to use your telephone normally for answering and dialing voice calls.

On the downside, a HomePNA network is slower than a standard cabled Ethernet connection, although it should be fast enough for multiplayer gaming and sharing an Internet connection. Most cabled Ethernet networks run between 100 Mbps and 1000 Mbps, but current HomePNA networking hardware is limited to about 100 Mbps. Also, the hardware is a bit more expensive than a typical Ethernet kit, running approximately $100 for a two-PC HomePNA kit. You should also consider how many telephone jacks are spread throughout your house. Because most homes have only a handful, you're somewhat limited with this option.

Use your AC wiring

Come to think of it, there's another network of wiring within the typical house — but can AC current and computer data coexist? You bet! You simply plug a *powerline adapter plug* (which acts as a network card) into any AC wall socket in your home and connect the other end of the cable to your PC's USB port. You probably have an AC outlet in just about every room of your home, so this system is a little more adaptable than a HomePNA network.

As you might expect, speed and cost are again the issues: A powerline network is somewhat slower than a home phoneline system, and it's much more expensive than a basic, twisted-pair Ethernet kit. I'd recommend this option for those who want only basic file and printer sharing because it's not really fast enough for multiplayer gaming or for sharing a DSL or cable Internet connection. It's also about the only option for homes with basements or walls that inhibit wireless signals.

Use your USB port

If you don't mind cabling things together, the USB 2.0 port — the jack-of-all-trades of the PC world — can act as a network portal for your computers. Like a powerline network, this option doesn't require network cards, and you don't have to remove the case on your computer. One end of each cable connects to the USB port on each PC in your network, and the other end of each cable connects to a black box called a *USB hub.* The hub both connects the cables and — surprise! — acts as a switch in a traditional Ethernet network.

A USB network is about the same price as a standard Ethernet network kit, so it's cheaper than a home phoneline or powerline network. At 10 Mbps, though, it's far slower than a full-fledged, twisted-pair 100 Mbps Ethernet network.

Unfortunately, the downside for a USB network is tied to the length of the cable. There can be a maximum of only 10 meters between computers on a USB network — which, coincidentally, is also the maximum length of a standard USB cable. Anything longer, and your network signal fades between computers. Of course, this isn't a problem if all your computers are in the same room, but I don't think that the Brady Bunch will be using a USB network.

Go wireless

If you eschew any type of wiring, hop on board the wireless Ethernet bandwagon! For this option, each PC in your network needs a wireless network adapter card (or built-in integrated wireless hardware). You also need a stand-alone piece of hard-ware — a *wireless base station* or *wireless access point* — which acts as the switch of your network, transmitting and receiving data from the computers. The two common wireless networking standards to choose from follow:

- ✔ **802.11g:** 802.11g is currently the most common standard, allowing maximum connection speeds around 54 Mbps. 802.11g is backward compatible with any "antique" 802.11b hardware that you might pick up.

- ✔ **802.11n:** This is the latest and greatest wireless standard, offering faster speeds of up to 300 Mbps. (Like a dial-up analog modem, don't hold your breath waiting for this "maximum theoretical" speed. You're more likely going to get about 150 Mbps.) 802.11n is a better choice than 802.11g for network applications that demand faster data transfer, such as copying and moving large files of 250MB or more between your laptop and your home network or for playing today's latest network games.

If you come across anything on the 802.11a standard, don't just run away — SPRINT away! You can't buy "a" hardware any longer.

Both Windows XP and Windows Vista can handle wireless connections with aplomb, maintaining the proper security so that your next-door neighbors don't use your Internet connection for free.

For a comprehensive look at wireless connectivity in your home, check out *Wireless Home Networking For Dummies,* 3rd Edition, by Danny Briere, Walter Bruce, and Pat Hurley (Wiley).

Installing Your Network Interface Card

Stuff You Need to Know

Toolbox:
- ✔ Phillips screwdriver
- ✔ Parts bowl

Materials:
- ✔ Network interface adapter card
- ✔ Screws

Time Needed:
15 minutes

So your motherboard doesn't have built-in Ethernet hardware? Not to worry. You picked up a PCI network interface adapter, so you're ready to add Ethernet support to your PC.

Before you get started, make sure that every computer on your network without built-in Ethernet hardware has at least one PCI slot open for a network adapter card.

1. If your computer chassis is plugged in, unplug it. And did you just finish polishing the silverware? Touch a metal surface before you install your card to discharge any static electricity on your body. Hop to Chapter 3 to read all about how important — and easy — this preventive step is.

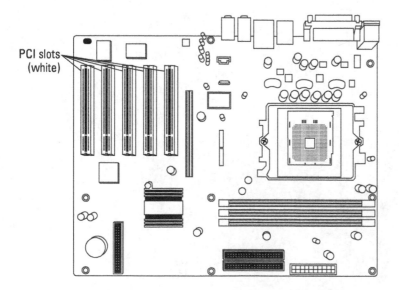

PCI slots (white)

2. Select an open PCI adapter card slot for your Ethernet network card.

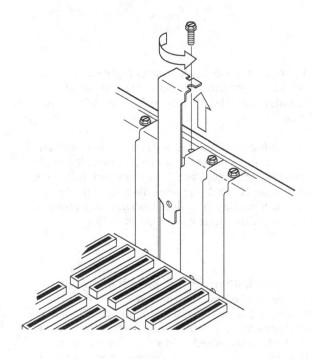

3. Remove the screw and the metal slot cover adjacent to the selected slot. Save both the screw and the slot cover in your spare parts bowl.

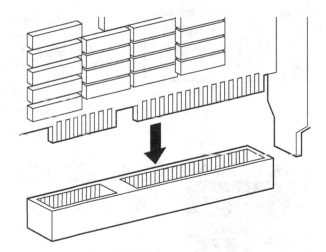

4. Line up the connector on the card with the slot on the motherboard. The card's metal bracket should align with the open space created when you removed the slot cover.

5. Apply even pressure to the top of the card and push it down into the slot. If the card is all the way in, the bracket should rest tightly against the case.

6. Add the screw and tighten down the bracket.

7. Connect the network cable to the corresponding port on the card. Your adapter card manual can help you locate the network cable connector on your card. Push the male connector into the female connector until it clicks. The connectors fit only one way. The connection is the same for both the ports on your switch and the ports on your adapter cards.

8. Install the network adapter card driver software. Check your card's manual for information on how to load the driver software for your particular operating system.

Turning Things On

After you install the network adapter cards in all your computers and connect your cables, all that remains to get things running is to install the driver software on each computer and "flip the networking switch" inside Windows XP or Windows Vista.

The exact steps and the order to follow in the network driver installation process vary according to the version of the software, the operating system on the computer, and the options that you select. Therefore, the following generic steps might not match exactly what you see onscreen. Luckily, the card's installation program should display complete instructions, so you should always follow the onscreen directions when things vary.

1. Run the driver installation software provided by your network adapter card manufacturer and then follow the onscreen instructions. After the drivers are installed, allow the installation program to reboot your computer. Watch the network start-up messages and write down any error messages that appear. These error messages and possible solutions should be listed in the card's manual.

2. After installation is complete, use the Windows wizards.

- **XP:** Use the Windows XP New Connection Wizard to automatically configure the computer as a good network citizen. To run the wizard, choose Start⇨ All Programs⇨Accessories⇨ Communications⇨New Connection Wizard, which displays the dialog box that you see in the figure.

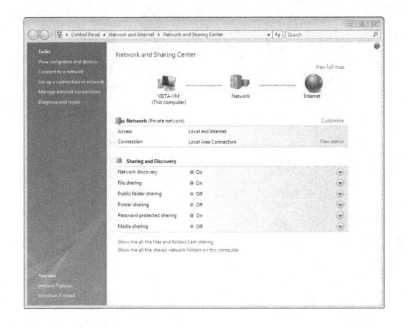

✔ **Vista:** Under Windows Vista, choose Start⇨ Network⇨Network and Sharing Center, which displays the dialog box that you see in the figure. Make sure that Network Discovery and File Sharing are turned on; then click Connect to a Network (Tasks section, left side).

3. Follow the wizard's prompts (which appear as a series of honest-to-goodness, understandable English questions), and Windows will configure itself for you. (If you feel the urge to hug Bill Gates afterwards, that's normal.)

Chapter 13

Input and Output: Scanners, Cameras, and Printers

Task performed in this chapter

✔ Installing a scanner or printer

Are you lagging somewhat behind Ansel Adams as a professional photographer? (I know I am.) Thanks to today's scanners and video capture devices, though, anyone can convert a kid's drawing, a photo of a ball team, or a small business logo into a digital image. You can even use a digital camera to snap your own original digital images or use a Webcam to record digital video. And don't forget that you can print your digital images with an inkjet or a laser printer. Go ahead — preserve family history by scanning treasured photos, or support your local charity with flyers you print at home. You can turn your PC into a print shop!

Although these peripherals aren't requirements for assembling a PC, they *are* requirements for joining the world of digital photography and digital video as well as just plain helpful tools in today's busy world. Just try creating a hard copy of your resume without a printer! Therefore, consider yourself warned: You'll likely be choosing at least one or two of these toys within a few months after you finished building your computer, so it pays to keep in mind the system requirements: a scanner, camera, or printer. (I'll keep you abreast of the situation, of course.)

The Wide, Wonderful World of Scanners

With the help of a *scanner,* which you use to convert a printed page to a digital image, you can digitize and input graphics from books, magazines, cereal boxes, CD covers, your children's doodlings, and even the daily newspaper. Anything that you can legally copy (and lay flat) is fair game for scanning (and using in your documents, or faxing with your PC's fax modem). I write more about copyrights in the sidebar "The lazy person's guide to copyrights," elsewhere in this chapter.

A color scanner with decent specs costs less than $200, making it an affordable addition to your PC. In this section, I discuss the various types of scanners on the market and what you should look for while shopping. You want to shop for the model that best fits your needs and budget, including its configuration, color bit depth, and resolution. Kinda like shopping for a camera, when you think about it.

Scanners eat hard drive storage for breakfast because today's scanners can produce awesome high-resolution images that can literally take up hundreds of megabytes for *each file* (depending on the type and size of the image). If you're going to be doing a lot of scanning, make sure you invest in a minimum of one 500GB hard drive to hold all those graphics! (Perhaps even 1TB — terabyte — if you're gaming and taking digital photographs at the same time.)

For a comprehensive look at scanners (including basic image editing, maintenance, troubleshooting, and a huge repository of scanning tips and tricks), I invite you to pick up a copy of another of my books, the bestselling *Scanners For Dummies,* 2nd Edition (Wiley).

Most scanners come bundled with various software programs, which should include the image-acquisition software that you need for scanning. You might also receive other software, such as an image-editing program, a desktop publishing application, or an optical character recognition (OCR) program. OCR software can "read" the contents of a printed page that you scan and then enter the text from the page right into your word processor, just as though you had typed the text yourself. Although OCR technology isn't perfect and you might need to correct some errors, you don't have to manually retype the entire contents of a page into your word processor.

Recognizing scanners in the wild

Scanners come in three flavors: flatbeds, sheetfed, and photo. (Some "all-in-one" units mix a scanner with a printer and fax machine, but they're generally more expensive and not as versatile as a dedicated scanner, and your scanning results from an all-in-one unit won't be as good.) For portability and convenience on the go, consider using a photo scanner. For everyday workhorse scanning, I vote for flatbeds, and here's why.

- **Flatbed:** "Yessir, this here's your Cad-ee-lac of scanners. Ain't she a beaut?" In fact, the flatbed scanner looks more like a copy machine than a luxury car. Flatbed models have dropped so dramatically in price that they're the clear choice for most shoppers. The large scanning area of a flatbed enables you to spread out an entire magazine or a book page, and many flatbed scanners also have the ability to scan film slides and negative strips. I recommend a flatbed scanner with at least an 8.5" x 12" scanning area — that's about the average — and don't forget to check for Windows Vista compatibility.

  Flatbed scanners typically offer higher resolutions and better color depth than sheetfed scanners (which I discuss in the following bullet). Even 8 x 10 glossy photographs are no problem. In other words, images scanned on a flatbed scanner (see Figure 13-1) offer greater detail and more true-to-life colors.

  One drawback to using a flatbed scanner is that they inherently take up more deskspace because of their configuration.

Virtually all late-model flatbed scanners use a USB 2.0 connection (although some of the fastest and highest-priced models use a FireWire connection). If your PC has USB connectors, a USB scanner is the easiest route for connecting a scanner. And, coincidentally, I discuss these ports in Chapter 5.

A flatbed scanner is your best choice!™

✔ **Sheetfed:** A typical sheetfed scanner, which looks similar to a fax machine, takes up less space on your desk than a flatbed. See Figure 13-2.

With a sheetfed scanner, you feed in letter- or legal-size sheets of paper, which the scanner draws in automatically. Unfortunately, this process limits sheetfed scanners to source material no larger than a single sheet of paper — not a sheet in a bound book or atlas. Unlike with a flatbed scanner, you have to tear a page out of a book or magazine (or photocopy the page first) to scan it. Also, if your source image is smaller than a standard sheet of paper, you might need to tape the image to a sheet of paper for the sheet feeder to pull the image in. (You can also use a clear plastic sleeve to hold smaller items for scanning, but a sheetfed is still not the best way to work with older, brittle photographs and documents.)

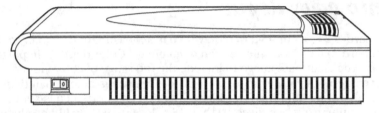

Figure 13-1: All hail the flatbed, the king of scanners.

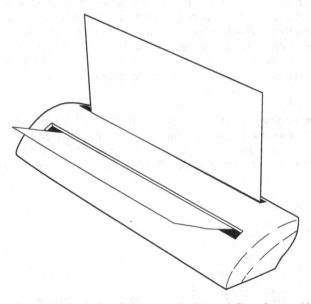

Figure 13-2: A sheetfed scanner looks much like a fax machine.

✔ **Photo:** Photo scanners are a relatively new breed of image scanner. They're available as external USB peripherals that you can carry with your laptop. These scanners scan individual pictures (or even small printed items, such as business cards or a driver's license). Most people use photo scanners to digitize prints that they've taken with a regular film camera. Because a photo scanner can't accept any original wider than a photograph, however, the size of the material that you can scan with one of these devices is limited. (Photo scanners should not be confused with dedicated _negative/slide scanners_, which produce incredibly high-resolution scans of film negatives and slides, but can't be used to scan regular film prints.)

On the other hand, photo scanners are automatic and fun to use. Just feed in the picture, and the scanner slowly spits the picture back out as it reads the image. Photo scanners generally offer the same scan quality as a sheetfed scanner, and they run on any PC with a USB connection.

Unless you're sure that your scanning needs will be limited to film prints, I recommend going with a flatbed scanner, which is far more versatile.

Diving into color depth

Most scanners feature 24-, 36- or 48-bit color, which is a measure of how many colors a scanner can record in the electronic version of an image. Color depth is important because you want the electronic image to include the full range of colors found in the original. For example, if you're creating a Web site featuring famous paintings, you would probably rather offer images with 16.7 million colors (which is about the maximum that the human eye can discern) than 16 colors (which would produce masterpieces that resemble paint-by-number pictures).

Any scanner on the market these days will be capable of a minimum of 24-bit color. If a scanner is advertised as _true color,_ it's probably a 24-bit model. A 30-bit scanner can record images in as many as 11 billion colors, and a 36-bit scanner can deliver more than 68.7 billion colors. Generally, the higher the bit depth, the better, and the larger the size of the file you create. Hence, the more RAM and the larger hard drive you install, the better. I would strongly recommend a 48-bit minimum color depth for your new toy.

This same 24-bit color figure comes up again when computer folks discuss their video adapters. In the world of video adapters, 24-bit color is equivalent to the 16.7 million colors that a modern video adapter card can display on a super video graphics array (SVGA) monitor. (You can find more about video adapter cards and monitors in Chapter 6.)

Resolving the right resolution

Many people tend to base their purchase of a scanner solely on the advertised reso-lution (usually in *dpi,* short for dots per inch). The higher the resolution, the better the quality of your scanned image. Most scanners available to normal human beings like you and me have these standard raw (or *optical*) resolutions:

- ✔ **600 x 600:** Appropriate for the kids and their school projects
- ✔ **1200 x 1200:** Good for scanning snapshots and photographs from books or magazines; images for Web sites
- ✔ **2400 x 2400:** The standard resolution for a good-quality scanner
- ✔ **4800 x 4800 (or better):** Suitable for graphics artists who need high-resolution detail at a higher price

It's true that the higher the raw resolution, the better the scanner. However, some manufacturers also advertise the interpolated resolution for a particular model. What's the difference between raw and interpolated resolution? The answer is in the software:

- ✔ **Raw:** The *raw resolution* value is the actual optical resolution at which the scanner reads an image. (Note that this has nothing to do with the RAW image format used in many cameras and image editors.)
- ✔ **Interpolated:** The *interpolated resolution* (the value of which is always higher) is calculated by the software provided with the scanner.

  In fact, the interpolated value adds extra dots to the scanned image without reading them from the original material.

Technoids would tell you that the interpolation step uses an *algorithm* (a mathemati-cal formula) to improve the quality of the image. In layman's terms, that's the equiva-lent of the imaging software inserting new dots by using an intelligent guess — but it's still a guess. (Call me old-fashioned.)

When you're shopping for a scanner, judge it by its optical resolution and forget about the interpolated value. If you don't see the raw or optical resolution in a scan-ner's advertisement, check with the manufacturer to get that crucial bit of informa-tion first . . . before you buy.

See the sections at the end of this chapter for the lowdown on installing a scanner.

Digital Camera Details

If you need to import a large number of original digital images and you want to avoid the drudgery of scanning them, look no further than the digital camera. Prices for digital cameras are less than $100 on some base models although higher-priced models with more features still hover around $500 to $1,000 (or more). Popular brands include Casio, Hewlett-Packard, Canon, Nikon, Minolta, Kodak, and Olympus.

In effect, a digital camera stores pictures you take and "develops" them. The images are stored in *flash RAM,* which is a form of memory with the neat ability to store information after you turn off the camera. More expensive digital cameras have more flash RAM onboard, so they can store more pictures. Not every digital camera uses flash RAM. Some use removable cartridges (memory cards or sticks), others have tiny hard drives, and some models of digital cameras even use mini-CD or DVD discs.

Loading the pictures from a digital camera into your PC couldn't be easier: You simply connect an appropriate cable between the camera and your PC's USB (or FireWire) port, run the camera's software, and the pictures download right from the camera into your computer. (I explain how to add these ports to your computer in Chapter 5.) The cable is usually furnished with the camera.

Most digital cameras look similar to their film-based cousins (including accessories such as a flash and that useless wrist strap). Point-and-shoot digital cameras are typically just as easy to use as the simple point-and-shoot 35mm film cameras available in any drugstore. Here's a list of features that can help you spot a better digital camera while you're shopping:

- **Higher resolution:** Just like a scanner, a digital camera has a resolution rating. In fact, many digital cameras can take pictures at more than one resolution. It's important to remember that the higher the resolution for an image, the more space the image takes in RAM. Therefore, cameras with multiple resolutions give you a choice. (You can choose between a smaller number of higher-resolution pictures or a larger number of lower-resolution pictures.)

Unless you spend a fair chunk of change on a digital camera (read that as $500 or more), you're not going to get anywhere near the fine detail of a 35mm film camera (even the cheaper point-and-shoot models). If you need to save money but you still want high-resolution images, you might decide to stick with the tried-and-true method of scanning film prints. (If you plan on scanning lots of photographs, check out the photo scanner information in the section "Recognizing scanners in the wild," earlier in this chapter.)

- **Compression:** Digital cameras can compress your images so that they take less space in memory. These images are similar to the highly compressed JPEG-format images common on the Web. Although you lose some detail when you use compression, it's usually not noticeable. These cameras can pack many more images into their memory, so your "roll" of digital film can carry twice (or even three times) the number of pictures. A camera with variable compression might enable you to turn off compression, too. (If a digital camera saves images in the TIFF or RAW formats, you'll get better quality, but you'll get fewer images on a memory card because images in these formats are far larger than the same images in JPEG format.)

- **Zoom:** The more expensive digital cameras have the same zoom capabilities found on standard film cameras. Zoom enables you to magnify your subject for more detail. The higher the optical zoom offered by a camera, the more expensive it usually is. (Just like the optical resolution on a scanner is more important than the interpolated resolution, the optical zoom level on a digital camera is far more important than the interpolated digital zoom.)

- **Special effects:** Most cameras now offer onboard special effects, just like the familiar special effects on a typical digital camcorder. Typical effects include automatic color palettes (which give your images a special look, such as sepia tone or pastel) and negative imaging (in which the image looks like a photograph negative).

Many digital cameras on the market today can do double-duty as a *Web cam*, which captures digital video for Internet video conferencing and display on Web sites. Remember that your camera must remain connected to your PC through a USB cable in order to use the Web cam feature.

One Word: Printers, Printers, Printers!

If you ask computer owners what one peripheral gives them the most value and fun for their money, most would probably say a printer. The printed page is still useful in today's world (at least for now), and the latest inkjet and laser printers can produce everything from T-shirts to transparencies, from greeting cards to stickers, CD and DVD labels, glossy photos, banners, and paper airplanes. Calendars, business cards, coloring books . . . you can see just how useful a printer can be, especially if you have kids.

The lazy person's guide to copyrights

Just because you can capture a video clip from a DVD or scan an image from a magazine doesn't mean that you can use it. Be careful when you're choosing material for your documents or your Web site. Although I'm not a lawyer, I can provide you with a few pointers that might steer you clear of original copyrighted material. Keep these guidelines in mind:

✔ **Beware the hidden copyright.** Under current law, copyright is granted immediately upon creation of an original work, and copyrighted text or images can be protected by copyright regardless of whether a copyright notice appears with the material.

✔ **Make sure permission is granted.** You must obtain permission to copy any original copyrighted work, even if the author has previously granted you permission for other work. For example, just because you obtain permission to use one of a series of pictures on your Web page does *not* mean that you can use the entire series of images: You must obtain permission for each individual image.

✔ **The source is important.** Most people think that images they receive from an Internet newsgroup or copy from a Web

site can be copied, but it doesn't matter where you obtained the material. If it's copyrighted, sticking the text or image on a newsgroup does not make it *public domain* (intellectual property that's not protected by copyright because it "belongs to the community at large"). You still need permission from the author to use the copyrighted material.

✔ **Alterations mean zip.** Another common misconception is that, "If I draw a mustache on this picture of Mr. Spock, it becomes my original work." Altering the original material does not reset or clear the copyright, and you still need permission.

✔ **A change in media means nothing.** If you scan a copyrighted image from an original on paper, the electronic image or document doesn't suddenly become your original work. (If it did, I would have claimed the works of Shakespeare, Edgar Allan Poe, and Mark Twain a long time ago.) You guessed it — the copyright still remains valid, and you need permission from the author to use the material.

✔ **Consult your lawyer.** Above all, if you're uncertain whether you can legally copy something, *ask your lawyer!*

In this section, I discuss what's available in a printer these days for less than $200 and how you can choose the right model for your needs.

Will that be laser or inkjet?

You have two breeds of computer printer to choose from these days:

✔ **Laser:** A *laser printer* uses heat to bond a fine powder (toner) to the paper to form characters and images. Although laser printers were once very expensive, the technology has dropped in price. Many black-and-white low-end models are now available for around $100; color laser printers still hover around $300.

✔ **Inkjet:** An *inkjet printer* shoots ink onto the paper. Inkjet printers (also known as *bubble jet printers*) are the most popular personal printers around these days. Inkjets can produce images ranging from standard black text to quality photographs. In fact, inkjet technology is used in high-resolution photo printers and in *multifunction printers* (which combine a fax, copier, and printer in one unit).

When you're shopping for either an inkjet or a laser printer, you should look for a number of features. Your new printer should be able to print legal- and letter-size paper, envelopes, and labels. The bigger the paper capacity, the better. The printer that you select for your system should also be able to handle at least 150 sheets of paper. And any printer that you consider should also come with additional software, such as a printing kit for kids (with software and blank paper) or a business printing kit, as well as the driver software you need for your particular operating system. (A *driver* is a software program that allows a specific hardware component — internal or external — to work with Windows.)

Other features are specific to the type of printer, so it's time to examine the advantages of both inkjet and laser printers.

Advantages of inkjet printers

Inkjet printers offer these advantages:

✔ **Less expensive:** Inkjet printers range from $45 and more, and the least expensive laser printers typically start at about $100. I should note, however, that laser printers produce a better looking black-and-white page for less money than a typical inkjet, and they can handle heavier printing loads. If you're looking for a heavy-duty monochrome printer with good quality for an office, a laser printer ends up costing much less in the long run when it comes to supplies.

✔ **Cheaper ink:** Ink cartridges for an inkjet printer are somewhat less expensive than a toner cartridge for a color laser printer. You can also refill your used black ink cartridges to save even more.

✔ **Cost-effective color printing:** Although laser printers also offer color, you can expect to pay at least $200 up to a whopping $1,000 for a color laser printer (depending on the quality and speed of the output).

✔ **Higher resolution:** A printer's resolution is measured in dots per inch (dpi). Most laser printers can produce 600 x 600 or 1200 x 1200 dpi resolution, but today's inkjet models under $200 can do much better, at 4800 x 1200 dpi. These printers are better choices for high-resolution graphics.

In general, inkjet printers are better suited to the home or to an office requiring quick color printing.

Advantages of laser printers

Thinking about a laser printer? Laser printers offer these advantages:

✔ **Faster printing:** Laser printers can hit anywhere from 12 to 40 pages per minute, which is faster than an inkjet's average of 8 to 20 pages per minute.

✔ **No smearing:** Because laser printers bond the toner to the paper, your documents are reasonably safe from water. The ink used to print pages on an inkjet printer usually smears if it gets wet.

✔ **True black:** Even a dual-cartridge inkjet printer can't deliver the true black of a laser printer, especially in graphics with large areas of black.

✔ **More pages per cartridge:** Black toner cartridges are more expensive than black inkjet cartridges, but they last much longer: You'll generally get about double (sometimes even triple) the number of pages from a black laser toner cartridge. Toner cartridges can also be refilled, thus saving you quite a bit of money over a new cartridge.

Laser printers are a better choice for offices of every size and any situation where the best-quality black print is required.

Installing a Scanner or Printer with a USB Connection

Stuff You Need to Know

Toolbox:
- Your bare hands

Materials:
- Cable
- Device installation CD

Time Needed:
5 minutes

If you're using a scanner, video capture device (such as a Web cam), or printer with a USB connection under Windows XP or Windows Vista, follow these steps:

1. If necessary, connect the USB cable to the device. Some USB peripherals have their own cables permanently attached, and others accept standard USB cables.

2. Plug in the peripheral's power supply and turn it on.

3. After you boot Windows normally, plug the USB connector on the cable into a USB port on your computer.

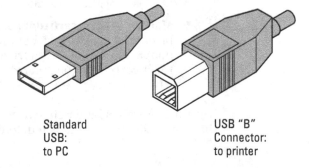

Standard
USB:
to PC

USB "B"
Connector:
to printer

Check whether you need to buy a USB cable for your new device before you leave the store!

4. Windows should recognize that you added a USB device. (If not, check again to make sure that your new device has been turned on. If the device is indeed receiving power and it's on — and Windows still doesn't recognize that it's been plugged in — check the connections from your PC's motherboard to your PC's USB ports. You may need to reverse the connector to the USB pins on the motherboard.)

5. When prompted, load the manufacturer's CD-ROM that came with your device so that Windows can install the correct drivers. If you're adding a USB printer to your system, a new icon for your new printer should now appear in your Printers folder, as you can see in the figure here.

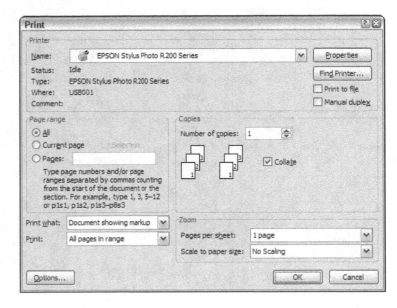

Chapter 14

Building a Gaming PC

It's common knowledge among PC techno-wizards that the two types of PC owners are gamers, and those who don't know they're gamers. Yet. And for this reason, gamers deserve their own chapter in this book because the latest 3-D games demand the *absolute* best performance that your PC can deliver if they're going to run smoothly (and shock your eyeballs with the best graphics). After all, hard-core gamers tend to take the same pride in their super-computers as sports car owners take in their automobiles — hence the customizing, or *modding*, that PC gamers undertake to create a truly unique look for their favorite computer. Hop on for the ride of your life in this chapter as I turn up the heat on your video card (literally) and add all the bells and whistles you need to supercharge your machine into a gamer's dream.

Exotic Video Card Stuff Explained

Of all the components in a gaming PC, the most important by far is the video card — or *cards* — that you install. (Yes, I did just say *cards* because you can boost performance to an unbelievable degree by linking more than one video card. More on this later in this section.) Although a fast CPU never hurts, the lion's share of the work performed by a gaming PC is putting that elaborate eye candy on your monitor; therefore, your video hardware takes center stage.

In this section, I cover what every gamer should know about a video card. And I would be remiss if I didn't mention upfront that you might also need a secondary 12 volt, 4-pin power connector to connect the power supply and motherboard to draw enough power for additional lights, fans, and some high-end video cards. You can read about this in Chapter 2.

Memory is number one

Today's visually stunning 3-D games need memory, and lots of it. Every subtle pattern — the bricks in a wall, the grass on the ground, the long flowing hair sported by the hero (or villain) is actually a texture. *Textures* are graphic designs that are "wrapped" around a 3-D model to create the intricate, realistic objects you see onscreen.

Textures have to be stored in memory, and that memory is actually part of your video card — not like the system memory installed on your motherboard. The current crop of gaming video cards typically offer either 256 or 512GB of onboard RAM; the more you can afford, the better. Your games will run faster, load quicker, and look better with more graphics memory.

What's a GPU, anyway?

Quite simply, a *GPU* (graphics processing unit) is the video card equivalent of your motherboard's CPU. A video card needs its own processing power to draw all those objects; juggle those textures; and produce realistic effects, such as clouds and rippling water.

Today's cards use either an NVIDIA or AMD (formerly ATI) chipset. These two companies are constantly battling each other, raising the bar with faster GPUs, so I won't go into specific recommendations on what models to look for. Literally, by the time this book is printed, what's cutting-edge has been supplanted by something new. If you're interested in the latest GPU performance figures, drop by Tom's Hardware online (`www.tomshardware.com`) and check out the newest reviews.

The minimum GPU speed (called the *core clock* in technospeak) I recommend for a midrange PC is about 500MHz, with the high-end gaming cards turning in over 750MHz.

Although most video cards have only one GPU onboard, some hard-core gaming cards carry two GPUs, allowing the two processors to share the load. (Naturally, these cards deliver unbelievable results. Think of a game like BioShock, which has literally dozens of video options, with *every* quality setting on maximum.)

Overclocking 101

Gamers take great joy in squeezing the absolute best possible performance from video hardware: tweaking their graphics settings, downloading the latest drivers and software updates, and running benchmarks that indicate just how many frames per second (fps) their systems can deliver. The higher the fps rate, the smoother the animation (and the more realistic everything looks in the game, from a flag waving in the breeze to a huge alien slashing at you with a correspondingly huge axe).

However, many hard-core gamers take an additional step to significantly improve the performance of a video card: overclocking. *Overclocking* allows a video card's GPU to run faster than the normal speed designed by the manufacturer. In simple English, faster operation means better performance, like a car with a well-tuned engine that's been modified for more horsepower.

In most situations I'm no fan of overclocking a CPU, but a graphics GPU is different. The GPU doesn't actually execute program instructions, so your PC is far less likely to lock up over time. Also, most gamers upgrade their video cards every two or three years, so the long-term damage caused by overclocking isn't a problem. (In other words, by the time a GPU fails because of overclocking, it's likely to have been replaced already by an avid gamer looking for better performance!)

Overclocking your video card will most likely void your manufacturer's warranty.

Just a few years ago, overclocking was a process best left to hardware techno-wizards, but today, there are Windows utilities that can automate much of the fine-tuning and testing required for a stable, overclocked card. For example, my NVIDIA GeForce 8400 GS card is overclocked using the RivaTuner utility shown in Figure 14-1. You can download RivaTuner from www.guru3d.com — it works with most of the current crop of NVIDIA video cards.

In the end, whether you overclock your video card or not is your decision. If you're satisfied with your PC's performance within your games, there's no reason to push your hardware beyond normal limits. However, if your card is nearing the end of its career or you're forced to lower the quality of your graphics in a game to keep things moving smoothly, overclocking might allow you to get another six months from your existing video hardware.

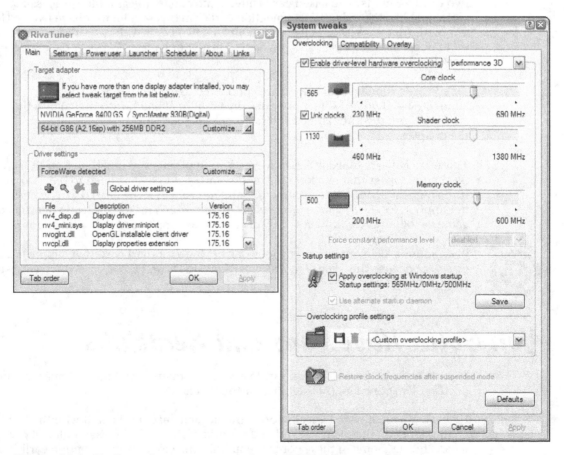

Figure 14-1: RivaTuner allows you to overclock your NVIDIA video card safely.

While testing your overclocking settings, keep these tips in mind:

- ✔ **Use the latest drivers.** Check your card manufacturer's Web site for the latest video drivers for your hardware. A bug-free, up-to-date software installation is easier to overclock reliably.

- ✔ **Start small.** Bump up the speed in small increments. If the card returns errors, you can fine-tune your settings by simply reducing the overclocking rate to the last stable point. (In fact, RivaTuner can help automate the testing process if you wish.)

- ✔ **Watch your heat.** Don't attempt to overclock your card unless your GPU has a heatsink or a built-in fan. Overclocking generates extra heat, and that heat has to be dissipated for stable operation.

Running multiple cards with SLI

If you have to push every single feature to the maximum in your games, you might want to consider adding a second (or even a third!) video card to your PC. NVIDIA calls this feature *SLI* (short for Scalable Link Interface), and it allows you to link two or three cards. The linked cards intelligently share the graphics processing tasks, just like the video cards I mention earlier in this section that have two GPUs onboard. (Heck, NVIDIA even supports linking two cards with two GPUs each, for a mind-boggling four processors devoted to just your gaming. We've come a long way from Pac-Man.)

Video cards running in SLI mode are connected to each other by a special connector — a *bridge* — that provides the additional bandwidth that allows the cards to work together at their full rated speed. You can see a bridge later in the chapter.

There are caveats to using SLI, however. Your motherboard must have an NVIDIA BIOS and chipset that supports SLI mode. And of course, you need to buy two or three high-end NVIDIA video cards to populate your system. (AMD card owners need not apply.) Not every game supports SLI, either, which makes sense; if your idea of a game is Solitaire, Civilization 4, or Sims 2, you just don't need that kind of power.

If SLI sounds like your salvation, consider buying a motherboard that supports SLI directly because this type of motherboard includes two PCI-Express video card slots instead of just one.

You Gotta Have Fans and Heatsinks

Sounds like a no-brainer, doesn't it? Every PC, no matter what the internal makeup, needs at least one fan. (At least one for the PC case.)

However, many novice PC techs forget that a game machine is built with the fastest components on the planet — and in the world of PC hardware, faster almost **always** means hotter! Some of those components (like the video cards I mention earlier) are even overclocked, which produces even more heat.

So, make sure that any gaming PC you're assembling has the proper number of fans. Your case should provide at least two fan cages (square boxes that look much like drive cages, typically with blades either 80mm or 120mm in diameter), as shown in Figures 14-2 and 14-3.

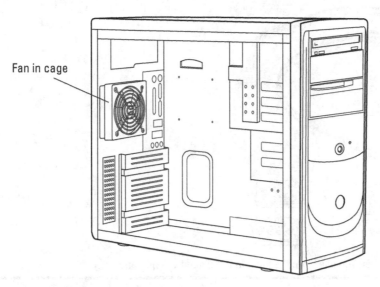

Fan in cage

Figure 14-2: A fan cage inside a case.

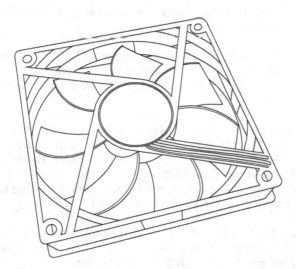

Figure 14-3: These cages allow you to add extra fans to your case for more cooling.

Fans that you add to your case use standard PC power supply connectors, so you'll need at least one free internal power cable (or a Y-splitter — as in Figure 14-4 — that turns one power connector into two).

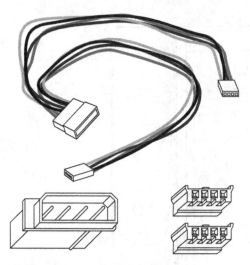

Figure 14-4: When you use more than one fan, you need a Y-splitter.

The best fans use ball bearings. They run faster, moving more air through your case, and are typically more quiet than cheaper "free-spinning" units. Most fan specifications include an airflow rating in cubic feet per minute (cfm). The higher the airflow, the better the cooling (and generally, the higher the price).

So how many fans should you add? If your PC has a single, high-end 3-D video card and a gaming processor, I recommend using two case fans. If you're using two or three video cards in SLI mode (or you're overclocking either your video card or your CPU), I suggest using three case fans.

As I said, today's CPUs generally use a dedicated fan, but that doesn't mean that every CPU fan is created equal! Like their bigger case-bound brothers, there are many price points and airflow ratings for CPU fans, and you should definitely invest in a better CPU fan for today's Phenom and Core 2 Extreme processors. (And as I mention earlier, overclocking also puts a strain on your CPU, so if you do decide to overclock your processor, you need the most airflow you can get.)

CPU fans are generally powered either from a set of pins on the motherboard or by a power connection from your PC's power supply. Make sure you know which type of power connector you'll need before you order that $50 CPU cooler.

Finally, the fastest CPUs also deserve a *heatsink* — a finned hunk of aluminum or copper that you can add under your fan (or, in some cases, in place of a fan). I generally recommend buying a combo unit (like the one shown in Figure 14-5) that integrates both a heatsink and a fan, offering the best possible cooling under heavy load. The heatsink/fan combo is separated from the CPU itself by a special thermal compound that helps transfer the heat evenly.

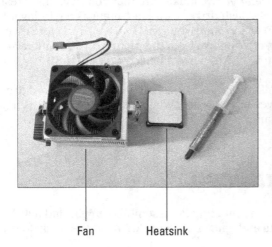 

Fan   Heatsink

Figure 14-5: A CPU heatsink/fan combination.

It's a RAID!

Gamers need more than just a super-fast video card, gobs of memory, and a performance CPU. What about all that data that has to be written to and from the hard drive while you're blasting away at those enemies? Enter another weapon in the ongoing war of high-performance gaming: the RAID array.

RAID stands for Redundant Array of Independent Disks, and most motherboards on the market today support RAID functionality. Like an SLI installation, a *RAID array* is a series of hard drives that work together to provide either faster read/write performance or a "mirror" backup that produces two copies of the same data. (As you might imagine, gamers are far more interested in the former. The only things they back up are their save game files. Go figure.)

The performance variety of the RAID standard is called RAID Level 0, and it's the most common implementation within the PC gaming community. RAID is supported within both Windows XP and Vista.

To create a RAID array, you need at least two hard drives; most PC owners choose two or more of the same model. Because data transfer speed is the goal here, you should consider high-performance 10,000 rpm SATA drives (like the Western Digital Raptor series, which I use on my machine). Your motherboard's BIOS settings must support RAID operation.

After you install the drives, you must create the array from the motherboard's BIOS setup screen. Because every BIOS chip manufacturer uses a different method, check your motherboard's manual for the procedure.

I recommend installing a fresh copy of Windows Vista on a new RAID array, allowing the operating system to automatically recognize the RAID installation and configure itself accordingly. Vista calls this a *clean install.* Make sure that you have the latest RAID driver handy on a floppy or USB Flash drive before beginning the Windows installation because Windows Setup will prompt you for the driver. You can download the RAID driver for your flavor of Windows from the motherboard manufacturer's Web site. (For more detail on installing Vista, check out Chapter 8.)

After Windows is installed, your RAID array works just like a single large hard drive. Even though there are multiple drives in your case, Windows displays them as a single logical unit, with one drive name.

Adding Lights and Gauges

Okay, I'm getting into an area that many budding PC assemblers might find a little amusing. Why should you add lights and gauges to your PC? What the heck do they add to your gaming experience?

The answer, honestly, is zero. Zip. Nada, nuttin', bupkis, goose egg. A cool, blue neon glow really doesn't add anything to the game. However, what it does add to is your reputation the next time you show off your PC, just like custom wheels on a '69 Dodge Charger. Visual extras add that cool touch to your PC — and, in some cases, actually add some functionality as well.

I call these PC mods "eye candy" because they're visible from the outside of the case. Eye candy includes

- **Lighted fans:** Because a gaming PC will likely need a second (or third) fan, why not invest in a fan unit that glows? I have to admit, these look pretty neat in motion. Other than the illumination, a lighted fan is just like any other PC fan, drawing perhaps just a little bit more power for the lighting effect.

  In case you're wondering, there are indeed lighted CPU fans. And naturally, you need a case with a transparent panel to see such visual splendor (see Figure 14-6).

- **Rope lights:** Another illuminated mod is the flexible rope light, which can be fitted to the interior of your case. (Again, a transparent panel is a must to receive the full benefit.) These lights come in a rainbow of colors, and some can be set to blink or animate. Like your other internal components, a rope light needs a power connection to your PC's power supply.

- **Cold cathode and UV lights:** These lights aren't flexible like a rope light, but they offer some neat effects. (Think neon. Really, really bright neon.) If your room is decorated with black light posters, one of these lights mounted in your case could lead you to a higher plane of existence. Anyway, these lights typically run the length of your case, and are affixed either with screws or double-sided tape.

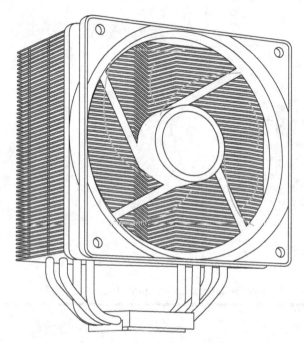

Figure 14-6: It's all about the glow. Lighted fans make a statement in a dark gaming cave.

✔ **Lighted feet:** No, I'm not kidding. You can buy illuminated plastic feet to replace those oh-so-mundane rubber feet on the bottom of your case. Still non-skid, but now lighted eye candy! Think of those cars you've seen on the road at night with a neon glow underneath — it's the same idea.

✔ **Temperature gauges:** Here's eye candy that actually provides you some information. These gauges provide real-time information about the temperature inside your case. (Some units can also be wired to report the temperature of your CPU or GPU.) Typically, a temperature gauge is mounted in a 3½-inch frame that allows it to be installed in a standard PC device bay (much like your optical drive). Figure 14-7 illustrates a typical, aftermarket temperature gauge.

Today's motherboards can report both the temperature of your CPU and the RPM speed of your CPU and case fans through software, so you don't really need a fancy external gauge. If you're running Vista Premium or Ultimate, for example, consider installing a Sidebar gadget that displays these figures.

✔ **Fan controls:** Need complete control over the amount of air moving through your supercomputer's case? Like a temperature gauge, fan control units are mounted in a drive bay: A twist of a knob can increase your airflow as necessary. (Personally, I think this is overkill because most of today's motherboards can control your fan speed automatically. But then again, eye candy is all about appearance and gadgetry.)

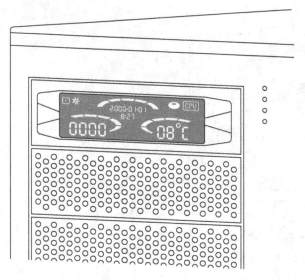

Figure 14-7: Gamers care very much about the internal temperature of their PCs.

Customizing Your Case

No chapter on modding a gaming PC would be complete without a mention of custom cases. Today's case styles range from the old-fashioned, sedate beige-and-cream variety — yes, they still do exist — to *complete* transparency. With a little searching on the Internet, you can locate cases sporting alien or demon faces, tribal graphics, hotrod flames, and even cases with physical characteristics modeled after the characters in today's hottest games. (Would a World of Warcraft case with Night Elf "ears" help my gaming experience? Probably not, but it might interest my cat.)

With so many designs, you can start your PC assembly with an attention-getting (and expensive) case that requires no extra modifications. But what if you're satisfied with your existing PC, and you just want to add a little pizzazz to your desktop? Luckily, it's easy to make your case stand out.

Probably the easiest mod you can perform on your case is a custom paint job, using stencils or even freehand airbrush work. Because most cases are metal, you can use a good-quality acrylic paint designed to cover metal surfaces. However, I do not recommend that anyone attempt to paint a case with components inside! A little miss-spray through the case's vents, and you'll end up with a lime-green hard drive, or (even worse) a damaged motherboard. Instead, paint your case while it's empty, either before you start assembly or after you disassemble your existing PC. (It's worth the time you take.)

I heartily discourage painting the inside of your case cover. Flaking paint is never A Good Thing when it comes to your motherboard and internal PC components. Also, heat from the inner components can melt the paint and cause it to further damage internal parts.

If you're considering adding decoration to the outside of your case, make very sure that your mods don't block any of the vents or drive bays. As I stress over and over in this chapter, airflow is extremely important, and you might need access to those empty drive bays in the future.

Color choices? Graphics? Heck, I've seen everything from automobile bumper stickers and baseball cards to neon paint and pinstripes. I've seen cases with actual cutouts (which might help air flow, but also probably result in a heavy accumulation of dust over time). If you're talented with metalcraft, you'll find that a standard PC case cover is a blank slate, ready for you to mold and shape as you like. Of course, the inside chassis must remain pristine — trying to force an internal optical drive into a mangled drive bay is a nightmare.

If you're shopping for a case and you're considering adding some of the internal "eye candy" I mention in the chapter, make sure you choose a case with at least one transparent panel.

The decorations you choose for your custom case are completely up to you although I wouldn't recommend a case decorated with refrigerator magnets. Too strong of a magnetic field is never a good thing inside a PC.

Will You Move the Joystick, or Will It Move You?

The Logitech Force 3D Pro joystick (www.logitech.com) is a power user's play toy. What sets this piece of USB 2.0 hardware apart from the pack is its ability to provide actual tactile feedback. In other words, when something happens in the game, you can feel an authentic sense, force, or impact through the joystick. For example:

- ✔ If you're flying a light plane with a flight simulator, you feel the stick resist your movements when you begin a turn and then relax gradually as the turn continues.

- ✔ If you're driving a tank, you feel the impact of each hit on your tank's armor as well as the recoil of each shot you fire.

- ✔ If you're playing a first-person shoot-'em-up, you feel your way around corners in the dark and recognize different wall textures.

- ✔ If you're bowling, you can tell whether your ball hit the lane too early or just right.

As a dyed-in-the-wool computer game fanatic, I can tell you that this kind of feedback adds that extra touch of realism. Much like how a sound card with 3-D support enhances the audio experience of a game, the Force 3D Pro enhances physical sensations of your game-playing experience. After all, a game becomes much more realistic when your World War II fighter plane gets harder to control when you're dodging bullets with an enemy on your tail. The Force 3D Pro reflects every hit on your plane as well as the force required to pull out of a power dive.

Like most of the more expensive joysticks on the market, you can program each button to perform a keyboard command. And the stick itself is specially designed for hours of hazardous flying through the enemy-filled skies of Planet SpeedBump without cramping your hand.

Before you tense your muscles to leap out of your chair and run to your local computer store for a Force 3D Pro, don't overlook the downside:

✔ **Pricey:** Compared with a standard joystick that costs $15 or $20, the Force 3D Pro is significantly pricier at about $70.

✔ **Game-dependent:** The game that you're playing must explicitly support the Force 3D Pro to enable the tactile-feedback feature. So, for older games, the Force 3D Pro becomes just another joystick (albeit a very good one).

Configuring SLI for Multiple Video Cards

Stuff You Need to Know

Toolbox:

✔ Screwdriver
✔ Parts bowl

Materials:

✔ SLI-capable mother-
  board
✔ Two PCI-Express video
  cards
✔ Bridge-connecting cable
✔ NVIDIA driver software

Time Needed:
15 minutes

If you decided to invest in more than one SLI-capable NVIDIA video cards, I salute you! You're a fellow hard-core gamer who demands the best graphics performance. To implement SLI, you need a motherboard with an NVIDIA chipset that offers this feature, as well as two NVIDIA video cards with SLI support. The SLI bridge connecting cable should be included with one (or both) of your video cards, as well as the Windows driver disc.

In this section, I assume that you already installed both cards into the PCI-Express slots on your motherboard, as I demonstrate in Chapter 6. Now the cards need to be connected and then the software installed.

1. If your computer chassis is plugged in, unplug it. Now that you've finished petting the family cat, touch a metal surface before you handle any components.

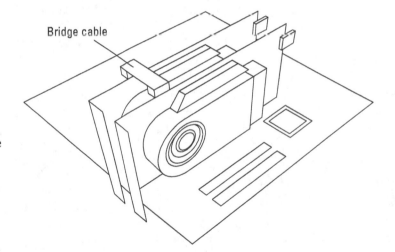

Bridge cable

2. Install the bridge cable between the two cards using the SLI con-nectors. The connectors are marked on each card, and are also identified in the manual for each card. Make sure you plug the cable in firmly — it only goes on one way, so there's no chance of installing it upside-down.

3. Plug your PC's power cord back in and make sure the monitor is connected.

4. Turn on your PC and allow Windows to load.

5. Windows displays a New Hardware notification, and then the SLI capable system notification message shown in the figure here. Click the notification to continue.

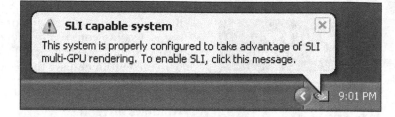

6. The NVIDIA Set SLI Configuration screen appears. Select the Enable SLI Technology (Recommended) option and then click Apply.

Keep your NVIDIA video card drivers updated to make sure SLI mode runs as fast as possible!

Part V
The Part of Tens

The 5th Wave   By Rich Tennant

"Hold your horses. It takes more than cadaver parts and sutures to build a computer."

In this part . . .

1 provide you with worthwhile advice and tips (and even the occasional warning) concerning a number of topics, ranging from the assembly process to maintaining your PC. Each chapter includes ten tips. Consider "The Part of Tens" as a quick dose of experience (without the hard knocks).

Chapter 15

Ten Tools and Tasks for a Power User's PC

. . . .

To me, a *power user* is a person who is perfectly at home at the computer keyboard. For example, a power user knows the keyboard shortcuts that can speed up a favorite Windows program. Experienced power users also know tips and tricks that can help make their computers run faster (such as defragmenting a hard drive), and they know how to diagnose problems with their computers. Power users are also more efficient, and this ability makes them more productive at work and at home. (Chapter 2 can help a power user build just the right PC.)

You can become a power user even if your computer isn't the fastest or most powerful PC on your block. Most people would say that it certainly helps to start with the best computer possible, and that's true in general: Speed and capacity never hurt. However, I've sat down in front of many a top-of-the-line retail computer system and noticed many features that could be added or improved.

In this chapter, I name ten computer hardware and software extras that help make your life easier behind the keyboard. They're not necessarily expensive; and each adds convenience, comfort, or efficiency that you might find worth the money.

If you're comfortable, confident, and productive with your computer — no matter *how fast it is* **— you are a power user!**™

Forget Your Mouse

The mouse has been the most popular computer pointing device for years now, but many power users favor other pointing devices. Power users dislike standard mice because they take up too much space on the desktop, they trail their cord "tails" behind them, and they get filthy after a few months of constant use. Mice are also terribly inefficient creatures because they require movements of your forearm, which often makes it necessary to pick up your mouse and relocate it to another area of your desk just to move the cursor all the way across the screen (and can contribute to carpal tunnel stress).

I heartily recommend that you select another pointing device instead of a mouse. These devices can include a touchpad, trackball, drawing tablet, or fingertip mouse. My favorite is the trackball, which offers precise control with movements of your thumb or fingers rather than your forearm. A trackball doesn't move across the surface of your desk, so it needs cleaning far less often, and it requires only a fraction of the desktop real estate necessary for a standard corded mouse. (For more information on these pointing devices, see Chapter 5.) Remember to try out your new pointing device at the store. Like a keyboard, a mouse is a personal device, and what feels comfortable to one person feels like a plastic brick to another!

If you're absolutely set on using a mouse, consider using an infrared *wireless mouse*, which at least eliminates that doggone tail. (Whoops! I mean *cord*.) I also recommend that you consider an *optical* mouse or trackball, which doesn't require cleaning like an old-fashioned model that uses a ball.

Guard That Power Supply!

It never fails. The moment that you finish the last chapter of your Great American Novel — you know, the one that you've been working on for the past 20 years — someone on your block decides to juice up a new electric car, and every transformer within three miles goes up in smoke. You get hit with a power failure, and the crowning chapter of your novel is suddenly headed to that home for unfinished classics in the sky.

What can you do? Unfortunately, the answer is a big, fat "nothing." If you saved your work often, you can at least back up to the last revision although the loss of power might have resulted in lost clusters on your computer's hard drive. In the worst-case scenario, you might have been burning a CD or DVD on your computer; if the recording process is interrupted by a power failure, you just created a dandy coaster for your cold drinks.

However, you can prevent such a catastrophe by adding an uninterruptible power supply (UPS) to your computer system. A *UPS* is essentially a giant battery that automatically provides power within a few milliseconds in case of a power blackout or brownout. A typical UPS provides your computer with another priceless 15 minutes or so of operation before it's fully exhausted, which should give you ample time to save your work and shut down your system normally (or finish recording that DVD movie). Believe me, it's a weird (but cool) feeling to see your computer monitor alive and well with every other light and appliance in your home as dead as a doornail. (After you finish saving your work, gather the family around for a computer game or two, but make it fast!)

Note that a UPS is different from a *surge protector,* which is essentially just an extension cord that self-destructs if it gets hit by a massive power surge. You don't get any additional power in case of a blackout with a surge protector.

A UPS is constantly recharged from your wall socket, so it's always ready. Most of these power supplies also filter AC line *noise* (small variations in line voltage caused by some appliances, such as vacuum cleaners and televisions) and provide some measure of protection against lightning strikes.

Back Up, Back Up, Back Up

Even if your computer is connected to a UPS, you can still lose data. Hard drives fail, viruses attack, and human error can result in deleted files. There's only one way to truly secure your computer from loss, so follow this Mark's Maxim to the letter:

Back up your data to tape or removable media — and do it on a regular basis!™

As a consultant, I've seen individuals, small businesses, and even one or two larger companies hammered by the loss of sensitive or irreplaceable data because of hardware failure. The sad part is that the data could have been backed up to a tape cartridge or a DVD-RW in just a few minutes. If you have important data that would take time or money to replace, remember the power user's secret weapon: *Back up your data!*

How often should you back up? It all depends on how often you significantly change your data. At a minimum, I back up my work in progress every week on DVD-RWs, and many companies run automated backups of their entire network every night. If time is tight, back up only your user data (such as documents, graphics, and spreadsheet files). If I'm in a hurry, I'll even create a copy of an important document on my removable USB Flash drive, just in case disaster strikes my desktop's hard drive. However, if you have the time, I recommend that you back up your entire system, including all your operating system files and application programs. This way, you avoid the hassle of reconfiguring Windows and reloading your programs on a new hard drive before you're back to normal.

Back up your data! (Did I stress that enough?)

Diagnostics Software to the Rescue

Most power users have at least one diagnostics program because they understand that hardware and system problems can lead to a slower computer, lockups, or even lost data. Unfortunately, these problems usually aren't obvious, so you need a program capable of both locating potential glitches and eliminating them (or at least identifying them and providing a possible solution or two). Some operating systems come with a simple disk-scanning utility — for example, you can scan a hard drive for errors under both Windows XP and Windows Vista — but these programs don't check for hardware problems and don't offer the range of features provided by commercial diagnostics software.

Probably the oldest and best-known diagnostics package for the PC is Norton SystemWorks Premier Edition, from Symantec (www.symantec.com). This suite of programs has been around since the days when DOS was king, and the utilities have saved my neck more than once! As of this writing, the Premier Edition also includes Norton AntiVirus 2008 (which I mention later in this chapter) and Norton Save & Restore 2.0 (which backs up everything on your hard drive with just a couple of clicks).

Stick Your Keyboard in a Drawer!

If you're going to remain comfortable at your computer, you need to consider ergonomics. Your keyboard should be at the proper height for comfortable typing, your wrists should be supported to avoid carpal tunnel syndrome, and your monitor should be close to your natural eye level to avoid cramping your neck.

One of my first additions to my desktop computer was a *keyboard drawer,* which is a metal case that holds a sliding drawer for your keyboard (as well as a place to store a pencil and paper clips). Your computer sits on top (or to the side) of the metal case, and you simply pull the drawer out and begin typing. The drawer keeps the keyboard at the proper height and saves desktop space that you would otherwise need for your keyboard. When you're finished at the PC, slide the keyboard back into the case. (Some drawers are designed to hold the keyboard and support the monitor instead, while the PC sits on the floor beneath the desk.)

If your computer's tower case sits on the floor (with only your monitor and pointing device on your desk), I recommend using a keyboard drawer that attaches to the bottom of your computer desk. If you're shopping for a computer desk, it's worth it to spend a bit more for a keyboard drawer.

Stop the Spread of Viruses

The latest wave of e-mail viruses might leave you thinking that computer viruses are hovering outside your Internet connection 24/7, just waiting to bite your computer like a rabid silicon dog. It never hurts to be prepared, especially if you receive lots of e-mail or try out lots of demo and shareware software on your PC. Every computer power user worthy of the title runs an antivirus scanning program constantly in the background.

The best-known virus scanning software for the PC is Norton AntiVirus 2008, which includes regular virus data updates downloaded automatically over the Internet. These data files enable the program to recognize all the new viruses that have been identified since the last update. You can learn more about this great program (which should set you back about $40) at www.symantec.com.

Most virus-scanning programs identify viruses present in your computer's random access memory (RAM) and on your hard drive including the files stored on your drive. Some scanners attempt to remove the virus from the program or data file, and other programs simply advise that you delete the infected file to guarantee that the virus is eradicated.

Be sure to update your virus signatures automatically (or, if you're doing manual updates, at least every week). Outdated virus protection is worse than no virus protection at all because you *think* you're covered and are likely to take risks, such as downloading and running software from the Internet!

If you do a lot of Web surfing, you should immediately install a spyware removal program. In my opinion, *spyware* is just one step below a virus: These programs work invisibly while you surf, collecting the addresses of sites you visit or displaying irritating banners. (Some spyware programs even go so far as to change your browser's home page to a sponsor site!) All spyware has one thing in common, though. These programs slow down your PC, so they should be eradicated. I recommend using the free spyware removal application Spybot Search & Destroy (`www.spybot.info`).

Organize Your Software

CDs and DVDs, Zip disks, and even that rare antique floppy . . . where do you put all this stuff? It's easy to throw everything into a shoebox, but can you find a particular disc when you need it?

A power user keeps software organized and within easy reach. For CDs and DVDs, I suggest an audio CD rack that stands on the floor or mounts on the wall. (Another good choice for discs that you've burned is a *CD binder,* which allows you to carry your gaggle of discs easily while protecting them from scratches and dirt.) You should keep floppy disks and Zip disks in a disk case, preferably with dividers that can help keep your games separate from that spreadsheet work you brought home from the office. If you need a little extra security, look for a disk case with a lock. You can also store backup tape cartridges in a special tape case. Although tape cases are a little harder to find, you should be able to buy one at your local office supply store.

Use the Power of Your Voice

Does the idea of controlling your computer with your voice seem like science fiction? How would you like to dictate your next report or memo to your computer — without typing a single character of the text? Thanks to programs such as Dragon NaturallySpeaking 10 from Nuance Communications (`www.nuance.com/naturallyspeaking`), you can dictate text without adding artificial pauses between words. These programs understand your normal speaking voice, and they can handle more than 100 words per minute (which beats touch typing).

 Although this technology has come a long way, you do still have to "train" the computer to recognize your speech patterns, and voice dictation on a computer is still nowhere near 100-percent accurate. And, unfortunately, using voice-recognition software doesn't get you out of proofreading your text. However, if you use a word that your computer doesn't recognize (such as a technical term or a phrase from a foreign language), it takes only a second to add that word to the computer's dictionary. Then, after you save the updated dictionary to the hard drive, your computer recognizes and types the new word in future sessions.

 At a minimum, your PC needs a sound card and a microphone to use a voice-recognition program, or a USB headset and microphone combo. (All are covered in Chapter 10.) Moreover, the more system RAM you have, the better.

Everyone Needs a Good Image Editor

"A picture is worth a thousand words." That adage is the foundation of today's World Wide Web as well as graphical operating systems, such as Windows Vista and Mac OS X. Power users add graphics to their documents, use images as a background for their operating system or their Web pages, build animated GIFs (*graphic interchange format,* one of the popular image formats on the Web), and demand high-resolution digital cameras for taking pictures of everything from the family dog to Stonehenge.

Because images are so important to today's computer power user, it's no accident that graphics editors, such as Paint Shop Pro Photo X2 (from Corel, www.corel.com) and Photoshop Elements (from Adobe, www.adobe.com), are some of the most popular applications available today. With an image editor, you can alter the size and shape of an image, crop it to enhance a particular element, and rotate it as you please. It's easy to add text or paste another image on top of an original. You can even edit the individual dots *(pixels)* in an image or draw on an image with a virtual paintbrush or spray can.

Keep It Clean!

What power user wants to sit at a dirty keyboard? After you've spent so much time and money building your own computer, it makes sense to clean the case, monitor screen, keyboard, optical drive, and pointing device from time to time (as well as your scanner and printer, if you have them). Dust and grime can interfere with the proper operation of your mouse or trackball. And if you don't clean the tray on your optical drive, don't be surprised if your PC encounters errors while burning discs!

Here are a few tips for keeping your hardware squeaky clean:

- **Case:** I recommend using a sponge dampened with mild soap and water to clean the outside of your computer case. Others have told me that they use an antistatic surface cleaner, which you can find at an office supply store.

- **Monitor:** For your monitor, use a lens-cleaning solution and a soft lens-polishing cloth, both of which you'll find at your local computer store, eyeglass shop, or camera store. Avoid using plain old window cleaner like you would avoid a case of pneumonia.

- **Keyboard:** For your keyboard, nothing is better than using a can of compressed air; it's great for cleaning hard-to-reach crevices. I've also used a cotton swab (sometimes soaked with a little alcohol-based cleaning solution) to clean the ridges on my keyboard.

- **Optical drives:** Again, compressed air works wonders to keep the tray within your CD or DVD drive clean and dust-free.

- **Mouse/trackball:** To clean your mouse or trackball, remove the retaining ring around the ball — usually you twist it in the direction indicated on the bottom of the mouse — and clean the contact points and rollers inside the mouse with a cotton swab soaked in alcohol. (As I mention earlier, optical pointing devices don't need this kind of maintenance.)

Chapter 16

Ten Important Assembly Tips

Assembling your own computer is a simple job if you're friends with Mr. Phillips — his screwdriver, that is — but, like just about every other human endeavor, you gain experience each time you build another PC. In this chapter, I present a list of ten tips and tricks that I've learned over the years that can help speed up the entire assembly process, help prevent accidents and mistakes, and generally make the assembly process more enjoyable.

Read the Instructions First! (Rule Number One)

I know, I know. . . . *Nothing* is more boring than reading the instructions for installing a hard drive or a video card; even techno-nerds dislike reading hardware and software documentation. However, every second that you spend reading about and familiarizing yourself with the installation process for a computer component will save you hours of frustration when you're knee-deep in your computer, trying to get that new part to work. It doesn't matter whether you read the instructions 15 minutes before you start installation or three days ahead of time, just *read them completely* first. Trust me on this one: Even the folks at NASA (and the techs in nuclear submarines) read instructions. If you don't have a manual for a component, check the manufacturer's Web site; often, you'll find a documentation archive for discontinued products.

Build the Perfect Workspace

Your kitchen table might be the most convenient place to assemble your computer, but is it truly the best workspace? Your work area must be large and sturdy enough to hold your computer's chassis and parts and your tools — and be secure and quiet (think kids and furry beasts). A well-equipped workspace also has these features:

- ✔ **Access to at least two or three power plugs:** During testing, you have to at least provide power to your computer and the monitor, but it never hurts to have a spare plug available in case you need to add and test an external device, such as a DVD recorder or tape backup unit.

- ✔ **An adjustable lighting source:** If you can't see it, you can't tighten it! I use an adjustable extension lamp. (The gooseneck variety — see Figure 16-1 — can be positioned perfectly.)

✔ **A smooth surface that won't scratch or mar your computer case:** Because the paint on a PC's case — especially a fancy, neon-green mod case — is easily scratched, it pays to cover your workspace with a few sheets of newspaper to keep your case looking new. And unlike a tablecloth, that newspaper won't build up static electricity.

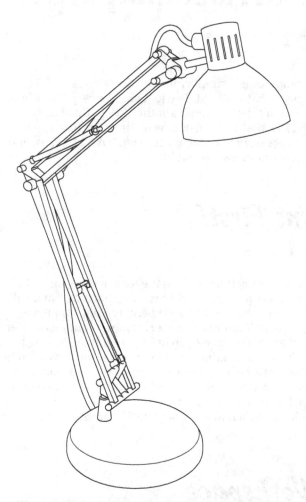

Figure 16-1: Use a gooseneck lamp for flexible lighting while you work.

Keep Track of UTOs (Unidentified Tiny Objects)

Why do some pieces of computer hardware have to be so doggone small? I'm talking about screws, jumpers, terminators, and other assorted tiny objects that you need to keep track of while you're assembling your computer.

Here's how you can make the perfect receptacle for these diminutive troublemakers: Glue a small magnet into the center of an old ashtray or ceramic bowl with a broad base and then keep this "parts basket" handy and near to you while you're assembling your computer. (Or, if you like, fasten it to your worktable.) The magnet will hold small screws, slot covers, and the like — and you won't be constantly digging in your pockets for small parts.

Make Sure That You Have Everything You Need

Before you start installing a new component, make sure you have all the cables, screws, and connectors required for finishing the job. When you open your new part, check that the box contains everything it should; If you end up with spare parts after the installation (screws, cables, or wires), make sure to add them to your parts box!

Similarly, it always pays to identify the requirements for a new part before you add it. For example, if you're going to install a new internal DVD recorder, does your power supply still have an unused power cable and connector of the right size? If not, you need a *Y power cable adapter,* which transforms a single power cable into two cables and connectors. If you're buying a USB printer, do you have a corresponding USB cable with the right gender connectors handy, or will you have to buy one? If you're buying an internal component, does your PC's chassis still have an open bay of the right height?

A little preparation goes a long way toward avoiding simple frustrations (for example, suddenly realizing that you don't have the required batteries for your new multimedia speakers) as well as big headaches (such as discovering that you don't have a spare PCI adapter card slot for your new internal eSATA adapter).

Yell for Help If Necessary

Some of the assembly steps that you encounter when building your own PC might make you nervous (installing a CPU or a memory module), whereas others might require additional configuration (fine-tuning your computer for use with a new DVD recorder or adding drivers for a new wireless network card). Always keep in mind that several sources of assistance are available and that there's no reason to be embarrassed about asking for help.

If you can't find the answers that you're looking for in the documentation that accompanied the new part, try these resources:

✔ **Query the manufacturer.** Most hardware manufacturers offer technical support over the telephone and also provide FAQs (lists of *frequently asked questions*) about their products on their Web sites.

✔ **Ask someone.** A friend, family member, or fellow computer club member with experience in computer hardware can come in very handy. (Don't forget to pick up the check the next time you have lunch together.)

✔ **Find a computer store/tech.** Most computer repair shops are happy to answer a few questions for free. If you find yourself completely unable to install a particular component, it's likely (of course) that you can pay one of the store's techs to install the part for you. (Hey, techno-types need new hard drives, too.)

Use a Magnetic Screwdriver

Carpenters have their hammers, and woodsmen are skilled with an ax, but the computer technician's tool of choice is a trusty magnetized screwdriver. Look for a reversible model that has both standard (straight) and Phillips (X-shaped) tips. With your magnetized screwdriver by your side, you won't panic when you inevitably drop a screw deep within the guts of your new PC. Just poke around in the general area and let magnetism do the rest for you.

Don't worry that the screwdriver will wreak magnetic havoc on your PC's circuits: The magnetic field from a screwdriver isn't powerful enough to damage these components unless you park your screwdriver on top of them for at least a weekend. Therefore, when your screwdriver is not in use, keep it in a drawer or on the wall. Some true techno-wizards keep their screwdrivers in a belt holder. Thankfully, a screwdriver or all-purpose, multifunction-style tool slung on your belt has replaced the pocket protector as the status symbol of the uber-tech.

Start Your Own Parts Box

The last time that you installed a computer component, did you find yourself with an extra unneeded screw, adapter card slot cover, cable, or connector? If so, **don't throw away those extras!** Instead, grab an empty cardboard box and throw all your unneeded computer parts in there (except for circuit boards and larger components, which should be stored separately in static-free plastic bags). *Voilà!* You created your own parts box. The next time you suddenly find yourself one screw short or you need an extra jumper block, check your parts box before you take off to your local Maze o' Wires electronics store. The more that you work with computer hardware, the more this box will grow. You'll soon have a comprehensive treasure chest of small computer parts. (Feel free to subdivide them into plastic bags.)

When you upgrade parts of your computer, you can always keep the older components as backup hardware in case of failure; as a general rule, however, I try to sell older components (or donate them to my local school or church if I can't sell them). Unlike the small parts in your parts box, older components that you've outgrown end up taking up too much room in your closet or garage.

Take Your Time: The Zen of Assembly

You might be excited about building your own PC, but rushing through an assembly step can lead to frustrating mistakes, such as mismatched cables and upside-down components. Follow the step-by-step instructions in this book and the documentation that comes with your hardware — and don't move to the next step until you completely finish every task in the current step.

If you're working on a particularly delicate assembly step (such as adding a CPU or a memory module to your motherboard) and it's not going well, take a deep breath or two. Then verify that you're trying to do the right thing. A friend of mine has a big sign above his workbench that reads "This isn't a race!" (That's good advice for any craftsperson.)

No one is timing you, so move at your own speed.™

Don't Cover Up Too Quickly

I would never use a computer on a day-to-day basis without its case because the components would get far too dirty too quickly, and there would always be a danger of spilling liquids on exposed components or touching a circuit board while the computer is on.

However, because everything changes when you're installing a new internal part in your computer, keep the case off until you're certain that the new component is working properly. Nothing is more irritating than attaching the case on a computer and then finding that you forgot to connect the power cable to your new DVD recorder or hard drive. Before I learned this important rule, I would sometimes remove the case on my PC three or four times until everything finally worked. As long as you keep liquids away from your computer and don't touch any internal components while it's on, you're in no danger. Save time and trouble by leaving the case off until you're sure that your computer is working.

The Cable Rule: Check and Double-Check

I've spoken to many computer technicians and hardware techno-wizards, and every one of them agrees: The number-one error that crops up while installing a new part in your computer is mismatched or disconnected cabling. Problems can even crop up with cables that are supposed to be foolproof, like SATA cables. Although internal power cables are designed to fit only one way, you have to remember to connect them in the first place. (This oversight is typically the cause of the classic line, "Hey, it doesn't act like it's getting power at all!" That's because it *isn't*. Around my shop, this discovery is typically followed by the sound of my palm hitting my forehead.)

On the other hand, many internal EIDE cables can be connected upside down, so remember the Pin 1 Rule, which you can see illustrated in Figure 16-2:

Pin 1 of the male connector on the component should always align with the marked wire on the cable (which is the cable manufacturer's way of identifying which wire on the cable is wire 1).

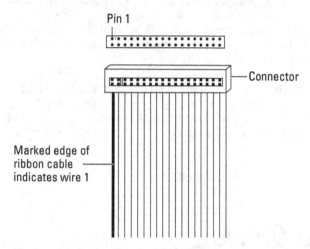

Figure 16-2: The Pin 1 Rule: Pin 1, meet wire 1.

Although it might take a few seconds extra when you install a new part, I recommend that you check each cable connection — including cables leading to other parts — before you test the new component. You can easily and accidentally unplug an existing connection while you're routing wires and moving things around inside your computer's chassis. If you install a new part and another part suddenly refuses to work properly, there's a good chance that you accidentally unplugged something.

Chapter 17

Ten Ways to Maintain Your PC

Every PC owner wants to keep that machine running smoothly. In this Part of Tens chapter, I outline several tricks that you can use to keep your machine reliable and stable. Some of these tips cost money (such as selecting faster hardware), but others won't cost you a cent. Go, Speed Racer, go!

Defragment Your Hard Drive

Over weeks and months of use, computers running any version of Windows XP and Vista will invariably slow down significantly because of hard drive fragmentation.

First, a quick explanation about fragmentation: When you delete a file from your hard drive, that area of your hard drive can then accept data from another file. If the file to be saved is larger than this open area, however, Windows must split the file into fragments. When your computer needs to load a file, Windows automatically (and invisibly) reassembles these fragments back into the complete file. However, the more fragmented the files are on your hard drive, the longer this step takes, and the slower your PC becomes.

When you defragment your hard drive (called a *defrag*), the program rearranges the data on your hard drive so that each file is *contiguous* (no longer divided up into individual fragments) — making it much easier and faster for Windows to read that file when you ask for it!

To defragment your hard drive, follow these simple steps:

Windows XP

1. **Click the Start button, and then choose Programs⇨Accessories⇨ System Tools⇨Disk Defragmenter.**

2. **From the list that appears, click the drive you want to defragment.**

3. **Click the Defragment button.**

4. **When the defragment is complete, click the Close button on the Disk Defragmenter window to exit the program.**

Windows Vista

1. **Click the Start button, and then choose All Programs⇨ Accessories⇨System Tools⇨Disk Defragmenter.**

2. **Click the Select Volumes button to choose which drive you want to defragment.**

3. **Click the Defragment Now button and then click OK.**

4. **When the defragment is complete, click the Close button to exit the program.**

Get Connected with the Speediest Data Transfers

For the fastest possible *throughput* (the data transfer rate between components on your system) from your internal hard drives and DVD drives, your computer cries out for a serial ATA (SATA) connection. For plugging in external devices, demand a FireWire, a USB 2.0, or an eSATA connection.

If you build your PC with an enhanced integrated drive electronics (EIDE) hard drive, you can still add any of these connections, either by using your motherboard's built-in hardware or by buying a PCI adapter with the correct connectors. (Chapter 7 describes more about your hard drives.) However, if you've done your homework and you're building a power user PC, it pays to build your computer around a motherboard with serial ATA, FireWire, and USB 2.0 built-in. "Just say *no* to EIDE!"

I recommend using a PCI-Express video card as well, especially if gaming is high on your list of applications! Chapter 14 covers gaming PC performance like a blanket.

Keep Your Backgrounds Plain

Graphical operating systems, such as Windows Vista and Linux, can be dressed up with 16 million–color photographs as backgrounds, animated icons, and other exotic eye candy. If you want your PC to run faster under one of these operating systems, however, select a simple, single-color background because your PC must use extra RAM to display true-color images or animated icons. Some full-screen background pictures that I've seen are nearly 6 megabytes (6MB) in size — 16 million–color bitmaps! meant for widescreen resolutions of 1680 x 1050 (and even higher)! If you use a high-resolution, full-screen bitmap with 16 million colors as your background, you might notice that your PC slows down significantly when it's loading the background image (or redrawing it after you close a window or quit a game).

Remove Resident Programs

Beware! Your computer might be harboring hidden programs that suck power and resources from your applications. No, I'm not talking about viruses. I'm talking about *resident programs,* which have been around since the days of DOS. (Yup, you win the secret prize if you remember DOS Days.) A resident program is loaded automatically when you boot your computer, and the program continues to work in the background while you run the applications that you want. Unlike a virus, a resident program is usually doing something you want, such as checking the status of your disk drive, polling your Internet service provider for your e-mail, or displaying stock quotes.

Unfortunately, if you load down your computer with too many resident programs, your PC has to devote too much processor time and RAM to maintain them; thus, your applications will slow down accordingly. To make sure that this slowdown doesn't happen, don't load more than two or three resident tasks. Also avoid installing programs that automatically start each time that you boot your PC unless you really need them to.

Under Windows XP and Vista, you can recognize most resident programs by their icons in the system tray, which occupies the lower far-right side of the status bar opposite from the Start button. To determine what each of these icons does, you can usually left- or right-click the icon to display a menu. (And most resident tasks have a menu item that you can select to shut them down.) If you don't need a program and it keeps loading a system tray icon, feel free to choose Start➪ Control Panel➪Add or Remove Programs (Windows XP) or Start➪Control Panel➪ Uninstall a Program (Windows Vista). This takes you to a dialog box where you can click the offending application and then click Change/Remove (XP) or Uninstall/Change (Vista) to delete it. Hurrah!

Although uninstalling a resident program is always the best way to banish it from your system, you can also stop a specific program from loading during startup under Windows XP and Vista. Here's how:

Windows XP

1. **Choose Start➪Run to display the Run dialog box.**

2. **Type** MSCONFIG **and then click OK.**

Windows Vista

1. **Choose Start and then click in the Start Search box.**

2. **Type** MSCONFIG **and then click the magnifying glass icon.**

3. **Click the MSconfig program.**

Either path opens the System Configuration Utility, where you can make changes to the behavior of Windows during the boot process. For both XP and Vista, do the following:

1. **Click the Startup tab.**

2. **When you see a list of the applications that Windows automatically runs during startup, locate the program that you want to disable in the list, clear the check box next to the program, and then click OK.**

Keep Your Drivers Updated

Although I mentioned this tip several times earlier in this book, it belongs here as well. I highly recommend that you make it a habit to check your hardware manufacturer Web sites every month for the latest and greatest versions of your drivers. These drivers should include your motherboard's BIOS, your video card, your sound card, and your network hardware. Not only will the latest drivers keep your hardware running as fast as possible, but you might even eliminate the occasional lockup!

Use a Native File System

When you use Windows (XP or Vista), Linux, or Unix, you'll find that you have at least one alternative format for storing and retrieving files: Each of these operating systems has a *native file system* that improves on the DOS file system. In every case, your operating system can save and load data faster from its native file system, which was designed for use in a 32- or 64-bit multitasking environment. I especially recommend using the NTFS file system if you're running Windows XP or Windows Vista.

When you install Windows, Linux, or Unix on a new hard drive, you're given the chance to reformat your hard drive for native file system support. I recommend that you use the native file system. See Chapter 8 for more.

Check Your Drives for Errors

I have no earthly idea why Microsoft continues to hide the Check Disk feature, but you should use it often. I check all the drives on my PCs every week. Checking the disk for errors ensures that no corruption has occurred because of power outages or misbehaving programs that don't load and save files how they should. If you don't check your drives often, a small problem can rapidly escalate into something far nastier, and you could end up losing data.

To check a disk for errors, follow these steps.

Windows XP

1. **Click the Start button and then click My Computer to display the drives on your system.**

2. **Right-click the drive you want to check and then choose Properties from the menu that appears.**

3. **Click the Tools tab.**

4. **Click the Check Now button and then select the Automatically Fix File System Errors check box.**

5. **Click Start.**

   If you're checking your boot drive, you'll see a warning dialog appear that tells you that Windows will have to check the drive the next time you reboot. This makes sense because you're currently using it.

6. **Click Yes to confirm.**

7. **Restart your PC.**

   Check Disk automatically does the deed.

Windows Vista

1. **Click the Start button and then click My Computer.**

2. **Right-click the drive you want to check and then choose Properties from the menu that appears.**

3. **Click the Tools tab.**

4. **Click the Check Now button and then select the Automatically Fix File System Errors check box.**

5. **Click Start.**

   If a warning appears, you'll have to reboot.

6. **Click Schedule Disk Check to confirm.**

7. **Restart your PC and allow Check Disk to run.**

Uninstalling 101

This one's common sense, but you'd be surprised how many PC owners simply don't remember to uninstall unneeded software! Over time, your Windows Program folder can become clogged with dozens of demos, shareware programs you tried but didn't buy, and even commercial software that you needed once or twice and haven't run in ages. Those unneeded applications take up space that you could be using for something you'll actually use.

Most applications now come with an uninstall program, which you can usually reach from the application's Start menu group. However, you can always display all the programs you've installed under Windows from the Control Panel:

Windows XP

1. **Choose Start⇨Control Panel⇨Add or Remove Programs.**

2. **Click the program you wish to uninstall.**

3. **Click Remove.**

   The uninstall program prompts you for confirmation.

Windows Vista

1. **Start⇨Control Panel⇨Uninstall a Program.**
2. **Click the program you wish to chuck.**
3. **Click Uninstall/Change.**

   The uninstall program prompts you for confirmation.

Maintain Your System Registry

Most of the settings for Windows XP and Vista — as well as the settings for the programs you run — are kept in a huge file called the Windows Registry. As you might imagine, over time the Registry can become clogged with entries for programs you're not even running any longer, as well as incomplete and corrupted entries that can slow down Windows (or cause errors, or even lock up your PC).

You can use any number of Windows Registry cleanup utilities to check your Registry for errors and then remove the inaccurate and unnecessary entries. My favorite is TweakNow RegCleaner Professional, from http://TweakNow.com. It's an inexpensive, $27 shareware program that keeps my Registry error-free, and it can also safely reduce the size of your Registry (resulting in faster booting and faster program loading).

Clean Up after Windows

Why do you have to clean up after Windows XP and Vista on a regular basis? You can save space by deleting the unnecessary (like the temporary files that many programs create) and compressing the stuff you do want to keep (like your documents). These tasks are performed in both XP and Vista by the Disk Cleanup program.

To run the Disk Cleanup program, follow these steps.

Windows XP

1. **Click the Start button and then choose Programs⇨Accessories⇨ System Tools⇨Disk Cleanup.**
2. **After the Disk Cleanup program displays the files that can be deleted, click each desired check box to enable it.**
3. **Click the OK button; then click the Delete Files button to verify.**

   Disk Defragmenter automatically exits when it's done.

Windows Vista

1. **Click the Start button and then choose All Programs⇨ Accessories⇨System Tools⇨Disk Cleanup.**
2. **Follow the preceding steps for Windows XP.**

Chapter 18

Ten PC Pitfalls to Avoid Like the Plague

- -

I n this chapter, I name a number of computer-related mishaps and mistakes that can lead to lost data, hardware headaches, legal hassles, and even physical injury — in other words, things that you should shun at all costs for the PC you spent so much money, time, and love building! Some things on this list should be avoided while you're building your PC, and others are dangerous practices that some people engage in with their computer after it's up and running. I recommend that you keep the following three sayings in mind; they seem to cover most situations in this chapter:

- ✔ If it seems too good to be true, it probably *is*.
- ✔ Let the buyer beware.
- ✔ **Warning labels are there for a reason.**™

(That last one is currently just a Mark's Maxim, but it ought to be as famous as the others.)

It's "Refurbished" for a Reason

You'll often see *refurbished hardware* for sale in computer hardware magazines, computer stores on the Web, and in catalogs for discount computers. Refurbished (or *recertified*) hardware was returned for some reason to the manufacturer — usually because it was defective. The company fixes the defect and then resells the hardware to another distributor.

By law, refurbished computers and hardware components must be identified as such in any advertising. The distributor usually trumpets the features offered on the computer, the fact that you get a warranty, and perhaps even that the merchandise is "like new." Usually, you do save a significant amount on refurbished hardware, so the prices that these companies advertise will indeed catch your eye.

However, I recommend that you give refurbished components a wide berth and buy only new parts (or use working parts from an existing computer). Personally, I would *never* purchase a refurbished computer or refurbished component, and here are the reasons why:

- ✔ You have no idea why the item was returned, but you can usually safely assume that it wasn't working properly.
- ✔ You have no way of knowing how the former owner treated the item.

✔ The manufacturer's warranty is typically less than 90 days, which is usually a much shorter length of time than the warranty on a new item.

✔ Many refurbished parts aren't completely retested before they're shipped back to the store.

✔ The sale is usually final, so if it breaks, you're stuck with it.

If you do decide to buy a refurbished item, here's another Mark's Maxim for you:

Always find out all you can about that refurbished bargain before you spend your money!™

Looking for an Antique? Buy a Pentium 4 CPU

Many computer hardware stores and mail-order companies still sell CPU chips and motherboards based on the Pentium 4 design. The Pentium 4 was a grand chip, and many of us techno-types with several computers in the house can point to at least one, but the days of the Pentium 4 are past us now. If you're building a computer to run any operating system other than Windows XP, take my advice and buy an Intel Core 2 Duo or Athlon 64 X2 CPU and motherboard. (I cover motherboards like a blanket in Chapter 3.)

Although a Pentium 4 CPU can indeed run Windows Vista, the older architecture simply isn't fast enough or advanced enough to offer anywhere near the performance of a multiple-core computer. Sure, these older components are much cheaper now, and you can save a considerable amount of money. However, you'll likely start looking for an upgrade CPU soon, and a Pentium 4-socketed motherboard doesn't accept a Core 2 Duo or Quad CPU.

When building a computer from the ground up, buy a multicore processor. You'll thank yourself (and maybe even me) for many months to come!

Never Depend on Floppies

Floppy disks and important data just don't mix. Floppies are susceptible to magnetic fields (*never* store them on top of a speaker or your PC's case); they have a low *shelf life* (the amount of time you can reliably store a floppy disk and then retrieve data from it); the exchange of floppies can spread viruses; they're easily mixed up or mislaid (even if you label them); and occasionally, one computer can't read floppy disks formatted on another computer. (Not to mention they will someday in the near future become obsolete.) In my years as a consultant and computer technician, I've felt the pain of literally dozens of folks who lost valuable data by trusting those familiar floppies.

Don't get me wrong: Floppies are fine for carrying a document or two in your pocket or sending a document through the mail — as long as you have a backup copy of that data on your hard drive, that is. From time to time, I even save a document on a floppy as a simple backup for a day or so, but I don't expect with absolute certainty to be able to read that document after six months.

If you need to store your data away from your computer or send it to someone else, *please* consider something more reliable. The best solution, however, is a favorite of mine: A CD recorder can archive information for more than ten years at 700MB on each disc, and CD-R discs are a much more permanent data-retrieval system than any magnetic method. If you opt for DVD, you can store 4 to almost 9GB of data, with the same reliability. (I discuss CD and DVD recorders in Chapter 9.) Of course, the person who receives your nomadic data will need the same type of hardware to read the media you send.

Another removable storage device that's swept the PC world is the USB 2.0 Flash drive, which plugs directly into your PC's universal serial bus (USB) port and provides anywhere from 32MB to a whopping 16GB of storage!

Under Windows XP or Windows Vista, a Flash drive requires no drivers or special software. Just plug it in, and your PC will recognize it as a removable media drive. The USB connection means that it's universally compatible with any late-model PC or Macintosh and that it transfers data much faster (and more reliably) than a floppy drive. Plus, these convenient solid-state drives aren't much bigger than a ballpoint pen. Because there are no moving parts, they'll last practically forever. Prices range from $25 to $200 for Flash drives.

Help Stamp Out Unnecessary Passwords!

Password protection is appropriate for sensitive files stored in an office network environment or connecting with your Internet service provider. However, passwords that you assigned to screen savers, archived files in .zip format, and even basic input/output system (BIOS) passwords that don't allow your PC to boot are nothing but trouble for the typical home computer owner. If you have no reason to be overly cautious about your computer and its data, for heaven's sake, *don't assign passwords that you don't need!*

Why do I despise unnecessary passwords? I've received countless calls from friends, family members, and clients who can't retrieve data from a disk or an archive file (or even log on to their own computer) because they forgot the password or typed it incorrectly. In effect, you're locked out from accessing your own data. In the worst-case scenario, all you can do is reformat that hard drive and bid that data good-bye. (And I can tell you that your memories of lost data will last a long, *long* time.)

Honor Thy Neighbor's Copyright

Computers and the Internet are the best tools ever invented for accessing and sharing information across the entire globe, and this dynamic duo also makes it extremely easy to cut and paste your way to plagiarism and copyright violations. If an image or a document is not your original work, you *must* be careful (and that includes quoting — even simple phrases).

Your PC Is Not a Kindergarten

If you're a parent, you probably want your children to be computer literate by the time they graduate from elementary school. And it's true that the earlier your children are exposed to a computer, the more comfortable they will be with a computer later in life.

However, I recommend that you keep very small children away from your computer until they're older; a good minimum age is about four years old. An active toddler can do a surprising amount of damage to a typical PC: jamming floppies the wrong way (or jamming toaster pastries any which way) into drives, spilling juice or milk on the keyboard or the case, yanking on wires and cords, and slapping the monitor. I've even seen a CD-ROM drive with peanut butter inside. To a one- or two-year-old, your PC is just another interesting toy with lights, and that child won't be learning anything useful about the computer for a while. Keep your computer safe until the kids are ready at three or four years old.

Don't Jump on the Pirate Ship

Programs illegally copied or distributed are *pirated* software. You can download such illicit commercial software — such as games, applications, and utilities — from a large network of Web sites and Internet newsgroups.

Besides being illegal, pirated software is an invitation for disaster; many renegade computer programmers use pirated software to distribute viruses and Trojan horse programs. Although a Trojan horse program is described as a useful application and might even look like one while it's running, it destroys data on your computer — or, in the worst case scenario, even allows a hacker to remotely gain control of your PC over the Internet!

Support the authors of shareware and the companies that produce the best commercial software: Buy their products and *don't pirate them!*

Keep Your Mitts Away from Monitors and Power Supplies

Most components used in your computer — such as the hard drive — are sealed. Even if you could open them, you'd never be able to repair them. Building a computer is a task of assembly, and you should never have to disassemble anything except for maybe removing components to make sure they're seating properly or to upgrade a part.

Two sealed components deserve an even wider berth: your computer's power supply and monitor. *Never attempt to open the case on either of these parts.* They can be repaired only by computer technicians or if sent back to the factory. They can also be quite dangerous if plugged in while uncovered.

Don't Lease a PC for the Long Haul

Maybe you're considering leasing a PC instead of building your own system. Or perhaps you decided to lease a PC while you save up the cash to build your dream machine. Leasing sometimes seems like a better deal; after all, you can start using the PC immediately, and if something breaks it generally gets fixed for free. Some mail-order companies and larger computer chain stores allow you to lease a computer for a monthly fee. Oh, and don't forget the "rent-to-own" stores that allow you to start leasing a new PC for a pittance.

If you need a computer for only a couple of months, leasing is fine. However, leasing a computer for more than six months is not a very good idea. PCs depreciate in value so quickly and advance in technology so fast that your leased computer will be significantly less powerful and worth less within just a year. As for "rent-to-own" PCs, make sure you check the bottom line to see just exactly how much the total cost (plus fees) will set you back. You're likely to find that you're paying far more in the end than you would by buying a new PC outright or assembling a PC from scratch.

By building your own computer, you end up with the most power for the money, and you can continue to upgrade your PC to stretch its useful life over many years.

Avoid Older Versions of PC Software

If you're a novice at buying computer software for your new PC, pay close attention to the version numbers of the software you're buying. Often, you see expensive applications being sold for far less than the going rate in a catalog or on a Web site. For example, an integrated suite of office applications might be advertised at $500 at one store but only $250 at another. Usually, the store selling the software for much less is selling an older version. For example, the more expensive office suite might be Version 7.0, and the cheaper version might be Version 6.0. The version number is usually listed in the advertisement, but it might be stuck down at the bottom of the ad.

I should note, however, that some PC owners prefer older versions of some software. For example, one of my editors for this book absolutely abhors Office 2007 and still prefers to use Office 2003 unless she has to use the newer version. If you need to buy a particular program and you have a preference for an earlier version (say, Photoshop CS3 instead of CS4), then by all means buy what you prefer! Just keep abreast of any industry-specific software to make sure you can work well with others.

If you're unsure about the latest version number of a particular program, talk with a vendor or research it online at the manufacturer's Web site.

Part VI
Appendixes

In this part . . .

Start out by reading about the companion DVD for this book. As handy as this book is, just wait until you play the DVD and watch it while I walk you through building your dream machine step by step. There's nothing quite like seeing someone do something, and that's why I wanted to create this video for you to follow. Use the book and DVD together; the parts of the DVD follow the same structure as the book. I take it nice and slow so you can really see what to do, when, and how to check your progress.

Also, I include a PC builder's glossary here you can refer to time and time again.

Appendix A

About the DVD

System Requirements

Make sure that your computer meets the minimum system requirements shown in the following list. If your computer doesn't match up with most of these requirements, you might have problems using the DVD.

- ✔ A PC running Windows 2000, Windows XP, or Windows Vista
- ✔ A Macintosh running Apple OS X or later
- ✔ A DVD-ROM drive
- ✔ A sound card and speakers
- ✔ 512MB of RAM or greater

If you need more information on the basics, check out these books published by John Wiley & Sons, Inc.: *PCs For Dummies,* by Dan Gookin; *Macs For Dummies,* by Edward C. Baig; *iMac For Dummies* by Mark L. Chambers; *Windows XP For Dummies,* by Andy Rathbone; and *Windows Vista For Dummies,* also by Andy Rathbone.

Using the DVD

- ✔ **On a PC running Windows XP or Vista:** If you have more than one media player installed on your computer, Windows might ask you to choose one to play the DVD. After you do, the DVD should start in that media player.

  To navigate through the DVD, use your mouse to select from the menu system instead of using your media player's navigation pane. Depending on the media player you choose, you might need to click once to select a menu item and then click again to play it.

- ✔ **On a Macintosh running Mac OS X:** When you put this DVD into the DVD drive on your Mac, the DVD Player pops up, complete with on-screen remote control.

  You can use the on-screen remote controls, your keyboard's arrow keys, or your mouse to navigate through the DVD's menu system.

- ✔ **On a DVD player connected to your television:** Use your player's remote control to navigate through the DVD's menu system.

What You'll Find on the DVD

The following sections are arranged by category and provide a summary of the software and other goodies you'll find on the DVD.

Installing Your Motherboard

Installing Your CPU

Installing Your RAM

Installing Your Ports

Installing Your Video Card

Installing Your Hard Drive

Installing Your Optical Drive

Installing Your Sound Card

Maintaining Your Hard Drive

Troubleshooting

If you have trouble playing the DVD, close all running programs. The more programs you have running, the less memory is available to other programs. Running video files can use a lot of memory, so if you keep other programs running, the videos might not play smoothly.

If the DVD does not automatically run after you insert it, here are some fixes:

✔ **On a PC:** Open My Computer and double-click the DVD icon on your desktop.

✔ **On a Mac:** The DVD icon should appear on your Desktop after you inserted it in the drive. Open DVD Player from the Applications folder to run the DVD.

Customer Care

If you have trouble with the DVD-ROM, please call the Wiley Product Technical Support phone number at (800) 762-2974. Outside the United States, call (317) 572-3994. You can also contact Wiley Product Technical Support at http://support.wiley.com. John Wiley & Sons will provide technical support only for installation and other general quality control items.

To place additional orders or to request information about other Wiley products, please call (877) 762-2974.

The PC Builder's Glossary

• A •

access time: How long a hard drive, an optical drive, or a memory module takes to read data. The faster the access time, the better.

adapter card: A circuit board that plugs into your motherboard to provide your computer with additional functionality. For example, a video adapter card plugs into your motherboard and enables your computer to display text and graphics on your monitor.

AGP (Accelerated Graphics Port): An older bus standard for 3-D video cards. AGP slots are rated by 2x, 4x, and 8x speeds. As you might guess, the higher the x factor in the speed rating, the faster the data flows to and from your video card. The AGP video card has been supplanted by the faster PCI-Express video standard. *See also* PCI-Express.

application: A program that performs a task on your computer. For example, an Internet application is a program that performs some useful function while your computer is connected to the Internet.

AT-class: An older, standard set of dimensions for a PC's motherboard and case derived from the original IBM AT-class computer. If your PC uses an AT-class motherboard, you must also have an AT-class case. AT-class cases and hardware are practically extinct (except to scavengers) because ATX-class cases and hardware have taken over the PC market.

Athlon Phenom: The fastest Advanced Micro Devices (more popularly called AMD) processor available at this time. The Phenom is the darling of gamers and also graphics professionals who edit digital video and create 3-D images. (It's also far more expensive than the Athlon 64 X2.)

Athlon Sempron: A lower-cost AMD Athlon processor, designed for the least-expensive entry PCs (like the kind you see offered by mail-order and department stores). The Sempron is not recommended for gaming or power user PCs.

Athlon XP: An older processor series from AMD. The Athlon XP is still a good choice for an inexpensive PC, but it's rapidly disappearing from the market and no longer offers the best performance for power user applications and computer games.

Athlon 64 FX: An older version of the Athlon 64 processor designed for games and high-end 3-D rendering applications. (64-bit operation allows you to add more memory and also provides faster disk and network access.) The FX series is being phased out in favor of the Athlon Phenom.

Athlon 64 X2 Dual-Core: The current mid-range Athlon processor, using two CPU cores that allow far superior efficiency and speed (especially when multitasking among more than one application). The X2 Dual-Core offers 64-bit processing.

ATX-class: Today's standard set of dimensions and features for a PC's motherboard and case, with support for standard built-in ports on the motherboard and simpler connectors for power, case switches, and case lights. If you buy an ATX-class motherboard for your computer, you must also use an ATX-class case.

• B •

bank: Another term for a RAM module socket on your motherboard. Most motherboards have at least two RAM banks. *See also* RAM.

BIOS (basic input-output system): Resides on one or two computer chips on your motherboard. Your PC's BIOS software controls many low-level functions of your computer, such as keeping track of your hard drive's characteristics and what type of monitor you're using.

bit: The smallest unit of information used by a computer. It can have a value of either 1 or 0.

Blu-ray: The latest standard in recordable optical discs. Blu-ray discs were developed to hold high-definition (HD) movies. Although Blu-ray recorders are still expensive compared with a mundane DVD recorder, they're likely to fall in price quickly, offering up to a whopping 50GB of storage (perfect for backups).

bps (bits per second): A common method of measuring the speed of a modem. Today's high-speed modems are usually measured in kilobits per second (Kbps), as in 56 Kbps.

broadband: A high-speed Internet connection that delivers data much faster than a dial-up analog modem connection. Common Internet broadband connections include DSL, cable, and satellite. *See also* DSL.

bus: A slot on your motherboard that accepts adapter cards. Bus slots on Athlon/Intel motherboards are generally 16-bit ISA slots, 32-bit PCI slots, AGP slots, or PCI-Express slots. *See also* AGP, ISA, PCI, and PCI-Express.

byte: A group of 8 bits that represents a single character of text or data stored in your computer's RAM.

• C •

CA (Commonsense Assembly): The technique of preventing mistakes during the assembly of a computer by using your common sense. First postulated by the author of this book.

cable modem: An external device that connects your computer to your cable TV company's coaxial cable. A cable modem is a requirement for connecting to the Internet through cable access. Although a cable modem really isn't anything like a traditional external analog modem, it looks like one.

cache: A special bank of memory that holds data that is often used or that will be required in a few nanoseconds. Storing data in a cache speeds up the operation of your PC because the data doesn't have to be retrieved from RAM or your hard drive. Many components have a cache, including your CPU, your hard drive, and your CD/DVD recorder.

case: The metal enclosure that surrounds your computer and holds all its parts. The case, typically held on with screws or thumbwheels, might have a separate cover that you can remove to add or remove parts; other cases are one piece and simply open up.

CD-ROM drive: An internal device that can read both data CD-ROMs (which store computer programs and files) and audio CDs (which store music). A typical CD-ROM can hold as much as 700MB of data. CD-ROM drives cannot write to a disc; they can only read data.

CD-RW drive: Also called a CD recorder. Enables you to record (and re-record) CDs. Discs made with a CD-RW drive can hold computer data and music. CD-Rs can be read on any CD-ROM drive but can be recorded only once. CD-RWs can be read on most CD-ROM drives and can be re-recorded.

Celeron: A less-expensive processor produced by Intel for the home market. Although a Celeron chip lacks the performance of a full Core 2 Duo-class CPU, it's a popular processor for low-end PCs.

CGA (color graphics adapter): The original IBM PC color standard. Programs with CGA support could display a stunning four colors at a time.

client-server: A network in which computers act as clients and retrieve information or services from a central server computer. Server computers can also hold common shared resources, such as modems or CD-ROM drives, or provide shared access to Internet services such as e-mail and a Web site.

CMOS (complementary metal-oxide semiconductor): CMOS RAM stores configuration data about your PC's hardware even after your PC is turned off.

coax: Standard Ethernet coaxial cable (also called 10Base2 or 10Base5); commonly used on simple peer-to-peer networks.

color depth: A reference to the number of colors in an image. Popular color depths are 256 colors; 64,000 colors; and 16 million colors.

COM port: A numeric designator for a serial port that uses standard hardware settings. Most PC serial ports can be set to one of four COM ports: COM1 through COM4.

component: The technoid word for a piece of computer hardware; a computer part.

compression: The use of a mathematical formula to reduce the amount of disk space taken by a file, a video clip, or an image. Some compression schemes can reproduce the original exactly; other compression schemes lose some detail from the original. Modems also use compression to reduce the time necessary to transfer a file.

Core 2 Duo: The current version of the midrange Intel CPU, offering dual-core performance. The Core 2 Duo is a good pick for any budget or family PC.

Core 2 Extreme Edition: The latest, fastest, and most expensive Core 2 CPU from Intel, offering the best results while multitasking applications or playing games.

Core 2 Quad: A quad- (four-) core version of the Intel Core 2 CPU, offering faster performance for gamers and power users.

CPU (central processing unit): The chip that acts as your computer's brain. The CPU performs the commands provided by the programs that you run.

DDR (double data rate): The standard RAM module used on Pentium 4 computers. A DDR memory module is effectively twice as fast as an older SDRAM module of the same speed. *See also* SDRAM.

DDR2: An improved standard for RAM modules developed by Intel, offering increased bandwidth and better performance with 64-bit hardware over DDR RAM. DDR2 modules are common on today's PCs.

digital camera: A camera that looks and operates much like a traditional film camera except that its finished images are saved in a digital format and uploaded directly to a computer rather than celluloid- (film-) based and processed into photographs. Digital cameras are more expensive than their film cousins.

DIMM (dual inline memory module): A specific type of RAM module usually used with current Intel and AMD-based PCs.

DIP (dual inline packaging) switches: A bank of tiny, sliding (or rocker) switches that enables you to set different features on your motherboard, some components, and many adapter cards. Use the tip of a pen to slide or push the switches into their proper sequence.

DirectX: An extension to Windows XP and Windows Vista that enables fast animation and graphics display in game and multimedia programs.

distinctive ring: A service from your telephone company that enables more than one telephone number to use the same physical telephone line. Distinctive ring is often used by PC owners who receive faxes using their computer's faxmodem.

DL DVD (dual layer digital video disc, or digital versatile disc): A dual-layer recordable disc with twice the storage capacity of the older 4.7GB media. DVDs can hold computer data, full-length movies, and several hours of audio in MPEG format. Dual-layer DVDs are often used for backing up larger hard drives.

DOS (disk operating system): One of the oldest operating systems still in use on PCs. This character-based operating system requires you to type commands to run programs.

dot pitch: The amount of space between pixels on a monitor. The smaller the dot pitch, the clearer and more detailed the display.

DPMS (display power management signaling): A feature that enables your computer to power down your monitor after a specified period of inactivity. This feature helps save energy and money.

drawing tablet: An input device that looks like a larger version of a touchpad. Although the drawing tablet can be used as a pointing device, it is typically used by graphic artists for freehand drawing in graphics applications.

DSL (digital subscriber line): A high-speed connection to the Internet offering top speeds of around 4–10 Mbps. Although DSL uses regular copper telephone line and is always on, it's still not available in some rural areas of the country.

DSL modem: An external device that connects your computer to a DSL line. The modem looks like a traditional external analog telephone modem but delivers data much faster.

DVD (Digital Versatile Disc or Digital Video Disc): The replacement for the older CD-ROM format. A single DVD can hold from 4.7–17GB. DVDs can hold computer data, full-length movies, and several hours of audio in MPEG format.

DVD-RW/DVD+RW drive: A DVD recorder that enables you to record (and re-record) DVDs. DVD-Rs and DVD+Rs can be read on any DVD drive (and virtually all DVD players designed for use with your TV set), but they can be recorded only once. DVD-RWs and DVD+RWs are not as compatible as DVD-R and DVD+R discs, but they can be re-recorded.

DVI (digital visual interface, or digital video interface): A high-performance port that connects your video card to the latest flat-panel LCD and older CRT monitors. A DVI connection provides the best-quality video signal and the fastest data transfer between your PC and your monitor — digital end-to-end, as the techs say.

EDO (extended data output): A standard type of RAM module used on older Pentium-class computers that provides faster operation than earlier types of RAM.

EIDE (Enhanced Integrated Drive Electronics): The standard hard drive and device interface technology in use on PCs. Standard EIDE controllers (which are built into today's motherboards) can handle as many as four EIDE devices, which can include additional hard drives and DVD drives.

Ethernet: A network topology in which data is broadcast across the network between computers. Although Ethernet is generally less efficient than other network architectures, it's less complex and less expensive to maintain.

external peripheral: A type of peripheral or device that sits outside your computer's case and is connected by a cable — for example, an external modem.

fax modem: A type of modem that has all the functionality of a standard modem but can also exchange faxes with either another fax modem or a standard fax machine.

female connector: A cable connector with holes that accept the pins on a male connector.

fingertip mouse: A pointing device that uses a small button. To move objects onscreen, you push the button in the direction that you want. Fingertip mice are common on laptop computers.

firewall: A program or device designed to protect network data from being accessed by a computer hacker. Most Internet and Web sites use a firewall to provide security for company data. Windows Vista (and XP) has a built-in Firewall.

FireWire: The popular name for the IEEE 1394 high-performance serial bus connection standard, developed by Apple. A FireWire connection is similar to a USB connection. Devices can be added or removed without rebooting the computer, and you can daisy-chain as many as 63 FireWire devices from a single port. Because of a FireWire port's high data-transfer rate of 400 Mbps and ability to control digital devices, it's especially well suited for connecting digital camcorders and external hard drives to your PC. The latest FireWire 800 standard (available for PCs) can transfer data at a mind-boggling 800 Mbps.

Flash BIOS: An advanced BIOS chipset that can be updated with new features by running an upgrade program (usually available from the manufacturer of your motherboard).

Flash drive: An external solid-state removable storage drive that connects to your USB port. These drives store data using the same technology as the memory cards that you find in digital cameras.

flat-panel monitor: A monitor that uses LCD technology instead of a traditional tube. LCD monitors have been used on laptop computers for years and are now the standard for full-size desktop computers. A flat panel is much thinner than a traditional tube monitor and uses less electricity and emits very little radiation.

floppy drive: An internal component that can save program and data files to floppy disks, which can be stored as backups or loaded on other PCs. Computers once used 3½-inch floppy disks that stored as much as 1.44MB of data on a single disk. However, floppies are unreliable and might not be readable on other PCs, and floppies have been rendered obsolete by USB Flash drives.

• G •

game port: A port for connecting joysticks and game peripherals. Game ports can be installed separately, although most sound cards have a game port built in.

GB (gigabyte): A unit of data equal to 1024MB (megabytes).

GHz (gigahertz): The frequency (or speed) of a CPU as measured in billions of cycles per second.

• H •

hacker: A computer user who attempts to access confidential information or steal data across the Internet or a network without authorization. Hacking is a criminal offense.

hard drive (or hard disk): A component that usually fits inside your case. Your hard drive acts as permanent storage for your programs and data, enabling you to save and delete files. Unlike the RAM in your computer, your hard drive does not lose data when you turn off your PC.

• I •

infrared port: An external optical port that allows fast, wireless transfer of data between your PC and another computer equipped with a compatible infrared port.

inkjet: A method of printing in which ink is injected from a cartridge onto paper to create text and graphics on the page. Color inkjet printers are relatively inexpensive but take longer to print a page than a comparable laser printer.

interface: A technoid term that refers to the method of connecting a peripheral to your computer. For example, printers use a parallel port interface or a USB interface; hard drives use EIDE, FireWire, or SATA interfaces. Some interface types refer to adapter cards; others refer to ports and cables. *See also* EIDE, FireWire, SATA, and USB.

internal component: A component that you install inside your computer's case — for example, a hard drive or an internal modem.

ISA (Industry Standard Architecture): Type of bus slots that accept 16-bit adapter cards to add functionality to your computer. ISA cards are typically slower than PCI adapter cards, and many motherboards no longer include an ISA slot.

• J •

joystick: An input device (for games) similar to the control stick used by an airplane pilot. Predictably, joysticks are usually used by game players who enjoy flight simulators.

jumper: A set of two or more pins that can be shorted with a tiny plastic-and-metal crossover. Jumpers are commonly found on motherboards, components such as hard drives, and adapter cards.

• K •

keyboard port: Where the cable from your keyboard connects to your computer. Most keyboards now use a USB connection, but older keyboards used the standard round PS/2 port.

KB (kilobyte): A unit equal to 1024 bytes.

• L •

LAN (local area network): *See* network.

laser: A printer technology in which a powder is bonded to paper to print text and graphics. Laser printers are fast and produce excellent print quality.

Linux: A 32-bit (or 64-bit) operating system similar to Unix; popular on the Internet for use with Web servers. Unlike Unix, Linux is freeware, and its source code is available. *See also* Unix.

• M •

male connector: A cable connector with pins that fit into the holes on a female connector.

MB (megabyte): A unit equal to 1024KB.

MHz (megahertz): The frequency (or speed) of an older CPU as measured in millions of cycles per second.

MIDI (Musical Instrument Digital Interface): Hardware standard that enables computers of all types to play MIDI music, enabling interaction between the computer and the instrument. MIDI music files are common on the Internet as "background music" on Web sites, and they are a very popular method of sharing music between musicians.

MIDI port: Enables you to connect a MIDI-compatible musical instrument to your computer. Notes that you play on the instrument can be recorded on your PC, or your PC can be set to play the instrument all by itself.

modding: Customizing a PC case or its internal hardware with lights, gauges, and other nonessential "eye candy." Modding can also refer to *overclocking* (where you make your CPU run faster than its rated speed to boost performance). Hard-core PC gamers are fond of modding their machines.

modem: A computer device that converts digital data from one computer to an analog signal that can be sent over a telephone line. On the opposite end, the analog signal is converted back to digital data. Modems are widely used to access the Internet, online services, and computer bulletin board systems.

monitor: An external component that looks something like a TV screen. Your computer's monitor displays all the graphics generated by your PC.

motherboard: Your computer's main circuit board. It holds the CPU, RAM modules, and most of the circuitry. Adapter cards plug into your motherboard.

mouse: The standard computer pointing device. You hold the mouse in your hand and move it in the desired direction to create movement on your screen. A mouse also has buttons that you can press to select items or run a program.

Mozart, Wolfgang Amadeus: My favorite classical composer, and a doggone good piano player to boot. He created the world's most beautiful music, and I'm happy to say that I now have a complete audio CD collection of every single note that he ever composed.

MP3: A popular digital sound format used to download CD-quality music from the Internet. Your computer can play MP3 files through its speaker system, you can listen to them with a portable MP3 player, or you can record MP3 files to a recordable CD and play them in any standard audio CD player.

MPEG (Moving Pictures Expert Group): A popular digital video format and compression scheme often found on the Web. MPEG-format video is used on commercial DVD movies.

network: A system of computers connected to each other. Each computer can share data with other computers in the network, and all computers connected to the network can use common resources such as printers and modems.

newsgroups: Also called Usenet. International Internet message areas, each of which is usually dedicated to a special interest. Reading and posting questions in these newsgroups is a fun way to find out more about a subject (as well as receive tons of unwanted Internet e-mail, which is lovingly termed *spam*).

OCR (optical character recognition): Software that can "read" the text from a fax or a document scanned by a digital scanner and "type" (or convert) that text into your computer word processing program.

overclocking: The process of increasing the memory and CPU speed on a motherboard or graphics card past the normal rate to improve performance. Overclocking requires special software, and is often used by gamers to deliver the best possible computing and video speed from a PC. Overclocking generates a significant amount of extra heat from your components, which can result in a shortened operational life for your PC's CPU and graphics card.

parallel port: A standard connector still found on most PCs that enables you to add peripherals. Parallel ports are still sometimes used to connect printers to PCs, but the parallel port has been almost completely replaced by the modern USB port.

PC card (or PCMCIA card): A device resembling a fat business card that plugs directly into most laptops. The card can perform the same function as a full-size adapter card, such as a modem, a network interface card, a SCSI adapter, or even a hard drive. A PC card can also be used on a desktop computer equipped with a PC card slot.

PCI (Peripheral Component Interconnect): A bus slot that can hold a 32-bit adapter card to add functionality to your computer. PCI slots are faster than older ISA slots, so they're used for everything these days: for example, Ethernet cards and sound cards. *See also* ISA.

PCI-Express: The high-performance successor for a standard PCI slot. A PCI-Express bus is most commonly used these days for adding the latest and fastest video card to your PC. PCI-Express cards have largely replaced the AGP video card standard.

peer-to-peer: A type of network in which every computer is connected to every other computer, and no server computer is required.

Pentium: The original Pentium CPU. Manufactured by Intel, successive versions include the Pentium II, III, and 4. The latest Pentium standard is the dual-core Pentium CPU.

Pentium Xeon: A version of the Pentium 4 CPU designed for network server computers and high-powered workstation PCs. It's considerably more expensive than the standard Pentium 4 CPU.

pixel: A single dot on your monitor. Text and graphics displayed by a computer on a monitor are made up of pixels.

port: A fancy name for a connector that you plug something into. For example, your keyboard plugs into a keyboard port, and your USB scanner plugs into a USB port.

power supply: The box that carries electricity to your PC's devices. Your computer's power supply provides a number of separate power cables; each cable is connected to one of the various devices inside your computer that need electricity. A power supply also has a fan that helps to cool the interior of your computer. *Never attempt to open or repair a power supply!*

printer: An external device that can print text, graphics, and documents from your computer on paper. Most printers sold these days use inkjet or laser technology.

PS/2 mouse port: A special port that first appeared on the IBM PS/2 computer (hence the name). Although mice and keyboards are rapidly moving to USB connections, today's motherboards still feature a port reserved especially for your mouse or pointing device.

RAID (Redundant Array of Independent Disks): A configuration in which drives work together to boost read/write speed (and therefore perform-ance) or provide an automatic "mirrored" backup on a second hard drive. Most of today's mother-boards allow multiple hard drives to be configured as a RAID array.

RAM (random access memory): The type of chip that acts as your computer's short-term memory. This memory chip holds programs and data until you turn off your computer.

RDRAM (rambus dynamic RAM): An older design for RAM modules that delivered better perform-ance than DDR RAM but is being phased out in favor of DDR2 memory.

refresh: The number of times per second that your video adapter card redraws the image on your PC's monitor. Higher refresh rates are easier on the eyes.

rendering: A technoid term for creating 3-D objects and full 3-D scenes on your computer. The Pixar films *Toy Story, Finding Nemo,* and *Wall-E* feature rendered 3-D characters.

resolution: The number of pixels on your screen measured as horizontal by vertical. For example, a resolution of 1024 x 768 means that there are 1024 pixels across your screen and 768 lines down the side of the screen.

rpm (revolutions per minute): The speed of the platters in a hard drive. The faster the RPM, the faster the drive can access your data.

SATA (serial ATA) interface: A popular hard drive and device interface technology that is easier to configure and faster than EIDE, SATA hardware is slowly replacing EIDE hardware in today's PCs.

scanner: A device that converts (or captures) text and graphics from a printed page into a digital image. Scanners are often used to "read" pictures from books and magazines; the digital version of the picture can be edited and used in documents or placed on a Web page.

SDRAM (synchronous DRAM): An older type of RAM module that was often used on Pentium II and Pentium III PCs. It offers faster performance than the standard EDO RAM modules used on orig-inal Pentium computers. *See also* RAM.

serial port: A standard connector on most PCs that transfers data to and from an external device. A serial port was once generally used to connect an external modem to your computer, but today's modems use a USB connection.

SIMM (single inline memory module): A specific type of RAM chip usually used with original Pentium-class computers.

SLI (Scalable Link Interface): Linking video cards. Two NVIDIA video cards can be installed in the same PC and linked via a special cable to boost performance and provide the best quality 3-D graphics for games and high-end applications. Your motherboard must use an SLI-capable NVIDIA chipset.

sound card: An adapter card that enables your computer to play music and sound effects for games and other programs. Sound cards can also record audio from a microphone or stereo system.

static electricity: The archenemy of all computer circuitry, especially computer chips. Before you install anything in your computer, you should touch the metal chassis of your computer to discharge any static electricity on your body.

subwoofer: A separate speaker that you can add to a standard two-speaker computer sound system. Subwoofers add deep bass response and can bring realistic depth to sound effects.

SVGA (super video graphics array): The most common graphics standard for PC video adapter cards and monitors now in use. The SVGA standard allows for more than 16 million colors (24-bit or true color).

• T •

tape backup drive: A type of drive that enables you to back up your computer's files to removable magnetic cartridges.

topology: The structure or design of a network.

touchpad: A pointing device that reads the movement of your finger across the surface of the pad. This movement is translated to cursor movement on your screen.

trackball: A pointing device that resembles an upside-down mouse. You move the cursor by rolling the trackball with your finger or thumb and clicking buttons.

twisted-pair cable: Also called 10BaseT, 100Base-T, and 1000Base-T, depending on the speed of the network. A form of network cable that looks much like telephone cord, twisted-pair cable is commonly used on Ethernet networks with a central hub or switch.

• U •

Unix: A 32-bit, character-based operating system. Like DOS, Unix is controlled from a command line, but graphical front ends are available. The Unix commercial operating system is well known for security and speed, and Unix computers have run servers on the Internet for many years. *See also* DOS.

USB (universal serial bus): A standard connector that enables you to daisy-chain a whopping 127 devices, with data transfers at as much as 12 megabits per second for USB standard 1.1 (and a respectable 480 Mbps for USB standard 2.0). USB connectors have become the standard of choice for all sorts of computer peripherals, from computer videocameras and scanners to joysticks and speakers. (By the way, a USB 1.1 device works just fine when connected to a USB 2.0 port.)

• V •

VGA (video graphics array): The IBM PC graphics standard that featured 256 colors. Replaced on most of today's computers by the SVGA standard. *See also* SVGA.

video card: An adapter card that plugs into your motherboard and enables your computer to display text and graphics on your monitor. Advanced adapter cards can speed up the display of Windows programs and 3-D graphics.

voice modem: A computer modem that can also act as an answering machine and voice mail system. Voice modems typically have a speakerphone option as well.

• W •

WAV: The Microsoft standard format for a digital sound file. WAV files are common across the Internet and can be recorded in CD-quality stereo.

wavetable: A feature supported by all modern PC sound cards. A wavetable sound card produces more realistic instrument sounds (and therefore more realistic sounding music).

Windows 2008 Server: The latest server version of the Windows operating system from Microsoft. The direct descendant of Windows 2000 and Windows 2003 Server, it comes in a number of flavors designed to appeal to small businesses. Windows 2008 Server makes a great network server or Internet server but, like 2003 before it, is more expensive than Windows Vista.

Windows Vista: The latest home and business PC version of the Windows operating system from Microsoft, offering superior graphics and a number of improvements over Windows XP. Windows is a multimedia, graphical operating system that relies heavily on a pointing device, such as a mouse. Unfortunately, Vista requires cutting-edge hardware to operate, so older PCs or slower processors may not be able to support all of Vista's features. Vista is available in both 32- and 64-bit versions.

Windows XP: The popular 32-bit operating system for the PC, replaced in 2007 by Windows Vista. Windows Me, the predecessor to Windows XP, had fewer features and lacked support for the latest hardware.

Windows XP x64: An advanced version of Windows XP designed to support the current generation of 64-bit processors from Intel and AMD. 64-bit functionality allows faster and more efficient multitasking, as well as faster hard drive performance.

wireless mouse: A pointing device similar to a standard mouse but without the cord that connects it to the computer. Wireless mice require batteries but are a little more convenient without the cord.

• Z •

ZIF (zero insertion force) socket: A socket that makes it easy to upgrade your computer's CPU in the future. The lever unlatches the CPU so that you can easily remove it from the socket and then drop in a new CPU.

Index

• W •

John Wiley & Sons, Inc.
End-User License Agreement

READ THIS. You should carefully read these terms and conditions before opening the software packet(s) included with this book "Book". This is a license agreement "Agreement" between you and John Wiley & Sons, Inc. "WILEY". By opening the accompanying software packet(s), you acknowledge that you have read and accept the following terms and conditions. If you do not agree and do not want to be bound by such terms and conditions, promptly return the Book and the unopened software packet(s) to the place you obtained them for a full refund.

1. **License Grant.** WILEY grants to you (either an individual or entity) a nonexclusive license to use one copy of the enclosed software program(s) (collectively, the "Software") solely for your own personal or business purposes on a single computer (whether a standard computer or a workstation component of a multi-user network). The Software is in use on a computer when it is loaded into temporary memory (RAM) or installed into permanent memory (hard disk, CD-ROM, or other storage device). WILEY reserves all rights not expressly granted herein.

2. **Ownership.** WILEY is the owner of all right, title, and interest, including copyright, in and to the compilation of the Software recorded on the physical packet included with this Book "Software Media". Copyright to the individual programs recorded on the Software Media is owned by the author or other authorized copyright owner of each program. Ownership of the Software and all proprietary rights relating thereto remain with WILEY and its licensers.

3. **Restrictions On Use and Transfer.**

    (a) You may only (i) make one copy of the Software for backup or archival purposes, or (ii) transfer the Software to a single hard disk, provided that you keep the original for backup or archival purposes. You may not (i) rent or lease the Software, (ii) copy or reproduce the Software through a LAN or other network system or through any computer subscriber system or bulletin-board system, or (iii) modify, adapt, or create derivative works based on the Software.

    (b) You may not reverse engineer, decompile, or disassemble the Software. You may transfer the Software and user documentation on a permanent basis, provided that the transferee agrees to accept the terms and conditions of this Agreement and you retain no copies. If the Software is an update or has been updated, any transfer must include the most recent update and all prior versions.

4. **Restrictions on Use of Individual Programs.** You must follow the individual requirements and restrictions detailed for each individual program in the "About the DVD" appendix of this Book or on the Software Media. These limitations are also contained in the individual license agreements recorded on the Software Media. These limitations may include a requirement that after using the program for a specified period of time, the user must pay a registration fee or discontinue use. By opening the Software packet(s), you agree to abide by the licenses and restrictions for these individual programs that are detailed in the "About the DVD" appendix and/or on the Software Media. None of the material on this Software Media or listed in this Book may ever be redistributed, in original or modified form, for commercial purposes.original or modified form, for commercial purposes.

BUSINESS, CAREERS & PERSONAL FINANCE

Accounting For Dummies, 4th Edition*
978-0-470-24600-9

Bookkeeping Workbook For Dummies†
978-0-470-16983-4

Commodities For Dummies
978-0-470-04928-0

Doing Business in China For Dummies
978-0-470-04929-7

E-Mail Marketing For Dummies
978-0-470-19087-6

Job Interviews For Dummies, 3rd Edition*†
978-0-470-17748-8

Personal Finance Workbook For Dummies*†
978-0-470-09933-9

Real Estate License Exams For Dummies
978-0-7645-7623-2

Six Sigma For Dummies
978-0-7645-6798-8

Small Business Kit For Dummies, 2nd Edition*†
978-0-7645-5984-6

Telephone Sales For Dummies
978-0-470-16836-3

BUSINESS PRODUCTIVITY & MICROSOFT OFFICE

Access 2007 For Dummies
978-0-470-03649-5

Excel 2007 For Dummies
978-0-470-03737-9

Office 2007 For Dummies
978-0-470-00923-9

Outlook 2007 For Dummies
978-0-470-03830-7

PowerPoint 2007 For Dummies
978-0-470-04059-1

Project 2007 For Dummies
978-0-470-03651-8

QuickBooks 2008 For Dummies
978-0-470-18470-7

Quicken 2008 For Dummies
978-0-470-17473-9

Salesforce.com For Dummies, 2nd Edition
978-0-470-04893-1

Word 2007 For Dummies
978-0-470-03658-7

EDUCATION, HISTORY, REFERENCE & TEST PREPARATION

African American History For Dummies
978-0-7645-5469-8

Algebra For Dummies
978-0-7645-5325-7

Algebra Workbook For Dummies
978-0-7645-8467-1

Art History For Dummies
978-0-470-09910-0

ASVAB For Dummies, 2nd Edition
978-0-470-10671-6

British Military History For Dummies
978-0-470-03213-8

Calculus For Dummies
978-0-7645-2498-1

Canadian History For Dummies, 2nd Edition
978-0-470-83656-9

Geometry Workbook For Dummies
978-0-471-79940-5

The SAT I For Dummies, 6th Edition
978-0-7645-7193-0

Series 7 Exam For Dummies
978-0-470-09932-2

World History For Dummies
978-0-7645-5242-7

FOOD, GARDEN, HOBBIES & HOME

Bridge For Dummies, 2nd Edition
978-0-471-92426-5

Coin Collecting For Dummies, 2nd Edition
978-0-470-22275-1

Cooking Basics For Dummies, 3rd Edition
978-0-7645-7206-7

Drawing For Dummies
978-0-7645-5476-6

Etiquette For Dummies, 2nd Edition
978-0-470-10672-3

Gardening Basics For Dummies*†
978-0-470-03749-2

Knitting Patterns For Dummies
978-0-470-04556-5

Living Gluten-Free For Dummies†
978-0-471-77383-2

Painting Do-It-Yourself For Dummies
978-0-470-17533-0

HEALTH, SELF HELP, PARENTING & PETS

Anger Management For Dummies
978-0-470-03715-7

Anxiety & Depression Workbook For Dummies
978-0-7645-9793-0

Dieting For Dummies, 2nd Edition
978-0-7645-4149-0

Dog Training For Dummies, 2nd Edition
978-0-7645-8418-3

Horseback Riding For Dummies
978-0-470-09719-9

Infertility For Dummies†
978-0-470-11518-3

Meditation For Dummies with CD-ROM, 2nd Edition
978-0-471-77774-8

Post-Traumatic Stress Disorder For Dummies
978-0-470-04922-8

Puppies For Dummies, 2nd Edition
978-0-470-03717-1

Thyroid For Dummies, 2nd Edition†
978-0-471-78755-6

Type 1 Diabetes For Dummies*†
978-0-470-17811-9

---

* Separate Canadian edition also available
† Separate U.K. edition also available

INTERNET & DIGITAL MEDIA

AdWords For Dummies
978-0-470-15252-2

Blogging For Dummies, 2nd Edition
978-0-470-23017-6

**Digital Photography All-in-One
Desk Reference For Dummies, 3rd Edition**
978-0-470-03743-0

Digital Photography For Dummies, 5th Edition
978-0-7645-9802-9

**Digital SLR Cameras & Photography
For Dummies, 2nd Edition**
978-0-470-14927-0

**eBay Business All-in-One Desk Reference
For Dummies**
978-0-7645-8438-1

eBay For Dummies, 5th Edition*
978-0-470-04529-9

eBay Listings That Sell For Dummies
978-0-471-78912-3

Facebook For Dummies
978-0-470-26273-3

The Internet For Dummies, 11th Edition
978-0-470-12174-0

Investing Online For Dummies, 5th Edition
978-0-7645-8456-5

iPod & iTunes For Dummies, 5th Edition
978-0-470-17474-6

MySpace For Dummies
978-0-470-09529-4

Podcasting For Dummies
978-0-471-74898-4

**Search Engine Optimization
For Dummies, 2nd Edition**
978-0-471-97998-2

Second Life For Dummies
978-0-470-18025-9

**Starting an eBay Business For Dummies,
3rd Edition†**
978-0-470-14924-9

GRAPHICS, DESIGN & WEB DEVELOPMENT

**Adobe Creative Suite 3 Design Premium
All-in-One Desk Reference For Dummies**
978-0-470-11724-8

**Adobe Web Suite CS3 All-in-One Desk
Reference For Dummies**
978-0-470-12099-6

AutoCAD 2008 For Dummies
978-0-470-11650-0

**Building a Web Site For Dummies,
3rd Edition**
978-0-470-14928-7

**Creating Web Pages All-in-One Desk
Reference For Dummies, 3rd Edition**
978-0-470-09629-1

**Creating Web Pages For Dummies,
8th Edition**
978-0-470-08030-6

Dreamweaver CS3 For Dummies
978-0-470-11490-2

Flash CS3 For Dummies
978-0-470-12100-9

Google SketchUp For Dummies
978-0-470-13744-4

InDesign CS3 For Dummies
978-0-470-11865-8

**Photoshop CS3 All-in-One
Desk Reference For Dummies**
978-0-470-11195-6

Photoshop CS3 For Dummies
978-0-470-11193-2

Photoshop Elements 5 For Dummies
978-0-470-09810-3

SolidWorks For Dummies
978-0-7645-9555-4

Visio 2007 For Dummies
978-0-470-08983-5

Web Design For Dummies, 2nd Edition
978-0-471-78117-2

Web Sites Do-It-Yourself For Dummies
978-0-470-16903-2

Web Stores Do-It-Yourself For Dummies
978-0-470-17443-2

LANGUAGES, RELIGION & SPIRITUALITY

Arabic For Dummies
978-0-471-77270-5

Chinese For Dummies, Audio Set
978-0-470-12766-7

French For Dummies
978-0-7645-5193-2

German For Dummies
978-0-7645-5195-6

Hebrew For Dummies
978-0-7645-5489-6

Ingles Para Dummies
978-0-7645-5427-8

Italian For Dummies, Audio Set
978-0-470-09586-7

Italian Verbs For Dummies
978-0-471-77389-4

Japanese For Dummies
978-0-7645-5429-2

Latin For Dummies
978-0-7645-5431-5

Portuguese For Dummies
978-0-471-78738-9

Russian For Dummies
978-0-471-78001-4

Spanish Phrases For Dummies
978-0-7645-7204-3

Spanish For Dummies
978-0-7645-5194-9

Spanish For Dummies, Audio Set
978-0-470-09585-0

The Bible For Dummies
978-0-7645-5296-0

Catholicism For Dummies
978-0-7645-5391-2

The Historical Jesus For Dummies
978-0-470-16785-4

Islam For Dummies
978-0-7645-5503-9

**Spirituality For Dummies,
2nd Edition**
978-0-470-19142-2

NETWORKING AND PROGRAMMING

ASP.NET 3.5 For Dummies
978-0-470-19592-5

C# 2008 For Dummies
978-0-470-19109-5

Hacking For Dummies, 2nd Edition
978-0-470-05235-8

Home Networking For Dummies, 4th Edition
978-0-470-11806-1

Java For Dummies, 4th Edition
978-0-470-08716-9

**Microsoft® SQL Server™ 2008 All-in-One
Desk Reference For Dummies**
978-0-470-17954-3

**Networking All-in-One Desk Reference
For Dummies, 2nd Edition**
978-0-7645-9939-2

**Networking For Dummies,
8th Edition**
978-0-470-05620-2

SharePoint 2007 For Dummies
978-0-470-09941-4

**Wireless Home Networking
For Dummies, 2nd Edition**
978-0-471-74940-0

OPERATING SYSTEMS & COMPUTER BASICS

iMac For Dummies, 5th Edition
978-0-7645-8458-9

Laptops For Dummies, 2nd Edition
978-0-470-05432-1

Linux For Dummies, 8th Edition
978-0-470-11649-4

MacBook For Dummies
978-0-470-04859-7

Mac OS X Leopard All-in-One Desk Reference For Dummies
978-0-470-05434-5

Mac OS X Leopard For Dummies
978-0-470-05433-8

Macs For Dummies, 9th Edition
978-0-470-04849-8

PCs For Dummies, 11th Edition
978-0-470-13728-4

Windows® Home Server For Dummies
978-0-470-18592-6

Windows Server 2008 For Dummies
978-0-470-18043-3

Windows Vista All-in-One Desk Reference For Dummies
978-0-471-74941-7

Windows Vista For Dummies
978-0-471-75421-3

Windows Vista Security For Dummies
978-0-470-11805-4

SPORTS, FITNESS & MUSIC

Coaching Hockey For Dummies
978-0-470-83685-9

Coaching Soccer For Dummies
978-0-471-77381-8

Fitness For Dummies, 3rd Edition
978-0-7645-7851-9

Football For Dummies, 3rd Edition
978-0-470-12536-6

GarageBand For Dummies
978-0-7645-7323-1

Golf For Dummies, 3rd Edition
978-0-471-76871-5

Guitar For Dummies, 2nd Edition
978-0-7645-9904-0

Home Recording For Musicians For Dummies, 2nd Edition
978-0-7645-8884-6

iPod & iTunes For Dummies, 5th Edition
978-0-470-17474-6

Music Theory For Dummies
978-0-7645-7838-0

Stretching For Dummies
978-0-470-06741-3

Get smart @ dummies.com®

- **Find a full list of Dummies titles**
- **Look into loads of FREE on-site articles**
- **Sign up for FREE eTips e-mailed to you weekly**
- **See what other products carry the Dummies name**
- **Shop directly from the Dummies bookstore**
- **Enter to win new prizes every month!**